The Divine Law of Cure

WARREN F. EVANS

COSIMOCLASSICS

NEW YORK

The Divine Law of Cure
Cover © 2007 Cosimo, Inc.

For information, address:

Cosimo, P.O. Box 416
Old Chelsea Station
New York, NY 10113-0416

or visit our website at:
www.cosimobooks.com

The Divine Law of Cure was originally published in 1884.

Cover design by www.kerndesign.net

ISBN: 978-1-60206-340-2

CONTENTS.

3

CHAPTER V.

CHAPTER VI.

CHAPTER VII.

CHAPTER VIII.

CHAPTER IX.

CHAPTER X.

CHAPTER XI.

CHAPTER XII.

PART II.

THE RELATION OF SPIRIT TO MATTER, AND OF THE SOUL TO THE BODY IN MAN.

CHAPTER VIII.

CHAPTER IX.

CHAPTER X.

CHAPTER XI.

CHAPTER XII.

CHAPTER XIII.

CHAPTER XIV.

CHAPTER XV.

CHAPTER XVI.

CHAPTER XVII.

PART III.

PSYCHO-THERAPEUTICS, OR PRACTICAL MENTAL CURE.

CHAPTER I.

CHAPTER II.

PREFACE.

No intelligent observer of the signs of the times can fail to notice among philosophical minds a marked reaction against the dominant scientific materialism of the past century, and a tendency to return to a more spiritual view of human nature and the world at large. Idealism, which has always had a strong hold upon the deepest thinkers of the world from Plato downward, is again coming into prominence, and many of the leading scientists of the day exhibit an inclination to adopt it as furnishing the most satisfactory explanation of the phenomena of nature. The system of Berkeley is undergoing a resurrection, and, in connection with the spiritual philosophy of Swedenborg, will have more influence than ever in shaping the metaphysical systems of the future, and in giving direction to the current of human thought. The present volume of the author is an attempt to construct a theoretical and practical system of phrenopathy, or mental-cure, on the basis of the idealistic philosophy of Berkeley, Fichte, Schelling, and Hegel. Its fundamental doctrine is that to think and to exist are one and the same, and that every disease is the translation into a bodily expression of a fixed idea of the mind and a morbid way of thinking. If by any therapeutic device you remove the morbid idea, which is the spiritual image after the likeness of which the body is formed, you cure the malady. The work lays no claim to originality except in the practical application of Idealism to the cure of the diseases of mind and body. It is the culmination of a life-long study of human nature, and to which the previous volumes of the author may be viewed as introductory. That its teachings will be fully accepted by all who peruse it is not to be expected. That there is a large and constantly increasing class of minds who are prepared to receive its doctrines, as a dry soil drinks in the vernal rain, he fully believes. To their thoughtful consideration the volume is dedicated, with the sincere prayer that they may find in it something more certain and satisfactory than the current materialistic systems of medication have been able to furnish.

8½ Beacon Street, Boston.

PART I.

THE

RELATION OF THE DIVINE LIFE

TO HUMAN LIFE,

OR

TRUE RELIGION AND HEALTH.

"There is one God and Father of all, Who is above all, and through all, and in you all."—Eph. iv: 6.

"He is not far from every one of us; for in Him we live, and are moved, and have our being."—Acts xvii: 27, 28.

"An indispensable requisite to a blessed life is that this living religion in us should at least go so far as to convince us entirely of our own nothingness in ourselves, and of our being only in God and through God; that we should at least *feel* this relationship continually and without interruption; and that, even though it should not be expressed either in thought or language, it should yet be the secret spring, the hidden principle, of all our thoughts, feelings, emotions, and desires."— *Fichte's Popular Works*, p. 437.

THE DIVINE LAW OF CURE.

CHAPTER I.

THE TRUE IDEA OF RELIGION.

In discussing the subject of Religion and Health, and the relation of the one to the other, it is necessary that we form some definite conception of what religion is, and what we mean by health.

Religion is certainly not a mere intellectual state, the belief of a creed however orthodox, or an assent to any number of theological propositions.

It does not consist in outward action,—the performance of the outward mechanism of forms and ceremonies, however grand and imposing, or however humble and simple, from the Roman Catholic ceremonial in the Gothic cathedral down to the forms, or want of forms, in the meeting-house of the Society of Friends. I do not affirm that either of these elements or both—the intellectual assent to some form of belief and the practice of some outward worship—may not enter into it, and be most intimately associated with it, but they constitute no necessary part of its nature and essence. They may be varied in form, like the colors of the cameleon, and are continually changing, while religion remains the

same.   It is very certain that there may be many gradations of
religious *intensity* in men whose creed is the same, and their outward forms of worship identical.   The intellectual state belonging
to religion is *intuitional*, and arises from feeling, and is not merely
an act of the logical consciousness.   This feeling, when left to
itself, like all other feelings, will spontaneously create its outward
and appropriate forms of expression.

There are two definitions of religion by two of the religious
thinkers of Germany, who knew from their own consciousness what
they were saying, both having been educated among the Moravians.   These two definitions, when combined, give us a clear conception of the essential nature of religion.   "Jacobi, who was
first to see the full worth and signification of *feeling* in the domain
of philosophy, defines religion to be a faith, resting upon feeling,
in the reality of the super-sensual and ideal.   The other is the
definition of Schleiermacher, than whom no man ever pursued with
greater penetration of mind and earnestness of spirit the pathway
of a Divine philosophy, and he places the essence of religion in
the absolute feeling of dependence, and of a conscious relationship
to God, originating immediately from it."   (*Morell's Philosophy
of Religion*, p. 71.)   When this feeling rises to a conscious union
with God, and to an intuitive perception of the spiritual truths
that underlie it, and are naturally associated with it, we have religion in its highest form — its Divine reality.   For religion (from
re and *ligo*, to bind together) is the conscious reunion of the soul
with God, after having been separated from Him by the disjunc-
tive agency of sin, or it is recovering the lost consciousness that
our life is inseparable from that of the Divine Being, and is identical with His.   If religion does not "bind" us to God, it is superficial and worthless.   It is valuable only so far as it does this.

Sectarian creeds and external and fixed forms of worship are no
more a necessary part of religion than warts, tumors, and fungus
growths are of the human body.   These may seem to have a connection with the body, but they are no essential part of it, and
they can be removed, and the patient be all the better for it.

In the religious history of every age and country, we find a certain class of minds who are impatient of ceremonial forms, technical distinctions, and dry, dogmatic formulas, and who have followed the yearnings of their own hearts for something better, and have yielded themselves to the instinctive impulses of the soul to rise from the shadow to the substance, from the sign to the thing signified, from the human to the Divine, the transient to the enduring, and from the non-essential to the essential in religion. Christianity, when properly apprehended, will meet the wants and satisfy the spiritual cravings of all such minds. Its constant aim is to unite the sundered link between man and God, and to bring the finite and infinite into a conscious harmony and felt oneness.

Religion may, and actually does, exist in a thousand different forms and degrees. The highest development of religious thought and feeling is that of a *Christian Pantheism*, not the cold, intellectual system of Spinoza, but one nearer to that of the warm and loving Fichte, who exhibited the blessedness of a life in God. The Divine inspiration and wisdom of Jesus the Christ, is seen in his placing religion in something above and beyond all ceremonial observances, and in teaching that the highest style of religion is found in the consciousness of God within,— the intuitive perception of the life of God in the soul of man. The system of Jesus and of Buddha here find a point of contact and flow together. The Buddhist Nirvana, or ideal conception of the *summum bonum*, the supreme good, was not originally a state of annihilation,— which is no state at all, much less one of happiness,— but was rather the rest of the soul in its complete union with God, and its harmony with the Divine Life. I cannot avoid this view, although Max Müller, in his Science of Religion, has seemed to prove to the contrary. It is that condition of union with the Godhead which Jesus so often affirmed of himself,— not a mathematical, but a spiritual oneness, which does not destroy the feeling of our individuality. It is that for which the mystics of all ages have longed. It was sought as a realization of their highest ideal of a state of blessedness by Eckhart, Tauler, Ruysbrock, Behmen, Guyon, and others. This is the essence of all religion; for a system that does not unite Divinity and Humanity does not answer to the fundamental idea of the word. In the evolution of the religious life of mankind we see what is the coming stage of its advancement. *It will be the revelation of God in the individual soul.* This is a stage of the religious consciousness to which the world is being borne by influences which it did not originate, and which cannot be suppressed. All genuine science and philosophy are drifting in that direction, and all church organizations will follow in their wake.

A spiritual science of religion, the philosophy of the relations of the finite mind to the Infinite Being, of matter to spirit, and of the body to the soul in man, will be the last to be worked out in the progress of human knowledge, but when it is elaborated according to the law of evolution, it will change the life of the world, and usher in a new and higher dispensation of Christianity. The great mistake of men is, *they seek without for what they can only find within.* Within the depths of the soul are infinite spiritual capabilities and possibilities. In every human mind is the hidden germ of an endless development. God dwells in man, and the body is the temple of the Holy Spirit. The Divine element in our nature is not there as an idle guest or spectator, but as an ever-operative force. God's activity is co-extensive with his presence. We cannot separate from the idea of his presence that of causation. The Divine Being is the *causa causarum*, the prime cause that lies back of all secondary causes. This doctrine was introduced into philosophy by an Arabian and a Mohammedan. Says Sir Wm. Hamilton: "As far as I have been able to trace it, this doctrine was first promulgated toward the commencement of the twelfth century by Algazel, of Bagdad, a pious Mohammedan philosopher, who not undeservedly obtained the title of the Imaum of the World. Algazel did not deny the reality of causation, but he maintained that God was the only efficient cause in nature; and that second causes are not properly causes, but only occasions of the effect." (*The Metaphysics of Sir Wm. Hamilton, by Prof*

Bowen, p. 540.) The subject was much discussed by the philoso-phers of subsequent ages, but the most distinguished advocate of the doctrine of Algazel was Malebranche. He believed and taught that God was the only active force in the universe, *and even in the body.* What we call second causes were only the *occa-sions* on which the Divine power acted. There is an important sub-stratum of intuitional and logical truth in this view. A cause is that without which something we call an effect could not exist or take place. But can anything exist without God? If not, then all secondary causes are but effects, and must be referred back to the great First Cause.

Some minds have so vivid a consciousness of God as to lose sight of everything else, at least everything else is thrown into the back-ground. Such was the mind of Fichte, Schelling, and Hegel. And this was emphatically true of Spinoza, who has been misunderstood and misrepresented. Novalis characterizes him as "the God-intoxicated man." The essence, or fundamental idea of his philosophy is contained in a single sentence of his writings, which is certainly in harmony with the Christian system. Its infi-delity consists in giving a more intense *reality* to God than most people have done, but not more than Jesus himself did. *Deus est omnium rerum causa immanens, non transiens,* God is the im-manent not transient cause of all things; or, in other words, God is permanently resident in nature, and not a power outside of it that has occasionally acted upon it.

We have seen in what has been said above that religion is a conscious union with God. All religions, however imperfect, are an instinctive seeking after this, and, in a measure, accomplish it. But it is a self-evident truth that what is the source of life must be the primal cause and fountain of health. The efficiency of any remedial agency must, in its last analysis, be referred to a Divine power and causation. But a soul, made in the image of God, may come into vital communication and fellowship with God, the only Life. This is, at the same time, both religion and health in their highest idea.   As religion, in its inmost essence, consists in an intuitive consciousness of a Divine life in the soul, so health is the Divine life within us coming to a *free* activity and expression in all our voluntary powers.

CHAPTER II.

RELIGION IS A DEVELOPMENT FROM WITHIN, AND NOT A FOREIGN
ELEMENT IMPORTED INTO OUR NATURE FROM WITHOUT.

The Divine element in human nature is not something of which
we are born destitute, and that is afterwards to be superadded to
our being by instruction and the religious propagandism of the
church, but is the seed, and the only vital germ, from which our
existence springs. This Divine germ is enclosed as in a pericarp
in every one of the human race,— the savage and the saint. It is
not the true function of *preaching*, and of religious instruction, to
import the Divine life as a foreign element into human nature,
for it is already there, but to bring men to a conscious realization
of this truth. The religious element in man is not something
communicated to him from without, but is an original constituent
of his nature, and one which may be drawn forth and modified in
its action by instruction and influences received from others. It
is not something entirely adventitious, but is inherent in the
essence of the soul. The universal prevalence of religion in the
world among all races and in all ages of human history would
militate against the theory that it is something extraneous, and
goes to prove that it is natural to man, and a necessary outcome
of his mental constitution, as much as language, or poetry, or
music, or civil government. This does not make it any less
Divine, for God is in all natural powers, susceptibilities, and laws.
Certain it is, I have never found a man in whom the religious
sentiments were utterly suppressed or annihilated. In many men

the religious nature is latent, and overlaid by a deep covering of externality, but there is still the vital germ in the depths of the soul that awaits the vivifying touch of the Divine Spirit to cause it to *sprout*, and to be unfolded into the flower and fruit of a religious consciousness and life.   It is only a question of the best means of developing this Divine instinct of the soul.   A seed may remain dormant for a long series of years without losing its vitality, and when exposed to the proper influences of moisture, heat, and genial sunshine, it starts into a manifested life spontaneously.   As we could never be taught morality without a moral nature and a moral sense to distinguish between right and wrong, and as we could not be taught music or mathematics without an inborn geinus for those sciences, so the same is true of religion.   All education (from *ex* and *duco*, to draw out) implies something in the hidden depths of the soul to be *educed* or developed into conscious activity.   On this principle is based the system of Fröbel. All moral and religious education consists in awakening and properly directing what is already *potentially* within us.   On this subject Mr. Morell justly observes: "We could never be taught religion by any external appliances unless there was some inward susceptibility which may indeed be aroused or regulated by discipline, but which has a prior existence as a primary element of our spiritual nature." (*Philosophy of Religion*, p. 65.)

This view, when fully recognized, must essentially modify our idea of the nature of regeneration.   It is no longer a new creation, but a development.   Religion will never be propagated with any great success unless this self-evident and fundamental truth is acknowledged, and the means of propagandism be adapted to it. The true religious life is an *evolution*, the unfolding of a latent and dormant power within us.

We must not confound religion with theology.   Theology is what we think *about* religion, and this is an ever-changing thing, but true religion remains the same.   The stars do not constitute astronomy, nor the rocky strata of the earth geology, but astronomy is what we know about the star , and geology what we know or

think about the rocks. Religion is the union of man with God,
or as Schelling defines it, "the union of the finite with the infinite." But this may be predicated of all men. If it be true, as
Paul affirms, that, "in Him we live, and move, and have our being"
(Acts xvii : 27), or in other words, that God is the inmost Life
of all that is, and the ground of our own existence, then no human
mind is or can be entirely sundered from the Divine Mind, or can
have any life that is not a manifestation of the One Life. We
may loose the consciousness of this, but there is a region of the
soul where God prepetually dwells, and in which our life is linked
to the Deity. The incarnation is not a solitary miracle in the
course of human history, and something outside of that fixed order
of things which we call the laws of nature, and confined to one
individual of the race, but a universal fact, without which the existence of the soul here, and its immortality hereafter, would be an
impossibility. The human soul is *distinct* from the Deity, but
not sepatate. It retains its self-consciousness and individuality
and never loses its personal identity in an all-prevading impersonal
Pneuma, or becomes a part of the abstract Reason. Though the
soul retains a connection with the totality of spirit, it is never
merged in it, like a drop falling into the ocean. The more fully
and consciously it is united to the All, the more it becomes *itself*.
The true theory is this,— that owing to the incarnation of God in
every individual soul, and in the whole of humanity, every man
has within himself a region of the soul where he may have direct
and immediate communication and converse with the Divine
Mind. Man is an individual endowed with free will, but in being
an individual possessing self-consciousness, he does not become
an *exile* from God. He is not banished from the Divine Presence,
but is still inclosed within the infinite circle of the Divine Life.
Through this medium he may learn all that is essential to his
highest interests in this world and the next, and may gain the
highest truths of wisdom in relation to health of mind and body.
All our knowledge of spiritual things comes from this source, and
is, in a proper sense, a revelation from God, and a ray of that un-

created and Divine Word that "lighteth every man that cometh into the world." All men, in favored moments, have experiences of this spiritual illumination, this awakening and quickening of the intuitive preception, and might have much more if they understood the laws and conditions of its transmission and receptivity. The reality of a present inspiration from God, both of life and light, in all human souls, can be established as a fact in mental philosophy, resting on a foundation of evidence far more substantial than that of most metaphysical theories.

One of the first results of this nearness of man to God is the revelation of God to man. The existence of God is a truth to be *seen*, not to be proved. There is no demonstration of the being of God that does not involve some logical absurdity, or, at least, a *petitio principii*, or begging of the question. The central sun of our system shines with his own light, and makes himself known to all the planets that revolve around this central orb. Their light is borrowed or imparted light, and not self-originated. God may be so very near to us that we cannot *see* him, but only *feel* him, and this is the highest possible evidence. Thus, Paul says that we should seek the Lord, if haply we might *feel* after Him and find Him, though He is not far from every one of us. (Acts xvii: 27.) Conscious *contact* of the soul with God, an all-satisfying communion and fellowship with Him, is the highest demonstration of His existence, for to *feel* anything to be true is to attain to a state of certainty and freedom from all doubt. It has been truly said by Immanuel Hermann Fichte that "God is not merely an object of faith, as is usually said; He operates faith *in us*, and gives in this very fact the most lively proof of His existence and care." He makes known Himself to the religious consciousness with more certainty and force of evidence than the external world is made known to our senses. He reveals Himself to the intuitive reason, — or, as Kant calls it, the pure reason, — which is the highest evidence the mind is capable of receiving. In the attainment of certainty as to the Divine Existence, so that the being of God is no longer a doubtful hypothesis, but He becomes to us the only

Reality, our pathway is opened to the fountain of all health and blessedness. As in the age of Augustus all the magnificent highways of the empire centred in Rome, and conducted the traveller from the provinces by an unerring route to the place whence emanated all subordinate authority and power, so to the man who has attained to the consciousness of God, and of our vital relations to Him, all remedies will conduct us to the central Life, and will bring the sick and bewildered wanderer to Him, from whom proceeds every sanative potency for soul or body. For it is the Divine alone that heals. There is one truth, of which we must never lose sight—*that there is but one Life in the universe.* As Fichte has said, "Being is simple and uncompounded. There is not a multiplicity of beings, but only one Being." Being and life are the same. This one Being, one Life, is what Jesus calls the Father, because from Him everything springs. By existence we mean manifested being. This is endlessly varied and multiplied. But all existences, from the atom to the world, from the insect to the angel, have their ground in the One Being and Life of which they are but manifestations to consciousness, that is, to sense and thought. All the millions of the race are but the rising into individuality of the ocean of being, but never lose their connection with it. They are a personal cropping out of the Primal Life, as mountains are an upheaval of the primitive rock, but are not sundered from it. The Father is in us, and we are in the Father. In the innermost root of our existence we are inseparably and perpetually connected with Him, otherwise we could not exist at all, and because of it we shall live forever.

"An insight into the absolute unity of the human existence with the Divine is certainly the profoundest knowledge that man can attain. Before Jesus this knowledge had nowhere existed; and since his time, we may say down even to the present day, it has been again as good as rooted out, at least in profane literature." (*Way Towards the Blessed Life, Lecture VI.*)

The grand error of the religious world has ever been in separating God too far from man. It has believed in a Divine Being who is somewhere, but not here, and indeed who is anywhere and everywhere except in man.

It is a fundamental doctrine of Swedenborg's spiritual philosophy, and one that comes continually to view in all his voluminous writings, that there is only one Life in the universe, and angels, spirits, and men are but recipients of it. (*Arcana Celestia*, 3742.) Our life is perpetually imparted from Him. His Being flows forth into our existence which is but a manifestation of it, and is continuous with it. Our individual life is identical with His, and is included as an item, or an atom, in the sum total of the Divine Existence. The thread of our life, without a break, is ever unwound from His.

Swedenborg also affirms (*Arcana Celestia*, 4525) *that man is so made that he can apply to himself life from the Lord.* In other words, as an individual existence, he can appropriate more of the Divine Life and make it his own, as you can enlarge the stream that flows from the lake in the mountains, and increase its volume by deepening the channel. In certain elevated states we become more highly charged with a Divine vitality, and become, in a more exalted degree, incarnations of the Deity. This fits us for the higher uses of life,— as the spiritual instruction of others, and the cure of their mental and bodily maladies. This is what is called, in the expressive language of the New Testament, being endued with power from on high. (Luke xxiv : 49.)

Descartes, the father of modern speculative philosophy, affirmed that God has accorded to created things no principle of subsistence in themselves, and that the existence of everything, from moment to moment, is due to the renewal each moment of the creative act of the Deity. (Med. iii. p. 23, ed. 1663.) Since his day, the tendency of philosophy has been towards a fuller recognition of a Divine Life and Force in Nature. To a truly religious and spiritual man the world is not a mere dead mass of material forces, but is everywhere seen to throb and pulsate with the life of God. It is everywhere inter-penetrated with a living Intelligence and Thought, of which it is the *ex*-istence or outward form and phenomenon.   By Fichte, one of the most profoundly religious men of any age or country, Nature is elevated into a living and sacred manifestation of the One Eternal, Divine Life. According to him, "Religion consists in regarding and recognizing all earthly life as the necessary development of the One, Original, Perfectly Good and Perfectly Blessed Divine Life." (*Characteristics of the Present Age*, p. 256.)

Especially is man, in a preëminent degree, a manifestation of God. "According to the meaning of *true religion*, and in particular of Christianity, humanity is the one, visible, efficient, living, and independant existence of God; or, if the expression be not misunderstood, the one manifestation and effluence of that Existence,— a beam from the eternal Light, which divides itself, not in reality, but only to mere earthly vision, into many individual rays." (*Characteristics of the Present Age*, p. 198.)

However strange it may seem, it is nevertheless true that this higher view of God and of our relation to Him, which arises naturally out of the profoundest religious consciousness and feeling, has almost always been viewed by more superficial minds as equivalent to atheism. Spinoza was ignorantly misapprehended, and has been maliciously defamed. The memory of the "God-intoxicated man" has been ignominiously buried beneath the stones that the ferocious zeal of shallow souls have cast upon it.   Every candid, religious mind will unhesitatingly adopt the language of Prof. Ferrier when he says: "This I will avouch, that all the outcry which has been raised against Spinoza has its origin in nothing but ignorance, hypocrisy, and cant. If Spinoza errs, it is in attributing not certainly too much to the great Creator, for that is impossible, but too little to the creature of his hands." (*Institutes of Metaphysics*, p. 554.)

Schleiermacher speaks of Spinoza as "that holy and yet outcast man, who was full of the sentiment of religion, because he was filled with the Holy Spirit."   Says Cousin: "Instead of accusing Spinoza of atheism, he should be subjected to the opposite reproach."   Prof. Saisset says of him: "He has been loudly accused of atheism and impiety. The truth is that never did a man believe in God with a faith more profound, with a soul more sincere, than Spinoza. Take God from him, and you take from him his system, his thought, his life."

Spinoza denied, as many great and pious divines have done, the free agency of man. Hegel escapes this charge by making the very essence of spirit to consist in freedom, and that of matter in passivity. (*Hegel's Philosophy of History, Bohn's edition,* p. 18.)

When Spinoza affirms that God is the only *substance*, he uses the word not in a physical but in a metaphysical sense. According to him, substance is that which does not depend upon anything else for its existence. (*Ethics, Part I.,* p. 3.) It is that which exists absolutely and of itself, and in this sense it is only another name for Pure Being. It is equivalent to the Hebrew Jehovah, which is derived from a substantive verb, and signifies *permanent being.* With that definition of it, he logically infers that God is the only Substance. He is the underlying, or, more properly, the *under-standing*, reality and support of all things. They do not exist separately from God, but in and from Him. Spinoza asserts "that whatever is is in God; and nothing can be, nor be conceived to be, without God." (*Ethics, Part I., Prop. XV.*) The world and all it contains are the *ex-istence* or out-standing of the Divine Being. This gives to the Universe its appropriate name (from *unum*, one, and *versus*, a turning), the το παν of the Greeks, the *mundus* of the Latin, the *welt* of the German, and the *world* of the English, which is radically the same as *whirl.*

Jesus affirms that God is Spirit,— not *a* spirit, which is contrary to the Greek; and spirit is essentially active and living. God is not merely an *extraneous*, isolated, individual Being,— though his personality, in any proper sense of the word, is not denied,— but the *internal*, collective, and intrinsic energy and Life of all things from the sparrow to the archangel. He is the ever-present, ever-acting, and indivisible Life of the world. Under the idea of the Primal Life he was apprehended by the Greeks as well as by the

Hebrews. *Zeus* and *theos*, and even the Latin *deus*, are all derived from a verb meaning to live. Kuss, a distinguished physiologist of Strasbourg, has defined life to be "all that which cannot be explained by chemistry or physics." But all the laws of chemistry and of every physical science are only modes of action of the One Life. Physiology and even Psychology are in their inmost essence only individual manifestations of the Divine Existence in man. As one has said, who will not be suspected of any heretical taint: "There is something grand in the idea of the *unity of all being*, and the connection of our life with the whole life of the universe." (*Christlieb's Modern Doubt and Chris·ian Belief*, p. 188.)

CHAPTER III.

The region of the religious sentiments and feelings is the seat of the kingdom of heaven in man. The religious emotions are the most powerful of all the principles to which our nature can appeal. They can hold the animal nature in chains, and control and restrain our hereditary bent from any wrong direction. Even when distorted by superstition, and directed into a wrong channel, they give a force of character which breaks down all minor opposition, and an almost supernatural energy to human nature, but when of a pure and elevated description, and united with a high moral sensibility, and under the guidance of an exalted intellectual state, they lend to our nature a power, a dignity, and a glory which shows its alliance with the Divinity here, and gives the clearest intimations of its exalted destiny hereafter. (*Morell's Philosophy of Religion*, p. 23.)

The history of the world is full of illustrations of the power of religion to move and control great masses of men. The conquests of the Jews under Joshua were effected by the animating influence of a religion by no means perfect, but better than that of the tribes they overran and displaced. The brilliant career of the Persian empire under Cyrus found its inspiring principle in the Zend-Avesta. The petty tribes of Arabia were galvanized into an irresistable life and conquering force by the Koran of Mohammed, which still maintains its hold upon millions of the human family

An hundred and fifty millions of Hindoos have been moulded and directed by their sacred writings, the Vedas and Puranas, for more than twenty-five centuries. The writings of the mild and gentle Buddha, who approaches in spirit the nearest to Jesus, hold sway over one-third of mankind, and have for many ages. The religion of Confucius, as contained in the "Kings" and the "Four Books," has given shape to the civilization and the every-day life of the millions of China. The power of religion to inspire to action great masses of men is seen in the Crusades, during which Europe was poured out upon Asia, under the preaching of Peter the Hermit, like a stream of lava from a volcano. What men can *suffer* for religion is illustrated in the lives and deaths of the martyrs and reformers of all ages and countries. All these things show the power of the religious nature, when developed into activity, over the life of man. It gives energy to all below it, the intellect and even the body. It is a power when properly educated and directed that, by its native Divine right, comes forth from the inmost depths and sublimest heights of our being, and assumes command of every department of our nature. From its throne, in the inmost palace of the soul, it reigns *dei gratia* over the whole external domain of mind and body.

In the system of the Christ, and in the apostolic Church, religion was a spiritual medicine and a means of cure. In the spiritual philosophy of Jesus, religion and health were viewed as one. Health of body was external holiness, or wholeness, and holiness was internal health. But the power of the spirit over disease was gradually lost sight of both in the doctrine and practice of the Church. As the religion of the Christ spread, it seems, except in scattered individual cases, to have lost in depth what it gained in surface extension, and at length the priests of religion, who were but a poorly-defined shadow of Jesus, stood in dumb and powerless amazement before diseases that yielded at once to the primitive spiritual power and Divine force.

Religion is influential over the life and health of soul and body in proportion to its depth, and powerless in an exact ratio to its shallowness. Genuine religion, and a true spiritual philosophy, raise the soul above all mere appearances, the surface of things, and all empty show, and penetrate to the very nature of things, and thus exhibit the most felicitous use of the spiritual powers, the greatest depth and acuteness of thought, and the highest *strength* of character. All these are favorable to a vigorous health of the mind, and therefore of the body. The religion of the day is too superficial, and has thus lost its sanative value. It is a sort of pious coloring stamped upon the external memory, the mere surface of our being. It does not strike through the tissue, and easily wears off. Its outward expression is a mechanical round of ceremonies, and posturing of the body, or a repetition of cant phrases that have lost their spiritual meaning,—a sort of parrot talking, where the words are too large for the ideas in the mind of the one who utters them, and which are consequently empty sounds. The religious zeal of such persons, full of sound without sense, seems to a thoughtful mind like acting in the pulpit, and in the conference room, instead of upon the stage, the drama of Shakespeare under another form of "Much Ado About Nothing." The faith of such a person, instead of being the *substance* of things hoped for, the evidence of things not seen, dwindles down, when closely examined, to an *opinion* borrowed from others. Its moral code, its Decalogue, is to do what most people do, and especially to ape the life of the ecclesiastical organization to which it belongs without much vital attachment to it. In their speaking in the "assembly of the saints," they use symbolic language which they have acquired in the same way as they learned to talk originally, that is, by imitation of others. The creed is a tradition, and not a present Divine conviction. They speak in riddles, with no power to interpret them, or to translate them into the definite language of a spiritual science. They dream dreams with no Daniel at hand to explain them. In this state of things, the trumpet of the Gospel gives an uncertain sound, and the creed to which the man has given an unintelligible assent is written in a spiritual tongue that has become a dead language, or, at least, a foreign one, which is no longer the soul's vernacular. All this is but the foam on the great current of the religious life of the world. Underneath it is a region of Divine life that has not been stirred.

A certain degree of mental activity is necessary to health, both of soul and body. It maintains the body in a state of perpetual youthfulness,— a constant juvenility,— for intellectual and spiritual growth is the mental state we call adolescence (from *adolesco*, to grow). In the other world we return to a state of perpetual youthfulness, because we enter upon a state of constant progress. The cause of old age and death is not a physical one; it is metaphysical. It is a cessation of growth,— a *stasis*, or standing still, in our intellectual life. Any creed, or form of religion, that demands for its acceptance a torpidity of the reflective and reasoning faculty, and that can exist only by suppressing all active thinking, is not mentally healthful. A religion, to be spiritually healthy, and to furnish any nutriment to the souls of men, must be co-existent in the soul with a *profound thoughtfulness*, in opposition to that light-hearted and shallow thoughtlessness which professes to believe so much,— and even the most absurd and incredible dogmas,— but does not in reality possess the power of realizing a profound conviction of anything. The bigotry and narrowness of such persons is always in an exact ratio with their shallowness and spiritual ignorance.

Religion being, as we have defined it, the conscious union of the soul with God, or at least an instinctive *conatus* to realize this, must bring us into closer and more vital and influential relations with the Central Life than anything else. To know God aright is eternal life. (Jno. xvii: 3.) It is only in union with Him that we live at all, and health is only a mode or condition of life. Religion, as thus defined, is that alone which can give to the soul the quality of immortality. Life, whatever it is, is only in the soul, and is a derivation and perpetual gift of God. The body neither lives nor dies. It lives from the spirit, and this from the Deity. From the cessation of the organic movements of the body, or what we call death, we are no more to infer that the spiritual force, which actuated that life, and those physiological movements, is annihilated, than we are to conclude that the spinning-girl is dead because the wheel stands still, or that the woman who runs the sewing-machine has passed out of existence because the machinery is found at night to be silent and motionless. There is but One Life in the universe. All else is derived, and not original. It is the true function of a religious and spiritual philosophy to teach men how to make this great truth available for the cure of all mental unhappiness and physical maladies.

God is the only Reality. On this subject Kant has said all that we can think or know in few words. It is absolutely impossible that nothing should exist. This is a truth of the intuitive reason. An absolutely necessary Being, therefore, exists, who is single, simple, and must be a spirit, for no idea that we can form of matter answers to this conception. This necessary Being comprises all reality, and is the Supreme Ground of all possible Reality. This Being is what we call God. This is a rational pantheism; it makes God the underlying Reality of all other things. Kant brought his transcendental view of God and of man's relation to Him up to the imperfectly drawn and separating line between an infinite truth and an essential falsity. Spinoza crossed the Rubicon, and, by losing sight of our *individuality*, carried his philosophy over on the wrong side of the line. Paul expresses in guarded language the highest truth,— that in God we live, and move, and have our being. (Acts xvii: 28.) No remedial device, or redeeming agency, can have any saving power that is not borrowed from Him who is the only Life and Supreme Reality. A union with God, which brings our consciousness of individuality down to the lowest point, and makes God the All in all, as exhibited in the life of Jesus, who could say "I and my Father are one," is the highest condition of health and blessedness.

Can we attain to a *consciousness* of God? Raymond Lull (born *anno* 1236, in the island of Majorca) speaks for all great minds when he says "The spirit longs after nothing as it does after God." But a Deity that I can never *find* is to me little better than none. The various churches claim to have a revelation *from* God, but they will never satisfy our spiritual cravings until they instruct us how to obtain a revelation *of* God. There is a power in the soul by which we may attain to an inward *sense* of the Deity. Bernard, of Clairvaux (A. D. 1091), affirms that in the third stage of the development of the spiritual life we reach a position where the soul has an *experience* of the Divine. (*Neander's History of Christianity and the Church*, Vol. IV., p. 372.)

To *know* God is eternal life, and He has not hidden Himself from us in an impenetrable darkness. There is a power in all human souls, call it what you will,— psychometry with Buchanan, intuition with Jacobi, or faith with Wesley,— by which God may become an object of *perception* or intuition. He is then no longer the *Great Unrevealed* of Basilides, nor the *Abyss* of the Gnostic Valentine. Wesley defined faith to be "a divine *evidence* and conviction of God and of the things of God." David Hartley, notwithstanding his materialism, recognized the power of the soul to attain to an inward sense of God, and calls it *theopathy*, and avers that it is a right and beneficial condition. Jesus declares that the pure in heart *see* God. And why not? Shall the material world alone be visible to us, and the only Reality be hidden from our perception? The pulpit is telling us what somebody has thought *about* God, and gives its hungry hearers for spiritual nutriment traditionary beliefs of the past, but we long to hear what it *knows* of God. It will ever be shorn of its power as long as its preaching is only a dogmatic history, and not like that of Jesus, an *original* knowledge of God and of a spiritual world.

In the system of the Christ it is made our highest duty not only to *love* God but also to *know* Him, for can we, in the highest sense, love a being or a thing about whom we know nothing? In Christianity the Spirit is promised to teach us all things, and to guide into all truth; it searches all things, yea, the deep things of God. (*Hegel's Philosophy of History*, p. 15.) The objects of nature are a Divine Theophany, or an appearance of God to the sensuous range of the mind's perception, as the body in man is a manifestation of the soul. That God is the All is no new truth, but is as old as religion. It was the *grand arcanum* of the Orphic theology. According to Dr. Cudworth, Orpheus taught that "this universe and all things belonging to it were made within God; that He is the beginning, the middle, and the end of all things." (*Intellectual System of the Universe*, Vol. I, pp. 108–112.)

There can be no profound religious life of the soul as long as we look upon the existence of God as a thing probable rather than certainly known. We know God as we know the existence of the *spirit* of man from its manifestation in the body. Every individual organism is an embodiment of the activity of the all-comprehending Life. The Whole, the All, is in each of the parts, or, as Goethe has it, "If you wish to appreciate the whole, you must see the Whole in the smallest." God does not impinge externally upon the universe. He moves the world from within. As he is out of time and space, there is an indivisible unity of God in every object of nature. This is true of the soul in the body. Every spot on the face of the earth is a Peniel or vision of God, where we meet Him face to face; and we need not go beyond the place where we are to find a Bethel or house of God. To sunder any part of the earth's surface from God, when we are there, is to be for the time being an *atheist*, or without God.

Bishop Berkeley, whose theological soundness has never been questioned, whatever may have been said of his idealistic philosophy, very truly says: "God is known as certainly and immediately as any other mind or spirit whatsoever distinct from ourselves. We may even assert that the existence of God is far more evidently perceived than the existence of men, because the effects of nature are infinitely more numerous and considerable than those ascribed to human agents. We need only open our eyes to see the Sovereign Lord of all things." (*Principles of Human Knowledge, Krauth's edition*, pp. 275, 276.)

CHAPTER IV.

The clergy, by a figure of speech, which represents what ought to be rather than what always is, have been called physicians of the soul, and religion has been viewed as a spiritual medicine. This idea is given us in the Scriptures. "Is there no balm in Gilead? Is there no physician there? Why, then, is not the health of the daughter of my people recovered?" (Jer. viii : 22.) If, then, souls in great numbers are diseased, and lost, and bewildered in the darkness, is it not because the physician is unskilful, and his medicine inefficient, even if it is not positively injurious? Let us search for the true remedy, the spiritual specific. The minister is a spiritual physician, and has medicine for the mind in proportion as he reproduces in himself the life of Jesus the Christ, and teaches the truths which he proclaimed.

All the various religions of the world are useful, and none of them could have been dropped out of human history and the general life of humanity without the race having suffered loss. They have all been factors in the progress and development of the human mind. They have all, in different degrees, accomplished the use of a *spiritual medicine*, in healing the hurts of the soul, and as preventives of something worse. The best medicine is that which prevents disease ; the next best that which cures it. Religion serves both these uses to the soul. Every style of religious thought and life that has gained any considerable degree of currency in the world has met some deeply-felt want of the human spirit. It has often but imperfectly satisfied the instinctive cravings of the soul for spiritual nutriment, but its dry, and perhaps mouldy, crusts have preserved the divinest realm of the soul's life from starvation, and kept an absolute famine from its door. The great religions of the world have been the system of Confucius, Brahmanism, Buddhism, the system of Zoroaster, Judaism, Christianity, and Mohammedism. Of more insignificant systems that have sprung out of these we need not speak. The most imperfect of all these religions have been a spiritual nutriment and a mental medicine to many millions of souls. To those who cannot live directly and immediately from the Divine Being, to which state Christianity elevates the soul, all other religions have served at least as a nursing-bottle to prevent complete spiritual death, and to furnish the means of spiritual growth. They have been as a gentle breath of wind from the heavens to keep alive the Divine Promethean spark in human nature, and to prevent the smoking wick from going entirely out. "All these religions," says S. Baring-Gould, " set themselves to respond to some craving of the head or heart of man, to satisfy some instinct, dimly felt and read ; and however various, however contradictory they were in their expression, they did fulfil their office in some sort, else they would never have lasted a day. They differ unquestionably, according to the stage of thought-development of the several peoples and nations which embraced them ; but their differences ought, if man is progressive, to be capable of arrangement in a series of progressively advancing truths. In every religion of the world is to be found distorted or exaggerated some great truth, otherwise it would never have obtained foothold ; every religious revolution has been the struggle of thought to gain another step in the ladder that reaches to heaven. (*Origin and Development of Religious Thought*, Vol. 2, p. 9.)

The Christian religion, as a medicine and a nutriment to the spiritual life of man, has the advantage, in one respect, over all others,—that it is in its nature *eclectic*. It is not in its spirit *exclusive* but is *inclusive* of that which is good and true in them all. Jesus defines the Word of God to be truth. It is the totality of all truth. So far as the sacred books of the different nations contain and record any spiritual truth, they are the Word of God, or a manifestation of the Logos,—"the light that lighteth every man that cometh into the world." The Logos, or Word, is the living principle of them all, and without it they could have had no permanent hold upon the souls of men, for "in it is life, and the life is the light of men." Christianity has in its spirit and teachings the elements of universality, and thus may properly be called the natural religion, or the religion of humanity, while other systems are adapted only to particular peoples or races. As one has said, "That which excludes or shuts out is not so great as that which takes in and receives. So Christianity has received into itself all the good of many systems,— the philosophy and arts of Greece, the laws of Rome, the mysticism of India, the monotheism of the Jews, the triad of Egypt, the war between good and evil taught by Zoroaster, the reverence for ancestors, and the conservatism of China, and the Scandinavian faith in liberty and progress. All the prophets, since the world began, and all the civilizations of the past, have, like the wise men of the east, brought their gifts to the infant Messiah. There is in this wonderful religion the power of assimilating to itself all that is true and good everywhere. It is like the sea, into which all rivers run, and yet is never full." (*Lecture by James Freeman Clarke on Essentials and Non-Essentials in Religion.*)

Jesus left no written creed, no unalterable system of ecclesiastical polity, and no fixed forms of external worship. Everything was left to be unfolded by the Spirit that was promised, the Paraclete that was to lead into all truth and duty. The Christian system is constructed on the principle of progress, and thus bears the mark of Divinity, and it cannot but administer to the healthy growth of all who receive it in its true spirit. Once in the soul, it is like the mustard grain that develops into a tree, or like a Divine leaven that transforms the whole nature. A truly catholic system

that receives into itself all that is of permanent value in the
world's science, philosophy, and religion, and that stimulates the
growth of all that is good and true in the souls of men, must have
a spiritually sanative efficiency.   It is God's "saving health,"
which the prophet prayed might be known among all nations.
(Ps. lxvii: 2.)   It is like the Apocalyptic tree of life, whose
roots drew fresh nutriment from the river of life, on the banks of
which it stood; its fruit is ever fresh and new, and the leaves of the
tree are for the healing of the nations.   (Rev. xxii: 1, 2.)   This
religion is everywhere in the Scriptures represented as a spiritual
medicine; and Jesus the Christ, as the founder and present life
of the best system of religion the world ever saw, rightfully claims
to be the Great Physician, a title the Church in all the centuries
has given him.

In the infancy of the race, and in the earliest ages of human
history, the sanative value of religion was fully recognized.   Mankind were then more in a state of nature, and governed by
instinct and intuition.   The priests were the only physicians, and
the temples were the place of cure,— a sort of spiritual pharmacy
where the body was affected and healed through the mind.   Civilization is in some sense an unnatural and artificial condition, as
was taught by Rousseau, and in it man is influenced more by
reason, which is a far more imperfect guide than instinct.   But we
must be converted and become as little children before we can
enter the kingdom of the heavens, or come into the closest sympathetic relations with the general sphere of life and light in the
world above.   When the religion of the Christ is divorced from
all the shams and counterfeits that pass current for it, and is
pruned of all that a priestly ecclesiasticism has grafted into it, and
it becomes what it was in its founder, a sympathetic union with
the living God and the ever-present angel-world, it will be the
power of God and the wisdom of God unto salvation to body and
soul.

CHAPTER V.

The fundamental ideas of all possible religions, so far as they are expressed by an intellectual belief or creed, seem to be the common possession of mankind. The radical elements of all religious belief, the essential faith of the universal church, which is older than Christianity, appear to have become a part of the original dowry of the human soul, and to have been deeply impressed upon the spiritual nature of man. St. Augustine, under the mistake that Christianity is a creed, affirms that " what is now called the Christian religion has existed among the ancients, and was not absent from the beginning of the race until Christ came in the flesh; from which time the true religion which existed already began to be called Christian. (*Augustine, Retr.* I, 13.) Religion has existed in all ages of the world, and always will exist as long as human nature remains the same. There is no absolutely new religion since the commencement of human history. There has been a singular pertinacity in the hold which the fundamental ideas of religion have had upon the human mind. In Christianity we behold the highest exhibition of religious life, and development of religious thought, which have sprung out of the nature of man according to the law of spiritual evolution. But it is not unreasonable to suppose that even Christianity itself may undergo a still higher development than the world has ever seen. Religion, as

39

represented by the Church in past ages, and by the Christian world of today, cannot be accepted as a finality. From the fruitful womb of the past will be born a still higher style of religious consciousness and spiritual life than the Church has ever realized in the brightest ages of its history.

The following remarks of Max Müller in relation to religion as an intellectual belief seem to me eminently true, and justified by the history of the human mind : "The elements and roots of religion are seen as far back as we can trace the history of man ; and the history of religion, like that of language, shows us a succession of new combinations of the same radical elements. An intuition of God, a sense of human weakness and dependence, a belief in a divine government of the world, a distinction between good and evil, and a hope of a better life,— these are the radical elements of all religions. Though sometimes hidden, they rise again and again to the surface. Though frequently distorted, they tend again and again to their perfect form." (*Essays on the Science of Religion*, p. 10.)

An examination of all the great religions of the world will clearly show that the most vital articles of faith and rules of life are the common property and inheritance of mankind, and they must have come from a common source,— a Divine inspiration, a radiation from the living Word, the light of life, the eternal Logos. Even the Christ himself is *more* a principle than a person,— not that we doubt the historic reality of his life, but we affirm that he was an embodiment of the Word, that found in him an organ of communication with mankind, and the Word is the light that lighteth every man that cometh into the world.

Justin Martyr (A.D. 139), in his Apology, uses this language : "One article of our faith then is that Christ is the first begotten of God, and we have already proved him to be the very Logos (or universal source of light and reason) of which mankind are all partakers, and therefore those who lived according to the Logos are Christians, notwithstanding they may pass with you for atheists." The Logos, or Word, which is an emanation of the

Divine Intellect to the receptive mind, is the primal source of all truth and the fountain of all mental illumination. Inspiration is not confined to the writers of the Old and New Testaments, but has been enjoyed by mankind in every age of the world, and in every clime where the life of an omnipresent God is felt. Clement of Alexandria goes so far as to affirm that "It is clear that the same God to whom we owe the Old and New Testaments gave also to the Greeks their Greek Philosophy, by which the Almighty is glorified (or his thoughts made known) among the Greeks." (*Stomata, Lib. VI., Cap. V.*)

There is a sacred and divine element in all religions that ought to command our respect; for in no age of the world has man ever been sundered from the Divine Mind and the illuminating Word that goes forth from Him. There has been, and still is, a secret yearning of the soul after Him who is the central point of our existence, and he has responded to this instinctive craving by giving life and light to men, as the sun pours its vitalizing beams into the flower that turns towards him. All souls, if they could express themselves in language, would say in the words of David, who speaks for us all, "As the heart panteth after the water brooks, so panteth my soul after thee, O God. My soul thirsteth for God, for the living God." (*Ps. xlii:* 1, 2.) Or, in the equally expressive language of one of the hymns of the Vedas, "Yearning for Him, the Far-Seeing, my thoughts move onwards, as kine move to their pastures."

Christianity, or the system of Christ, differs from all other religions in making the union of man with God a more *practical* reality, and not a mere speculative hypothesis. In the Gospel of John we have the best presentation of the ideas of Christ and the essential nature of Christianity. The preface which exhibits the doctrine of the Logos, or Word, the Light and the Life communicable directly to men's souls, is to be taken as the essence, the fixed standing-ground of Jesus the Christ, in all his discourses and teaching. It is the spirit, the innermost root, of the whole doctrine and philosophy of Jesus. The other Gospels contain a somewhat dry chronicle of the *doings* of the Christ,—especially is this true of the first and second,—and of his conversations with the sensuous multitude, in which he brings down celestial truth veiled in parabolical representations, so that some spark of its heavenly fire might reach and animate their carnal minds.   The Gospels of Matthew and Mark push the *miracles* of Jesus into prominence, which are of secondary importance.   A miracle, in the ordinary theological use of the term, as an event outside of the ordinary laws of nature, can by no possibility be made to prove anything but itself.   It is an isolated fact, standing alone, and having no fixed connection with the uniform mode of the Divine procedure.   A doctrine that requires a miracle to prove it is not true.   There is a natural adaptation of the mind of man to the reception of all real truth.   Spiritual truth requires no external evidence, nor does it admit of it.   It shines by its own inherent, Divine light. It is axiomatic, or self-evident, for you can find nothing clearer than itself with which to construct an argument to prove it.   It is very generally supposed that John had the writings of the other evangelists before him, and only designed to supply what they had omitted.   It is thought to be the supplementary Gospel.   "If that is the case," as Fichte has said, "then in our opinion the supplement is the best part of the whole, and John's predecessors had passed over that precisely which was of essential importance."   (*Way Toward the Blessed Life, Lecture VI.*)

The *conscious* realization of a life in God, and not as a speculative thesis to be argued and disputed, is the fundamental thought in the system taught by the Christ,—a union with God so complete in every department of our being that we can say: "The Father is in me and I am in the Father," and "I and my Father are one."   A Christian Pantheism which does not destroy the individuality of man, nor separate God from the universe which he continually creates out of Himself, nor sunder Him from the activities of the human soul by the intervention of second causes, is the highest development of religious thought.   An intuitive perception of the unity of the human with the Divine existence is the highest attainable spiritual intelligence, and one which raises man above disease and the possibility of death. Before Jesus, this knowledge had nowhere existed; and through the dreary, dismal centuries of the history of the Church, it has been covered with a deep layer of externalism, and well nigh lost sight of. But a great original truth has a Divine vitality in it, and cannot die, because it becomes a part of the life of God in the soul of man.

Such was the conjunction of Jesus the Christ with the Deity that a sympathetic union with him brings us into a receptive relation with the Eternal God and his Life. At every moment of time, he who is thus linked to the Godhead comes into a present possession of Eternity, and lives everlasting life.

The life of Jesus has been viewed by the Christian world as an unattainable ideal of a perfect human development, after which we should strive, but with no hope of reaching the goal towards which we were to run, or of hitting the mark at which we are expected to aim. His character and activity are presented to us by the Church as an example having the force of a moral law, and yet we are told that they lie beyond the possibility of a full realization. This is thought to be especially so as to his union with God, his perfect conquest of evil, and his power over diseases of mind and body. In consequence of this view, the Church has come so far short of the true Christian standard, for men will make but a feeble, sickly effort—a mere pretence to exertion—in aiming at the impossible, and in seeking for what is deemed unattainable. But a slight glance at the teaching of the Christ will convince us how far this doctrine—which was at the same time the result as well as the cause of the spiritual poverty of the Church—was from the ideas of him who introduced Christianity into the world, not as a speculative metaphysical system, but as a practical religion and attainable state. To follow Christ, that is, to reproduce his life and experience, was made by him the essential condition of discipleship. (Mat. xvi: 24.) Every true disciple or scholar was expected to be a repetition of the Master, and not a faint and

unrecognizable imitation or caricature of him.   Wherever Christ
stood was one greater than the temple of Solomon. (Mat. xii.: 6.)
So every human body was made to be a living temple of God, as
was the personality of Jesus.

That the union of God with Jesus is something unattainable by
the soul of man is contradicted by the prayer of Christ (John
xvii: 21–23), where he prays that all his disciples in every age
might be one with God, as he and the Father were one.   The
works that he performed, which have been called *miracles* by an
unauthorized substitution of a word of Latin origin for the Greek
term employed in the Gospels, were to be repeated by his followers   " Verily, verily, I say unto you, he that believeth on me, the
works that I do shall he do also, and greater works than these
shall he do, because I go to my Father."   (John xiv: 12.)   In
proportion as a man is consciously united to God, he comes into
conjunction with the central Life and Power of the universe, and a
Divine energy will burst forth from him, and exhibit itself in works
of healing the souls and bodies of men.   An individual soul in a
state of union with God, and with its natural powers augmented
and reinforced by a conjunction with the Central Life, will expend
its activity in doing the works of God, as naturally as water
descends from a higher to a lower level.   It is a belief that has
been more or less current in the world that one person may be controlled by another, and the phenomena of animal magnetism has
proved it.   When a spirit out of the body takes possession of one
in the flesh it is called *obsession.*   This has been witnessed in all
ages of the world, and was common in the time of Jesus.   But it
is self-evident that we may be influenced by a good as well as by a
bad spirit.   The union of the soul with God as a *practical reality* is
the central idea of Christianity.   The true Christian is one who is
obsessed of God, if we might be allowed to use the term in that sense,
and he acts from an inward Divine impulse in resisting evil and
doing good.   As Paul expresses it, " he is strengthened with might
by God's spirit in the inner man, and is filled with all the fullness of
God, and is thus strong in the Lord and in the power of his

might." (Eph. iii: 16, 19. Eph. vi: 10.) "Nearer, my God to Thee" is the song that leads to a higher wisdom and to a power from above as surely as the Marseillaise hymn nerved the arm to victory in the struggle for freedom.

Jesus introduced into the current of the world's thought, from which it had disappeared, the idea of the nearness of a higher realm of being which he calls "The kingdom of the heavens," — an orderly world of spirit-life that is intermingled with this, and that acts and reacts upon it That higher world does not merely border on this, it is everywhere present in this. It was one of the aims of the life of Jesus to bring the two realms of life, that are not separated by distance of space, into *conscious* contact. It was the key note of his preaching. "Know ye that the kingdom of God is nigh at hand." (Luke xxi: 31.) In the Church the moral force of this primitive Christian idea has been well nigh lost sight of, but will again be restored. An ever-present spiritual realm, with God as its Central Life, is being interfused with this world, as the light of the sun is mingled with the darkness at break of day. It is coming into available nearness to men's souls, as a source of inspiration to a higher knowledge and nobler deeds. A religious or scientific system that leaves this out becomes like an ocean without water. In the mud at the bottom the mind may find some intellectual treasures, but they are only relics from the wreck of higher truths. Materialism, in religion or science, can never satisfy the soul of man any more than the husks that the swine did eat could the belly of the prodigal son. The ancient Persian Magi, and the Chaldeans, who represent the creed of an older civilization, believed, according to Cudworth, that there was a certain *vital sympathy* between the superior and lower orders of being. This is demonstrably true by psychometry. Communion with God involves communion with the angel-world, for there is a common Life that connects all existences in one chain of being.

On this subject Kant remarks: "I confess I am much inclined to assert the existence of immaterial beings in this world, and to class my soul itself in the catalogue of these beings."

"We can imagine the possibility of the existence of immaterial beings without the fear of being refuted, though, at the same time, without the hope of being able to demonstrate their existence by reason.   Such spiritual beings would exist in space, and the latter notwithstanding would remain penetrable for material beings, because their presence would imply an acting power in space, but not a *filling* of it, i.e., a resistance causing solidity."

"It is, therefore, as good as demonstrated, or it could easily be proved, if we were to enter into it at some length, or, better still, *it will be proved in the future* — I do not know where and when — that also in this life the human soul stands in an indissoluble communion with all the immaterial beings of the spiritual world; that it produces effects in them, and in exchange receives impressions from them, without, however, becoming humanly conscious of them so long as all stands well."   (*Kant's Works*, Vol. VII., p. 32.)

CHAPTER VI.

"As science progresses, it draws nearer in all its forms to the proof of the spiritual origin of force, that is, of the Divine immanence in natural law." (*Biology, by Joseph Cook*, p. 320.) If matter is entirely passive, or, in other words, if inertia is one of its essential properties,— and this is a fundamental principle in physical science,— then it cannot be self-moved.   Its condition always sustains to some power, distinct from itself, the relation of an effect to a cause.   It requires a force, outside of itself, or at least something that does not belong to itself, to generate its movements and all the phenomena it exhibits.   The material universe is the periphery of a circle of which God is the living Centre, and nothing occurs in the boundary that does not by a creative and controlling influence proceed from the inmost.

God was not transiently present in nature, that is, in a mere creative moment, and has now left the world in a state of orphanage, bereft of a deific influence and care, but he is *immanent* in nature or permanently present, as Spinoza affirmed.   On this subject extremes meet.   Here Joseph Cook and Theodore Parker find a divine point of union in their apparently antagonistic systems. The latter affirms that God is not idly but actively present in nature,— that he penetrates and pervades the world as a spiritual force.   "Our Father worketh hitherto, and for this reason nature

works, and so has done since its creation. There is no spot on
which the hoary foot of Time has trod that is not instinct with
God's activity. He is the ground of nature,—what is permanent
in the passing, what is real in the apparent. All nature is but
an exhibition of God to the senses,—the veil of smoke on which his
shadow falls, the dew drop in which the heaven of his omnipotence
is poorly imaged. Endless and without beginning flows forth the
stream of Divine influence that encircles and possesses the all of
things." (*Discourse on Matters Pertaining to Religion*, p. 161.)

There is truth in the old theory of an *Animus Mundi*, or Soul
of the World, for God sustains to the material universe a relation
analogous to that of mind and body in man. All of nature's
action is God's action, and the uniform mode of the Divine activity
and procedure is what we call a law of nature. All theological
systems, and all religious philosophies, meet here and embrace,—
Spinoza and Cudworth, Hegel and Schleiermacher, Berkeley and
Locke, Renan and Neander, Fichte and Tholuch, Parker and
Channing. They all believe, however cautiously they may express
it, that nature is an apparition of the Deity,—God in a mask.
This gives to this great truth, that God is the only Reality of
nature, the character of an intuition, or inspiration, which means
the same.

But is it reasonable to suppose that God is everywhere present
in matter and not in mind or spirit? .The realm of mind is one
degree nearer to the Central Life than matter, and it is here that
the Divine Presence is most clearly seen, and His activity dis-
played. If He is present in matter, and is the hidden force in all its
phenomena, then the law of analogy would require his immanence
in spirit also. If He is immanently active, and thus totally and
essentially present in every material atom of creation, then He is
universally present in all mind. Even *fetishism*, or the adoration
of external objects, rises to the dignity of being, in some measure,
an instinctive acknowledging of a Divine Presence in nature, as in
the worship of idols, the sun and moon, rivers and mountains, or
the worship of the *host*, or bread of the Sacrament, in the Catholic

Church. The external object was viewed by the better class as a symbol or manifestation of a Divine power in nature, although this intellectual elevation was seldom reached, but only dimly *felt* by the multitude. But God's ubiquity is not confined to matter and to space, but can be predicated of all spirit as well. As His presence in what we call nature, not as a slumbering, inoperative and latent power, but as an active force, is the basis of His direct influence there, so His presence in the soul is the foundation of our belief in His constant influence there, and is the source of a never-ceasing inspiration. He acts through the natural powers of the soul, which are perpetually derived from Him,— instinct, reason, conscience, and intuition. " Through these channels, and by means of a law, certain, regular, and universal as gravitation, God inspires men, and makes revelation of truth, for is not truth as much a phenomenon of God as the motion of matter? Therefore, if God be omnipresent and omniactive, this inspiration is no miracle, but a regular mode of God's action on conscious spirit, as is gravitation on unconscious matter. It is not a rare condescension of God, but a universal uplifting of man. To obtain a knowledge of duty, a man is not sent away outside of himself to ancient documents for the only rule of faith and practice; the Word is very nigh him, even in his heart, and by this Word he is to try all documents whatever. Inspiration, like God's omnipresence, is not limited to the few writers claimed by the Jews, Christians, and Mohammedans, but is coëxtensive with the race. As God fills all space, so all spirit; as He influences and constrains unconscious and necessitated matter, so He inspires and helps free and conscious man." (*Parker's Discourse of Matters Pertaining to Religion*, p. 203.)

The above is the view of one of the most profoundly religious men of modern times, however much he was misunderstood. In a certain sense mind is no more self moved than matter. There is an *inertia* of spirit as well as of matter. From the possession of free will mind has the *appearance* of an automatic activity, but every thought, or, at least, the ability to think, and every volitional effort requires a Divine aid as much as the movement of a planet in the heavens, or the motion of my arm. Paul declares that there is no such thing as self-originated thought,—that we are not able to think anything of ourselves, but all our sufficiency is of God. (2 Cor. iii: 5.) All thought, and the advent of an idea to the soul, are in reality an inspiration. What we call the Bible, or, as it means, the Book, is not God's last word, or a farewell, to the human soul when He was about to retire to an unapproachable remoteness and unhailing distance, and to withdraw Himself from the minds of men into the silent and unfathomable depths of His own being. The Divine Life can never become dormant and latent, or pass into a comatose state. His life is action, and His activity is the only life. God is as near to our souls as the material world is to our bodies. Our being forever touches His, and separation from Him would be annihilation. Our life is a circle, or, at least, a point somewhere in the inclosure of the Divine Being, and we are always in speaking nearness to Him and He to us. The voice of God and the Word that came to the prophets was never designed to be a forgotten sound in the soul of man,—a thing of history, a Divine phenomenon of a past age, but a reality of the eternal *now*, the ever-living present. The *Word of the Lord*, which was the primitive Hebrew form of expressing the creative will and thought of God, and the communication of His thoughts to men by a direct impression upon the mind, was never intended to be like a repeating echo that was to expend its audible force in a few brief centuries, and then die away in an eternal silence, but man, as an image of God, must forever, in a finite measure, repeat the thoughts and activity of the Divine Mind. We cannot *live* or exhibit any of the phenomena of life without God, and He cannot *ex-ist* without us. Our life is bound up in His, and a constant *inspiration* from the primal source of being follows from the necessary relation of the perpetually-created to an ever-present Creator. To the truly spiritual mind an *atheist*, or a man or thing without God, is an impossible conception. It would be like a *something* or a somewhat pro-

ceeding from nothing, or an effect without a cause,— a contradiction of the intuitive truth, *ex nihilo nihil fit.* The highest functions of the human mind, such as reason, instinct, intuition, are a
constant inspiration of God, and there is nothing of permanent
value in the whole realm of literature and art, in law and medicine, that is not an expression of God's thought and feeling,— the
laws of Minos, of Moses, of Numa, Lycurgus, and Rhadamanthus
the poetry of Homer and Isaiah, the works of Phidias and
Michael Angelo, the patriotism of Washington and Lincoln, and the
philosophy of Socrates and Plato, and the religious systems of Confucius, Zoroaster, Buddha, Jesus, and even Mohammed. This is
only reducing the religious *creed* of all men to a fact. It is making real what men pray for, if they pray at all. For it is as natural for the religious nature of man to pray for a Divine influence
and aid as it is to breathe. A prayer that does not spring from a
desire and expectation of receiving an *influx* from God is a solemn
mockery, a cloud without rain, a well without water. But we
should never forget that health or wholeness, as the word signifies,
the perfect union of a sound mind with a body in correspondence
with it, is a Divine gift, an inspiration of God. It is, as the
devout Scougal would call it, "the life of God in the soul of
man." In fact, God and man cannot be separated, but it lies
within the compass of that apparently self-acting power we call free-
will, or faith, or imagination, to give *intensity* to our consciousness of this truth, and to make it available as a redemptive influence and a spiritual medicine.

CHAPTER VII.

SAVING AND HEALING GRACE, OR MEDICINE A SACRAMENT.

In the foregoing chapter it has been shown that God is present in nature and is the primal source of all its active powers. The material world and all it contains is a perpetual manifestation and revelation of the Divine Being, both in its greatest and least parts and particles. Paul teaches that "the invisible things of Him from the creation of the world are clearly seen, being understood by the things that are made, *even* His eternal power and Godhead." (Rom. i : 20.) All the forces of nature are but manifestations of a Divine energy. This is true of the action of medicines on the human body. Hence all curative agents are of the nature of a sacrament or " means of grace."

There is an underlying truth in the Church dogma of grace, though limited in its application. Grace has been defined to mean favor. In the religious parlance of the Church, it is made to signify an unmerited favor or gift. In the Epistle to the Ephesians, Paul, in a single verse, gives us the whole doctrine of grace. " By grace are ye saved, through faith, and that not of yourselves : it is the gift of God." (Eph. ii : 8.) The idea of grace, as it exists in the mind of most people independent of all theological definitions, is that of a help, or influence, imparted to us directly or indirectly through means, from the Divine Being. It is an augmentation of our powers by a force given us from our vital relation to God, so that we are able to do, or to bear, what otherwise would be impossible to us. By grace we are saved or *healed* morally and physically.

52

Grace, as a Divine principle in nature, and as a spiritually sanative force, may be imparted to us directly from God, or through some
intervening medicine. That it may come to us through more external means is the idea on which the doctrine of the efficacy of the
sacraments is based. But it is a mental law that it is only through
faith that any benefit is received from these. In the Catholic
Church extreme unction has often turned out a means of cure.
But, without faith, a few drops of oil has no healing efficacy, and
one piece of bread, or a few drops of water or wine, is no better than
any other bread or water or wine. If our faith in God and the
universality of His life — the idea that we live in God and that
everything else has its being in Him — is to us a religious consciousness and a certainty, then we have no need of any sacramental or intervening agency between us and Him. Crutches are
of no use, but rather a hindrance, to one who is not lame. The
Divine Love and Life need not to be materialized, or come to us
through any outward forms of manifestation. To the ignorant
Catholic, or the feeble-minded Protestant, the sacramental elements,
the bread and the wine, represent the presence of God, and are the
visible medium through which saving grace is imparted. The
more active their *faith* in these outward symbols the more benefit they receive from them, for they are saved by a grace of which
they are made receptible through faith. It is the same with medicine ; for if one cannot come into a direct communication with the
Infinite Life, let him connect himself with the Divine Being and
his " saving health " by means of visible and material remedies.
It matters little what they are, provided they bring the patient
into communicative contact with the primal source of life and
health. The sacraments are supposed to be a spiritual medicine,
or a means through which the Divine Life is made communicable
to us. In them, as in all medicinal preparations, God descends
from the unapproachable, and, to many minds, the inconceivable
region of the absolute, to the lowest depths of the spiritual needs
f men. They are an exteriorization of the Love and Life of God,
and thus it brings them within the grasp of the sensuous mind, so

that they may become appropriable to that range of the intellect
But to the spiritually enlightened mind God is everywhere, and
consequently in all things, and there is not a point in the wide
universe where we may not come into communicative contact with
the whole undivided and indivisible Deity.   His presence is not
recognized by the spiritual mind only in the sacramental elements
of bread and wine, but everything becomes a sacrament of good
and means of saving grace to us.   It is the office of Christianity
to make general what has been considered as limited and partial.
Thus the sacraments are not the only point in the material universe
where man can meet God.   It is better to meet Him there than
nowwhere.   Every material thing may be to us as God made visible and accessible, and consequently as a sacrament, -- the food we
eat, the water we drink, the medicine we take, every object of
beauty and grandeur around us, the mountain summit, the flowing
stream, the dew-gemmed flower, the waving field of grain, the
summer cloud, the morning song of the birds, the vernal shower,
and the autumn leaf,—all these and many more are, or may be,
sacraments to the soul and means of communion with God.

As God is the only Life, everything that has any therapeutic
value or healing influence is of the nature of a sacrament,—that
is, it is the communication of a Divine saving grace through an
external medium which in itself is of secondary importance.   We
need the Divine help every moment, but never so consciously feel
it as when sick and unhappy.   And that through the medium of
which the desired aid comes to us is to us a sacrament, let the
remedial agency belong to whatever school of medicine it may.

Protestantism reduces the sacraments to two; but the Papal
Church has been more liberal and given us seven channels through
which a saving or spiritually healing grace may flow.   But a genuine Christianity is *Catholic* in its spirit and nature, which, as the
name primarily signifies, is that which is universal and inclusive, and is opposed to that which is particular and exclusive, and
comprehends all that is good and true in every religion, past, present, and future.   Its sacraments are not fixed at two or seven, but

are all those external things that are or can be the means through which a spiritual aid and influence may come to us, and through which the feeble and ignorant may mount upward, as on a ladder, to communication with the Divine Life.

In the light of this truth, it is easy to see that medicine is a sacrament to those whose faith needs some external support on which to lean, and the more spiritual the remedy the more of a sacramental efficiency it has in it. For it is an eternal and necessary truth, that it is by grace or an impartation of living force from God that we are saved and healed, and that comes to us through *faith*. Any remedial agency that places the sick in body or mind in vital communication with the Central Life is a holy sacrament and means of grace. The word sacrament (from *sacramentum*) originally signified the oath that a Roman soldier took of fidelity to the government, but has been employed in Christian literature as "an outward and visible sign of an inward and spiritual grace," or influence. All material things are only the outward expression or correspondence of some spiritual reality or essence which represents it to the senses. In the case of a medicine, it is the spiritual essence of the drug that gives it all its curative value and its power over that *dynamic* disturbance which, according to the system of Hahnemann, constitutes the disease for which it is given. This makes it of the nature of a sacrament. If a drug is not this, it has no therapeutic efficacy. This gives to the administration of medicines a sacred character, and the real physician is elevated to the dignity of a priest, and even a *vicar* of God. As God is love, and, as Swedenborg taught a century ago, love is the life of man, all remedies administered by the hand of kindness, and are charged with its spirit, have an efficiency and spiritual power that they could not otherwise possess. They are, when viewed in the light of these truths, no longer like the goods and chattels that the merchant sells behind the counter, but they have a principle of spiritual life in them, and the physician executes the function of the priesthood in its divine reality. The ministerial and medical professions should never have come under the influence of the modern tendency to a division of labor, but should have remained one; and the priest, as in the older civilizations, should have been the physician of both soul and body.   It is in accordance with the *usus loquendi* of the New Testament, or usual mode of speaking, to employ the words *to heal* and *to save* as equivalent and interchangeable expressions.   "The prayer of faith shall save (or heal) the sick." (James v: 15.)   To the blind man, whom he restored to sight, Jesus said: "Thy faith hath saved thee." (Luke xviii: 42.)   The Greek verb *sozo*, answering to our English word to save, is usually rendered to heal or make whole.   (See Mat. ix: 21, 22; Mark v: 23, 28, 34; Mark vi: 56, and many other places.)   A scheme of salvation that leaves out the restoration of the body to health, as is done in the churches of today, comes short of the primitive *Christian* idea, and brings the pulpit under the reproof of the prophet, that it heals the hurts of humanity slightly or in part only. (Jer. vi: 14; Jer. viii: 11.)   A religious system that sunders what God has joined together, and does not furnish a medicine for soul and body both, will be deprived of more than half its salutary influence.   The Church should at once come back to the original Christian method. It is well known that no missionaries are more successful than those who combine with the preaching of the gospel a successful medical practice.

The fundamental error in religion has been in separating God too much from nature.   Nature, as the word means, is that which is perpetually begotten and born of God, and is permanently attached to Him.   There is not on one side a solitary God, and on the other an isolated universe, for the Creator is incessantly incarnated in each of His creatures, and they become each in a degree manifestations of Him, and their life is His Life.   According to this, as Saisset has said, God sleeps, as it were, in the mineral, dreams in the animal, and comes to consciousness in man.   The presence of God is not confined to the narrow limits of the holy of holies in the temple, where the Jewish anthropomorphism (or view of God as a man) located Him on earth, nor to some distant world in the starry heavens, where the childish thought of the

Church has placed Him. There is in all created things (what shall I call it?) a Divine internal virtue or essence. All things go forth from God into an outward expression, but never break away from Him, or lose their connection with Him. Under this view of the Divine Being and his Ex-istence in nature, every common bush is ablaze with God, as was that of Horeb to Moses; every mountain is as holy as Sinai; every river as sacred as the Jordan; and the food we eat, the water we drink, the air we breathe, and the medicine we take have in them the sanctity and virtue of a sacrament, and may be to us a means of grace.

CHAPTER VIII.

ORIGIN AND CONSERVATION OF LIFE-FORCE.

It is now a well-established principle in philosophy that all life is a force, and it is equally certain to the intuitive reason that all force in the universe is a manifestation of some primal Life, some central living Power, call it by what name we may. We may consider it a fundamental truth that life is a spiritual force, and not, as formerly supposed, a fluid, but it is a force different from the ordinary forces of the physical universe. It is now admitted that all force is indestructible, though it may be changed into other forms of manifestation, and this constitutes the highest scientific evidence of the immortality of man.

The grand source and central fountain of all physical energy is supposed to be the sun. Here is the origin of all motion on the globe we inhabit. Take that away, and universal darkness, stillness, and death would be the result in the physical world we inhabit. All the movements of nature would cease at once, the streams would no longer flow, the tides would come to a perpetual pause in their inward and outward motions, the successions of the seasons and the alternations of day and night would come to an end, and all the one hundred thousand species of plants would perish; and Byron's dread picture of a sunless world, in his poem of Darkness, would be a realized fact and not a fancy. Scientific men have felt the need of some *central spiritual power* that should sustain the same relation to the souls of men that the sun holds to the material world. On this subject Prof. Trowbridge remarks: "Looking, therefore, at the problem of life and mind from a purely scientific point of view, we seem to require a source from which can come the principle of life, and which can create moral and intellectual growth in suitable soil and under fitting conditions. In case of the energy derived from the sun's heat, we have a cycle of operations in which there is no annihilation of force. If we grant that there is a source of life and mind independent of mere chemical changes produced by the sun's heat, and if we adhere to the notion of the conservation of force applied to this principle of life and mind, we are led to adopt the idea of a cycle of operations in which there is no annihilation of spiritual force. The doctrine of the existence of the spirit after physical death seems to me not to be foreign to the scientific ideas of the conservation of force, which have now obtained such complete supremacy in the science of physics; or to the doctrines of Darwin, which are accepted by so large a body of eminent naturalists. Without the sun there would be an annihilation of force. When energy is dissipated, we find the sun exalting it again by processes which we cannot completely follow. The idea of a great source of life and mind, the prototype of our physical sun, which sets in motion a vast scheme for the survival of the fittest and the exaltation of energy in vast cycles, is not inconsistent with the doctrine of the New Testament, and seems to be required in a philosophical theory which shall endeavor to account for the differences in that great spiritual world which are continually suggested to the human mind by the various types of mental growth." (*Popular Science Monthly*, April, 1877.)

This primary and exhaustless source of life and spiritual energy we have in the sun of the spiritual world, as described by Swedenborg in the treatise on the Divine Love and Wisdom. He affirms that the proximate emanation of the Divine Essence assumes to the inhabitants of that realm of life the form of a sun, and that it sustains the same creative relation to that world that our solar orb does to its planetary system. This is one of the original concep

tions, or revelations, of Swedenborg, and which, under a modification of language, is being adopted by scientific men. The "solar
radiance," and the "sun above the sun," which are favorite expressions of the Rev. Joseph Cook in his lectures on the relation of
science and religion, are borrowed from the Scandinavian Seer.
From this one source come forth all life and spiritual force, and
all creations. No life can perish, because it is uncreated, and is
eternally supplied from this central fountain.

Can we have access to it, and come into voluntary receptive
communication with it? It is the source of all inspiration of life
and light in the souls of men, and what is called the Word of the
Lord that *came* to the prophets, and the Holy Spirit in the system
of the Christ, are modifications of it. We see its most intense
form of reception in the transfiguration of Jesus on Mount Tabor,
and in the shining of the face of Moses. In fact, we are never
sundered from it, for it is to us "the light of life." If we can say
with Whittier,

> " And all the windows of the soul
>   I open to the sun,"

we may come into a conscious appropriation of its life and light.

The existence of God and His ceaseless influence is as necessary in
science and philosophy as it is in theology. Every scientist can
say of science as Robespierre said of France : " If there is no God,
we must make one; France cannot do without God." Prof.
Lionel S. Beal, one of the highest authorities in the use of the
microscope in histology and physiology, in his " Theories of Vitality
and Religious Thought," says, " that all vital power affects the
molecules of matter, and makes them take up certain positions, and
so arranges them that certain definite combinations shall take place.
This vital power is capable of causing the particles it guides to be
so arranged as to form at length complex, and it may be very
elaborate, structures, performing the most delicate work, and in a
most perfect manner." All this, as I. H. Fichte has demonstrated,
is effected by an unconscious, or, as he calls it, a preconscious, men-

tal action, a subject we shall have occasion to discuss hereafter.
Beal affirms that "mental action is the highest manifestation of vital
power of which we have any cognizance," and that it is reasonable
to conceive that the highest form of vital power of which we have
knowledge and experience is in some way closely related to the
Deity. (*Theories of Vitality and Religious Thought*, pp. 92, 97.)
This is only a reproduction in other language of the doctrine of
Paul that "in Him we live, and move, and have our being."

One thing is certain that the vital functions are performed without any conscious volitional effort on our part. A state of unconsciousness and of perfect passivity is not necessarily, and as a matter of fact, a cessation of existence and of mental activity. We
still live. In a dreamless sleep, and in a trance, we are unconscious of the external world, and have no voluntary control of the
bodily organs, and yet we are alive. The spiritual principle and
force that animate the body, and are the spring of all its vital
activity, still move the physiological machinery with undeviating
regularity, and with an unerring intelligence. Something beside
our own conscious intelligence and a vital activity not under the
control of our individual will, a higher life in our personal existence, must then reside within us, and there must be some power
distinct from our volitions that executes these important functions.
Call it by what name you please,— we will not dispute about words,
— it will ultimately refer itself to our connection with the Divine
Being, the common Life of the universe.

The primary movements of the body, and those on which all
others depend, viz., respiration and the action of the heart, are for
the most part involuntary and unconscious movements, yet they
take place according to a fixed law, and are under the guidance of
intelligence. The force that creates and maintains these movements must lie in the preconscious region of the soul's activity,
and this must be related most intimately to the Divine Life. It
is the nature and property of spirit to produce motion, and of matter to receive it. Dr. Darwin says, "I am ready to allow that
the ultimate cause of all motion is immaterial, that is, God"
(*Zoonomia*, Vol. I., Sec. 14.)

It is a truth that science in the future will be compelled to
recognize, that we live in God and He in us.   Yet the more closely
we are consciously united to God, the more *real* becomes our own
life, and the more distinctly defined to our perception is our own
individuality.   For as God has life in Himself, so He *gives* to us
to have life in ourselves.   In His infinite love, and the exuberance
of His goodness, He imparts life to us so freely and fully that it
requires an effort to make it seem otherwise than a self-originated
life of our own.

Creation is a genesis, or begetting, and the life of the Creator is
prolonged, extended, multiplied, and manifested in the beings that
go forth from Him.   The primary meaning of the word creation,
in all languages, is that of an act of generation.   It seems to be
deeply imbedded in the consciousness of mankind that creation is
a genesis or begetting.   Hence the first book of the Pentateuch
of Moses, though without a title in the Hebrew, was named by the
Septuagint translators, Genesis, from γεννάω, to procreate, because
it was supposed to give an account of the creation of the world
and of man.   In the preface of the Johannean Gospel, where it is
said that all things were created by the Word, or the Divine
Thought, the verb is γίνομαι, to be born, as creation is represented as a birth.   The Hebrew *bara* signifies not only to create
but primarily to bring forth, to give birth to.   The Saxon word
beget (from *be* and *getan*) signifies not only the generative act, but
more literally to cause to exist.   That the generating principle of
creation, or that which causes all things to *ex*-ist, or come to a
manifested being, is the Divine Word or Thought of God is
clearly stated in the Scriptures.   (Ps. xxxiii: 6; John i: 3; 2
Pet. iii: 5.)   It is also recognized in common language in the
use of the word *conception.*   To conceive signifies not only the
vitalizing of an ovarian germ, but also to form in the mind, or to
think.   In Pneumatology, or the science of spirit, when we have a
sensation of an object, the idea which is awakened is called a *perception.*   When the same object is presented to the mind in
thought, it is denominated *conception.*   It is then a spiritual *gene-*

sis, a mental procreation. By thought we *beget* it, that is, get it to be, or cause it to exist. But in both cases the thought is the inmost reality of the thing, and is all that of which the mind knows anything. For, as Plato taught, the only objects of knowledge are ideas. God conceived the world, or generated it from Himself, by thought, and a thought is never disconnected from the mind that thinks. When a thought assumes an outward form, so as to be conceivable by the mind, it is a word or thing, which, in the Hebrew language, are one and the same. Plato and Hegel both agree with Swedenborg in making the Word or Thought of God the verimost reality and the verimost essential in the universe, or, as the latter expresses it: "The very real itself or the very essential itself of the universe" (*Arcana Celestia*, 5272), where the idea struggles to find an appropriate form of outward expression.

The inmost ground of all beings and things is Divine. It is what is called in the first chapter of Genesis, and the first chapter of the Johannean Gospel, the *beginning*, the first principle, or proximate out-going of the Divine Life. This principle is the inner essence of all things, because they have the *radix* of their being in God. Their tap-root extends downward to the Divine Essence, and springs from it. Consequently, all souls, as to their inmost self, finding their *immediate* principle, beginning, or ground of existence in God are *consubstantial* with Him, and also with one another. In and from this first principle ($\dot{\epsilon}\nu$ $\alpha\varrho\chi\tilde{\eta}$) God created and ever creates the world and all that is in it; or, as it is in the Latin Vulgate of the first verse of Genesis, *in principio creavit Deus*, in the beginning God created, which has no reference to time. He creates all things in this first principle by the Word, or expressed Thought of the Divine Mind. This Word, as it was represented by the Christ, is *the beginning of the creation of God*, or that which is the beginning and substance, or underlying reality, of all things. (Col. i: 15; Rev. iii: 14.) Because all things are manifestations of this one principle is the reason why all are as one, and the state of the least effects the whole; or as Whittier, in his "Quaker of the Olden Time," says: —

" With that deep insight which detects
    All great things in the small,
He knows how each man's life affects
    The spiritual life of all."

In the system of Hegel the underlying reality of all existence, or that from which all manifested being springs, is the Divine Reason. By him reason is viewed as substance as well as Infinite Power, underlying all the natural and spiritual life it originates, or that by which and in which all reality has its being and subsistence. It is the Infinite Energy of the universe; it is the infinite complex of things, their entire essence and truth, which amounts to about the same thing as Swedenborg's doctrine that God created all things by the Divine Truth. (See *Hegel's Philosophy of History*, Bohn's edition, pp. 9, 10.) In the philosophy of Schopenhauer (in his great work, " World and Will,") this underlying principle of existence is Will, but will as a force unconscious of itself, and separate from a Divine personality, which makes it atheism, which he openly professes. By a misunderstanding of Buddhism,— which he accepts as the oldest and best religion,— his system is an idealism that leaves out God. For as there is in the universe only the All and the nothing, if you subtract God from it there is nothing left.

In Hartmann's philosophy, he gives to the force that originates and actuates the world and all things in it the indefinite name of the *Unconscious*. This includes both will and intelligence, but acting blindly, and, as it seems, separate from personality, which is a contradiction and impossibility. In the system which I adopt, the Logos, the Word, the Divine Thought, is that which creates and governs all things, and the universe as a whole, and in its parts is a manifestation of it, and a permanent expression of it. In a way analogous to this, when an artist thinks or imagines a landscape, it is an ideal and real creation of it, and lacks only a permanent expression on the plane of sense which God gives to his creative thoughts.

CHAPTER IX.

Everywhere in the Jewish and Christian Scriptures our relation to God is represented as a vital one. This idea was not pushed to such prominence in the Greek philosophy, but is one which the science of the present age tends to demonstrate. That there is a God is a necessity of thought, for we cannot conceive of the finite without at the same time having the idea of the infinite. Time limited leads to the conception of unlimited time, or endless duration. Space bounded and definite suggests the thought of boundless space or immensity. The same is true of wisdom, goodness, and power. Thus, as Cousin, the French metaphysician, shows, the finite necessarily leads to the conception of the Infinite. Thus, the prevalence of theoretical atheism to any great extent will be an impossibility. The existence of God is a necessary truth and a fundamental verity of the intuitive reason. But the fundamental idea of Christianity as a system of religious philosophy, and one that distinguishes it from all other religions of the world, is the prominence it gives to the consciousness of God within, the incarnation of God in man, the indwelling of the Deity in the inmost depths of the human soul. But He does not reside there as an inoperative principle, or as a metaphysical idea, but as the hidden spring of our life, the very ground of our existence, so that without this connection of our souls with Him, our own existence, since it is not eternal and self-derived, and all our activity of body and mind, would be an impossibility.   Paul, as the representative of Christianity, affirms before the supreme court of the Athenian Republic that "in Him we live, and move, and have our being, and that it is He who giveth life, and breath, and all things;" and he quotes the poet Aratus to show that this is a truth recognized by the religious consciousness of the world: "for we are all His offspring."   We are children of God, that is, our existence is derived or springs from His, and is continued or perpetuated by our filial relation to Him.   (Acts xvii: 25–28.)

This must have sounded strange to those who looked for God in something without, and not in the depths of their own being.   In the city of Athens there were thirty thousand idols, and, as one has said, it was easier to find a god than a man, but it was only an intensifying of the tendency to externalize the Deity, which we see even at the present time.

The doctrine of Paul was drawn from the Jewish Scriptures, or, at least, is in perfect harmony with their teaching.   In one of the Psalms of David there is a passage equally explicit as that of the utterance of Paul before the Areopagus: "With Thee is the fountain of life; in Thy light shall we see light." (Ps. xxxvi: 9.) Here our life is viewed as a stream that issues from the inexhaustible fount of being, and consequently having no independent existence of its own.

Under a clear apprehension of the intuitive truth that life, and consequently health, which is only a mode of life, are from the primal source of being, the inspired Hebrew poet prays that God's "saving health"—an expression full of meaning—might be known among all nations. (Ps. lxvii: 2.) Under the influence of an influx of life and light from the world above, the Psalmist was raised out of the plane of Jewish selfishness and exclusiveness, and prays that an emanation of the Divine Life, as an efficient spiritual remedy for all disturbed conditions of mind and body, should become universally known.   The moment a man comes into a sympathetic conjunction with God he feels as God does, and is actuated by an irrepressible desire to impart all possible good to others.

David, in one of his Psalms, says of the man who considers the poor,— that is, of one who is of use in the world as an organ of expressing the Divine Love,— that the Lord will preserve him and keep him alive. The Lord will strengthen him upon the bed of languishing, and will make, or, according to the marginal and more literal rendering, will turn, all his bed in his sickness, and will not deliver him over to his enemies, or those spiritual influences that cause the disease. (Ps. xlii: 1–3.) In the Jewish religious consciousness the idea that life and health were from God seems to have been deeply rooted. This was often expressed in the prophetic state, or when the mind was under the influence of a Divine afflatus. Jeremiah prays, "Heal me, O Lord, and I shall be healed: save me, and I shall be saved." (Jer. xvii: 14.) In this passage we see the parallelism between the words "save" and "heal," which are identical in meaning. In that age of simple, child-like faith medical science had taught mankind no better way for the cure of disease than to apply directly to the source of all life for relief. It might have been as well for the world in this respect if it had remained in that stage of blissful and healthful ignorance. The trade in drugs would have been less, and the public health improved thereby.

All genuine poetry is an inspiration, and its tendency is to bring the soul nearer to God. It gives prominence to that which is ideal and divine. There is a marked likeness in the spirit of the hymns of the Vedas and the Psalms of David. Both give *reality* to the Divine influence in human life. There is a very beautiful passage in the Hebrew sacred poetry expressive of the relation of the Divine life to the cure of all mental and bodily maladies: "Bless the Lord, O my soul, and forget not all His benefits: who forgiveth all thine iniquities; *who healeth all thy diseases;* who crowneth thee with loving kindness and tender mercies, who satisfieth thy mouth with good things; so that thy youth is renewed as the eagles." (Ps. ciii: 2–5.) No comment on this could add to its force or beauty. It expresses one of the profoundest practical truths in the universe,— the life of God in human nature.

So fully convinced was the great religious poet of the Hebrews that the Lord was the source and the "strength of our life" (Ps. xxvii: 1) that he believed He could save us from the most fatal epidemics,— from the pestilence that walketh in darkness, and from the destruction that wasteth at noonday. (Ps. xci: 3–6.) When the ocean tide flows back and takes possession of a river, it gives to the stream the qualities of the ocean. So when a man attains to the consciousness of the immanence of God in his individual being, and that his "life is hid with Christ in God" (Col. iii: 3), he is an incarnation of the Deity, a divine theophany, a manifestation of God in the flesh. He is a partaker of the divine nature (2 Peter i: 4), and thus is strengthened with might in the inner man. (Eph. iii: 15.)

The idea of the indwelling of God in man as the source of life and health, which was so deeply rooted in the religious consciousness of the pious Jews, was carried over into Christianity, and received there a more philosophical expression. The whole life of Jesus the Christ was the highest exemplification of the power of this idea ever witnessed in the history of the race, and a demonstration of its theoretical and practical truth. He cured diseases of mind and body by bringing men into conscious contact with the one and only Life. Thus we see that the higher forms of the religious life, and the state of mind and body which we designate by the name of health, are closely associated. The radical significance of the word religion is that of reunion, or a binding together of what has been sundered. When realized in its full import, it unites the body to the soul in a living correspondence, and consciously connects the soul with God in an influential sympathetic union. In this state of conjunction with the Lord of life, and the Father of spirits, the boundary line between our individual existence and the Divine Being becomes more dimly defined, and each soul becomes in a degree a repetition of the Christ in another personality, and the answer of the prayer of Jesus is fulfilled, that we might become one with God as he and the Father were one. (John xvii: 21–23.) In this state we lay hold of eternal life; death is annihilated, and disease loses its reality. Our life is so linked with the Divine Being that because He lives we live also. The Divine incarnation thus becomes, in a proper sense, a universal and continuous fact, for it is this alone that makes man a spiritual being, and kindles in the depths of his individual being the unquenchable spark of immortality. We are thus made into the image of God, or are finite copies of the Divine Life. No one has life in himself, self-originated and underived, but it is the perpetual gift of God. It is also intuitively certain that the same is true of health. Vital force in its last analysis is the life of God in man, and every man can say, in the language of David, that the Lord is the "health of his countenance." (Ps. xlii: 11; Ps. xliii: 5.)

CHAPTER X.

The eloquent Balmes has well said : " The mysterious hand which
governs the universe seems to hold in reserve for every great
crisis of society an extraordinary man." This truth finds a complete illustration in the birth and life of Jesus the Christ.

An infant in the arms of its mother, in a cradle or in a manger,
is one of the most beautiful objects in nature, and no doubt a very
Divine thing. I hope to make this appear in what I shall have
to say in the brief compass of this chapter. An infant is the
Divine flower that is to ripen into the mature fruit of manhood.
But it is not suggestive of absolute but only of derived Divinity.
With regard to the infant Jesus, if we free ourselves from the
enchantment that distance lends to the view, and from the influence of all dogmatic theories which are the creation of subsequent
ages, and see him as he lay in the manger of the caravansary of
Bethlehem, we might be moved at the sight, but it would be difficult to conceive of him as a God. There is something Divine in
all infancy, and no man ever looked into the face of a new-born
babe without a certain feeling of respect and veneration amount-
ing almost to worship. Hence the Divinity most adored in the
Roman Catholic Church is an infant. Maternity is the divinest
function of human nature. The worship of Mary by millions of
people is a blind instinctive recognition of this truth. It is only

secondary to the Divine operation that goes by the name of creation, and a genuine motherhood stands next to the Godhead. And what shall I say of the product of this proximity? Only, that there is a point in our lives where God and man, Divinity and humanity, most intimately meet and blend into one; and that is infancy and childhood. There is an eternal meaning in the words of the prophet, "Unto us a child is born; unto us a son is given; and the government shall be upon his shoulders; and his name shall be called Wonderful, Counsellor, the Mighty God, the Father of Ages, the Prince of Peace." (Isa. ix: 6.) In every child we behold a divinely human power, born of woman, but conceived by the Spirit of God, and a multiplication in an individual form, and under finite limitations, of the Divine Life. In adult age, in order to get into the closest proximity to God and union with Him, we must return to the divine innocence of childhood. For unless we be converted and become *as* little children, we cannot enter into the kingdom of heaven. (Mat. xviii: 3.) As Wordsworth has expressively said,

"Heaven lies around us in our infancy,"

or, as another has said, "The child who lays on its mother's breast is nearest to the portals of heaven."

The sexual instinct is not an unholy and depraved action of the human mind, but is a finite image of the irrepressible *conatus* of the Divine mind to *create*,—a Divine impulse to add something to the sum total of happy existence. Creation is a necessity of the Infinite Love. God can no more help creating, or begetting, as the word means, than He can avoid living. His *being* must have *ex-istence*, or an outward manifestation. And the same loving Omnipotence to which we owe the commencement of our being will, if we consent, renew and restore our natures impaired and damaged by sin and disease.

Whatever we may think or believe of the human nature of Jesus, one thing is certain, God was never born or begotten. We are

born of God, and so was Jesus the Christ.   The name the child
of Mary received was familiar to Jewish ears, being the Greek
form of the Hebrew Joshua, by which he was known among the
Jews.   It was a common name among that people, and by it they
perpetuated the fame of their great warrior in the same way as
we do honor to the memory of Washington by giving his name to
our children.   He was, undoubtedly, a remarkable child,— we can
readily believe this,— and endowed with active spiritual instincts,
but he *grew* in wisdom as well as in stature, and from infancy to
manhood he seems to have undergone a perfectly *human* development.   His intellectual and spiritual precocity exhibited at the
age of twelve shone all the brighter for the dark back-ground of
Jewish stupidity on which the picture appears.   But all the phenomena of his childhood, and of his manhood's brief career, will
appear plain and natural if we can form a true idea of his conception and the influences of the circumstances under which it took
place.

   It matters little who the father of Jesus was, since in the
Divine paternity we have the origin of all human life.   With
regard to Jesus there is but a slender basis of fact on which to
erect a theory.   The Church dogma of his conception involves the
monstrous — I had almost said the blasphemous — absurdity of
the infinite God begetting *Himself* in the womb of a virgin. Who
the father of Jesus was is a question I have no disposition to discuss, much less to enter into any controversy about it, since all
human life finds its origin and paternity in God.   In the highest
sense, none of us have any father but God, the One Life of the
universe.   In the profound oration of Paul on Mars' Hill he
quotes with approval the line from the poet Aratus, that *we* are all
God's offspring (γένος, of His begetting).   Our individual existence is a sprout from a Divine underground root and always connected with it.   From the meagre array of facts which anyone can
give, it might be allowable to indulge in some "guesses at truth,"
since absolute knowledge with regard to it is out of our reach.
The current orthodox doctrine is one it is difficult to accept, as it

places the birth of Jesus so far out of the ordinary course of nature as to be inconceivable, and, consequently, cannot be made an article of faith. Most thinking people within the pale of orthodoxy feel that the less said about it the better; while those outside are disposed to look upon it as they do upon the Greek myth of the birth of a full-grown Minerva from the brain of Jupiter. There may be a substratum of truth in both, and in the case of Jesus we shall try to find it. If we examine the more extended account of Luke,—for Mark and John are both silent respecting it,—all that can rationally be made out of it is that he was begotten under a high degree of spiritual influence and Divine afflatus, which gave character to his whole life. It is a well-established principle in the physiology of generation that the circumstances and influences under which conception takes place give a permanent shaping to the character of the new being. I choose to interpret Matthew by the more rational view of the physician Luke. (Luke i: 35.) Perhaps we have in this passage the true theory of all conception. As all individual life is a derivation from God, the vivifying of the ovarian germ may always be ultimately referred to the operation of the Holy Spirit, or the emanating sphere of the Divine Life. If it be accomplished through an intervening medium and agency, it is still the same. If I move a rock from its place with my hands alone, or by the instrumentality of a lever turn it over, I am still the cause and origin of the movement. If this theory of conception is true, and the cohabitation of the sexes is only the *occasion* and not the cause of the impartation of soul-life to a preëxisting germ, it takes the generation and birth of Jesus out of the clsss of miraculous events, and brings them into the compass of the uniform laws of nature, or the undeviating mode of the Divine procedure. It seems to me that to impart the soul-principle to an ovarian germ, so as to constitute it a distinct and living *individual*, demands a Divine power as much as the creation of a world. If it be true, as Paul affirms, that in God we live and have our being, it must be equally predicable of the commencement of our existence. The beginning of spiritual life in the germ-cell must be from a Divine Promethean spark.   Then we are all, in a proper sense, sons of God, and begotten of the Holy Spirit, and, having one Father, we are all brethren.   In the birth of Jesus we have an illustration of the general law of conception and generation.   There may be much of truth in the saying of Emerson that "the history of Jesus is the history of every man written large."   His life shows what every one was made to be, and what undeveloped possibilities there are in human nature. This does not make him any less, for he remains still all that he ever claimed for himself, but it gives a Divine dignity to the whole of humanity.   He claimed to be the son of God, and called God his Father, but he taught us to address the Divine Being as "our Father, who is in the heavens."   The universal Fatherhood of God, and consequently the universal brotherhood of men, is an idea that he introduced into the world.   In the Sermon on the Mount all those who are peace-makers as well as those who do good for evil are called "sons of God."   (Mat. v: 9, 44, 45.)   In the Gospel of Luke all who do good, especially to the unthankful and the evil, are called by the Christ the "sons of the Most High." (Luke vi: 35.)   The belief that Jesus had only a one-sided earthly parentage, that of the Virgin Mary, rests on a slender foundation.   It is based on the evidence of a *dream*, a kind of proof that would have no weight in a civil court, and would not weigh as much as a feather in the scale in settling any doubtful question in theology or philosophy in the present age.   It has the disadvantage of not being our own dream, but that of another man more than eighteen centuries ago.   And it only affirms that the conception of Mary was from the Holy Spirit, which may, as we have seen, be perhaps predicable of the origin of all men.   (Mat. i: 20.)   Mary asserts that Joseph was the father of Jesus (Luke ii: 48): "Thy father and I have sought thee sorrowing."

In the genealogy of Jesus, in the beginning of the Gospel of Matthew, he is traced back through *Joseph* to Abraham.   Why is this?   What has that to do with it if Joseph was not his father in the ordinary acceptation of that term?   In the third chapter of the Gospel of Luke the line of succession runs back through Joseph to Adam, who is called the son of God; and it is said that Joseph was his *supposed* father. This is a feeble translation of the original term, which rather signifies that such was the current and unquestioned belief. It was taken for granted, and never doubted, that such was the fact. If this was a mistake, Jesus never corrected it. In the common speech of the day he was called the son of Joseph. "Is not this the carpenter's son? Is not his mother called Mary?" (Mat. xiii: 55.) "And they said: Is not this Joseph's son?" (Luke iv: 22.) "And they said: Is not this Jesus, the son of Joseph, whose father and mother we know?" (John vi: 42.) "Philip findeth Nathaniel, and saith unto him: We have found him of whom Moses in the law and the prophets did write, Jesus of Nazareth, the son of Joseph." (John i: 45.) The simple fact, unadorned by any theological fables, seems to be this: A young woman named Mary had been *espoused* at the age of sixteen, as the Church legends say, to a man much older than herself, by the name of Joseph, whose business it was, as Justin Martyr records, to make yokes and plows. In those days, as every Jewish scholar knows, espousal was in fact a marriage. *It gave to the man all the rights of a husband.* The law recognized it as a legal wedlock, and separation could be effected only by a writing of divorcement. Though no fruit of this virtual marriage was looked for, yet she "was found" in the incipient stage of a not undesired maternity, and Jesus was their first child. (*The Birth of Jesus*, by Henry A. Miles, D.D., p. 45.)

This is as likely to be true as any theory that we can construct, and is perfectly consistent with the idea he so often expresses that God was his father. He was at the same time the son of man and the son of God.

I have no disposition to pursue the discussion of the subject further, and the sacredness of the subject restrains me from employing the *reductio ad absurdum*, which would be a most effective, logical weapon to be used against the current theological belief. To one who loves Jesus it is more important to know that he still *is* and what he is than to understand how he came into existence. He represents the highest type of manhood, and, consequently, the highest manifestation of the Godhead. The Grecian gods, as Jupiter and Apollo, were all men; but Jesus the Christ is far more *human* than any of them, and, consequently, more Divine. A vital, sympathetic union with him cannot but elevate us to a more exalted plane of spiritual existence, whoever was his father, or even if he had no known earthly parentage. The nearer we get to him by a moral likeness, and the more we assimilate the Divine life that was, and still is, in him, and which is even now communicable to us through his personality. the closer is our proximity to the Deity. Happy is the man who realizes the conscious fulfillment of his promise : " Lo, I am with you always," and, " If I go away, I will come to you." His presence is to be sought and found not in the eucharistic elements but in our own spiritual nature. As he was never mentally or physically diseased, a sympathetic conjunction with him must bring to us a healthful and renewing influence. Nothing but a sanative influx, a spiritually therapeutic emanation can go forth from him. Let us remember that a sincere invocation of aid from him unites the severed link between our being and his, and puts his life in God in vital communication with ours. Jesus the Christ is the highest incarnation of the Logos, or the Word, as an inward light, and, consequently, union with him places us in a receptive relation to the Divine Life and Light. Bonaventura speaks of the Word as incarnated in the personality of Jesus as an interior light to mankind: " He is the interior teacher, and one can know no truth except by this Word, which speaks, not vocally as we do, but by an interior illumination. He is himself in our souls, and diffuses the light of true, and living ideas over all the abstract and dark ideas of our intellect." (*Lumen Ecclesiæ*, Vol. I., p. 42.) In the preface to the Gospel of John, the Logos, or Word, is said to be the light that lighteth every man that cometh into the world, and as many as receive it, to them it gives the power — or, as it is rendered in the margin, the right, the privilege,— of becoming the sons of God." (John. i: 9, 12.)

In closing the discussion of this subject, the question arises, when viewed from this stand-point,— that of a real, but exalted, humanity,— can Jesus be to the diseased and sinful what we all need, a Saviour? I unhesitatingly answer, yes, far more so than when we view him from the position in which the creeds of the Church generally place him. Untold myriads of souls have found in him all that his name implies. He is a Divine manifestation in the flesh, a human being intensely conscious of the identity of his life with God's Life, and through him and in him we may have access to the illuminating and vivifying Word. What more can any human soul need? The pure and lofty mind of Jesus, his deep and living spirituality, his irrepressible love for humanity, of which he was a part, his desire to make known God, and to impart to all the Divine Life and Light that were in him, is what lifted up those who intimately knew him to a higher stage of existence, and the same inspiring and elevating influence can be received by all who come into a vital sympathy with him in his true humanity today. He may become to us the highest mental and spiritual guide to health and happiness. The *man* Christ Jesus, in his glorified humanity, is a mediator. (1 Tim. ii: 5.) He bridges the chasm which our ignorance and sensualism have opened between the human soul and God, and in him and through him the finite spirit may meet and mingle with the Infinite Life. A genuine faith — a faith that is a divine conviction of God and the things of God — is one of the greatest moral forces in the universe. It summons into activity all there is of life and power in man, and develops all that is good in germ in human nature. Faith in Jesus, not as a theological myth, a mere theoretical and unsubstantial, divine *apparition*, but as a personal, human, living, and ascended but still present Christ, places the soul through the overflowing fullness of his spiritual being in communication with the unfathomed depths of the One Life. According to Paul, Jesus is exalted above all principalities and powers, and every name that is named, not only in this age, but in that which is to come. (Eph. i: 20, 21.) This was the untroubled, all-satisfying faith of the apostles and primitive believers. Of the incomprehensible metaphysical puzzle and contradictory jargon of the Athanasian Creed they were blissfully ignorant. To them the Christ stood at the summit of all created existences, below the Absolute and the Infinite, but above all that is finite, as the upper link in the chain of being, where it fastens to the Uncreated Mind, and conjoins all below to Him. Yet he was, and is, a *man*, — "the man Christ Jesus." As such he still lays down his life for men, that is, consecrates his blissful existence to the good of all. And we are saved (or healed) through him not so much by his death as by the sphere of his life. (Rom. v: 10.) When on earth, in his fleshly manifestation, those who came to him he directed to the One Life. He is today more accessible to the souls of men than when his presence was limited and restrained by a material body. If as a human personality he was ever a Saviour to the bodies and spirits of men, he can be more to us now. The self-styled and pseudo-evangelical view of Jesus takes him so far out of the sphere of human sympathy and removes him so far from us that he becomes inaccessible and unapproachable by the souls of men. There is an almost impassible gulf between us and him. If it had been the studied design of the Church to exclude men from the saving influence of Jesus, I know of no way in which this could have better been accomplished in harmony with the laws of mind than by the method adopted. They took away the keys of the kingdom of heaven, and neither entered in themselves nor suffered those who would to enter in. The dark and bloody history of the Church has been the result of this. For many ages they took away from the faith of men the humanity of the loving Jesus, and the result was an *inhuman* religion, a relentless and persecuting bigotry. In our language the word humanity is used for kindness, benevolence, and, especially, a disposition to relieve persons in distress and suffering. It is a fact to be accounted for by some spiritual law that in proportion to the extent in which the idea of the *true humanity* of Jesus has been banished from Christianity it became an *inhuman* bigotry. So far as the humanity of Jesus retired into the background in the creed, a cruel, implacable, and merciless spirit came to the front in the life of the Church. It is thus today, and always will be. But the true idea of Jesus is gradually but surely being rescued from the theological falsities beneath which it has been buried, but not suffocated, and men will find him again as a true, but exalted, humanity, and in all the inner virtue of his name Jesus, that is, Saviour or Healer.

We must accustom ourselves to make a distinction between Jesus, the name of his person, and the Christ, which is a designation of a state and character which he attained at an age long subsequent to his birth. Jesus was not born the Christ any more than Abraham Lincoln was born president of the United States. Owing to the spiritual influences and conditions under which he was conceived, the soul of the child Jesus was, by an ante-natal predisposition, open to the reception of the living Word, or illuminating Spirit. And he seems to have been educated from *within*, and not from without. His mind, as a *tabula rasa*, or clean slate, was not preoccupied by the study of Jewish literature, and he affirms that his doctrine was not his own, or self-originated, but received by influx from the Father. (John vii: 15, 16.) His spiritual nature, by the vivifying influence into it of the life and light of the Word, was *fully* developed instead of remaining, as in most men, in a dormant, chrysalis state. Thus, he gradually became the Christ, the anointed, or knowing one, just as Gautama, who was born of the Virgin Maia, is said to have become a Buddha, or, as the Sanscrit word means, "one who knows." Something analogous to this has often been exhibited in the history of the world, and especially in the development of Emanuel Swedenborg into seership. He became "one who knows" far more than Gautama. In the case of Jesus there was witnessed a perfectly normal evolution, or unfolding, of the deific soul-germ, or, as Swedenborg calls it, the Divine internal that is in all human souls. (*Arcana Celestia*, 1999.) I look upon Jesus the Christ as the highest illustration in the history of mankind of a fully and harmoniously developed *humanity*. In such a being there must of necessity be such a blending of the Divine and the purely human that it is difficult to tell where the boundary is that separates the one from the other. The individual man becomes so mixed with God that it is next to impossible to disentangle them. But this is no miracle, but only a higher order of nature.

I believe as much in the Divinity of the Christ as the most so-called evangelical and zealous orthodoxy ever did, but only in a different way. *The way in which the child Jesus was developed into the Christ is the law of the highest education, or unfoldment, of the innermost nature of man.* There is an infinite meaning in the saying of Jesus to his disciples, as the pioneer of a higher and diviner development of man : " I go to prepare a place [or attainable state and spiritual position for you]. And if I go and prepare a place for you, I will come again [in the influx of the sphere of my life] and receive you unto myself [or elevate you to the spiritual position I occupy]; that where I am, there ye may be also." (John xiv : 2, 3.) In this he teaches that his state is not unattainable by others, and that he is willing to share it with others. This makes the exalted *man* Christ Jesus more of a Saviour, Restorer, and Redeemer than the Church creeds have ever done. In this we see an illustration of the principle laid down by the Christ, and engraved, as it were, over the entrance gate of a genuine Christianity, and which the sounding-line of the Church has been too short to fathom, that the true disciple is to be a copy of the master or teacher. (Mat. xvi : 24.) The disciple, the scholar, *follows* the master to suffering, to active usefulness, and to the glorification of his humanity, and by a spiritual likeness becomes a repetition of him, and an echo of him. If any soul of man needs more a Saviour in Jesus than this view of him gives, he will search far and long through all the creeds of Christendom before he can find him. If this is a heresy, may it rapidly spread over the entire globe until, by beholding Jesus *as he is,* all may be changed into the same image from glory to glory *by the Lord as a Spirit* (which is the marginal and literal rendering). (2 Cor. iii : 18.) Through a sympathetic union with him, an affectionate melting of our souls into his, a fusion of our life with his life, and a blending of our mode of thought and feeling with his, may the world advance to the realization of a higher incarnation of God in the whole of humanity. This will be the fulfillment of the words of the Christ: "If I be lifted up [or exalted] from the earth, I will draw all men unto me." (John xii : 32.)

CHAPTER XI.

One of the mistakes of the religious world has been that men have sought without for that which they can only find within. The drowning man can be saved by a plank or a rope that a friendly hand throws to him, and he will even grasp at a straw; but there are circumstances of mental suffering and anxiety when the metaphorical plank and rope will not save us. How much better for a man to learn that somewhere in the compass of his own being, and the enclosure of his own nature, is to be found the principle of buoyancy that will keep him afloat, and then the rope and the plank will be serviceable but not indispensable. Tradition, the dogmas of the Church, the authority of an external book, and the outward machinery of worship, are the plank, the rope, and the straw thrown to a man in a flood of doubt and spiritual distress. But all these have become water-logged, and can barely keep themselves afloat in the public mind, and are fast sinking out of sight. And must we sink? By no means. The principle of Christianity, and of every true religion, is *within* the soul,— the recognition of the incarnation of God in every human being. Let us grasp this truth in all its fullness of meaning, and strike out and gain the shore. God is to us the fountain of life, and in his light we see light (Ps. xxxvi: 9.)

As a guide to duty, and in the discovery of spiritual truth, some higher faculty and diviner light than mere reason is needed. This has been felt and acknowleged in all ages of the world. In the Alexandrian schools of philosophy, which reproduced with modifications the speculations of Plato, and in the modern idealistic systems of Germany, and even in the metaphysics of Sir William Hamilton, and in the mystic writers of all ages, the incapacity of reason alone to solve the problems of philosophy and morality is fully confessed. The infallible and unerring guide of men's souls is not, and cannot be, an external book, but an *interior light* which quickens our spiritual intelligence, so that it becomes the light of life. The state of illumination in which spiritual truths are clearly seen has received different names. Plotinus denominated this higher faculty *ecstasy*,—a state in which the mind becomes freed from the trammels of sense and of the body. St. Bernard calls it *contemplation;* George Fox, *the inward voice.* Schelling called it the *intellectual intuition*, and Kant, *the pure reason;* Jacobi called it *faith arising from feeling.* Pythagoras designated it as *the great light and salt of ages.* Plutarch called it *the interior guide and everlasting fountain of virtue.* With Socrates it was the *good demon* or spirit. This was not, as has been generally supposed, an individual spirit or guardian angel. The word he uses will not bear that construction. It is not δαίμων (*demon*) but δαιμόνιον (*daimonion*), which properly signifies a Divine or spiritual influence. In the system of Confucius, the Chinese philosopher, it is spoken of as " that principle by which simple and ignorant men and women, of the most ordinary capacity, may know all that appertains to their ordinary actions and conduct every day of their lives." In its highest form of experience, Swedenborg calls it *perception* and a state of *illustration*, or interior illumination. In the New Testament this inward, Divine light is called *the Comforter* or Paraclete, the inward teacher, the Spirit of truth, which is to guide us into all truth. (John xiv: 26; xv: 26; xvi: 7, 13.) In the Old Testament it is called the *Word of the Lord* that *came* to the prophets and to Moses, and which in the first chapter of John is called "the true light that lighteth every man that cometh into the world." It is the source of every genuine inspiration. Under its influence the mind is raised in its action far above the decision of the senses, and even of the logical consciousness or the reasoning faculty. In this interior illumination all truth becomes self-evident. It is seen in its own light and loved for its own divine self. As a guide in life, it is far above the letter of the Word, and is that without which the external book would be of little use. It is of higher authority than any system of rules drawn from the Bible. For, as Paley long ago said, "Whoever expects to find in the Scriptures a specific direction for every moral doubt that may arise, looks for more than he will there find." We need every day, and every hour, the same inspiration by which they were written. In our interpretation of the Book, we need some divine illuminating power to break the seals and open the volume. (Rev. v: 5.) The answer of the eunuch to Philip, when he was asked, "Understandest thou what thou readest?" will always have its application to us,—"How can I, except some one guide me?" (Acts viii: 30, 31.) This interior light, this Paraclete, or Divine instructor, is always available. For, as I. H. Fichte has truly remarked, "Inspiration is a far more universal idea than its theological acceptation has admitted, while the ordinary systems of psychology have wholly ignored it."

That there is such a thing as an immediate revelation of truth from God to the human soul has been admitted and taught by nearly all theological writers, and those of the most diverse opinions on other doctrines. Jonathan Edwards, in a sermon on Mat. xvi: 17, proves "that there is such a thing as a spiritual and Divine light immediately imparted to the souls of men by God." (*Works*, Vol. IV., *Sermon* XXVII.) This is a doctrine that has always been maintained by the Society of Friends, and is the characteristic tenet of their system of religion. John Wesley taught the same thing in his two sermons on the Witness of the Spirit, in which he affirms that God directly impresses the spirit of the believer with the fact of his pardon, and with the assurance of the Divine favor. This is the distinctive doctrine of Methodism, according to Dr. Abel Stevens. But why confine Divine revelation to this one point? Can God speak to us only on one subject, that of our pardon and the forgiveness of our sins? Paul takes a broader view, and declares that we can have no knowledge of spiritual things except it be imparted to us by the Spirit of God, which reveals them to us. (1 Cor. i: 9–12.) Theodore Parker extends the idea of inspiration further than Edwards or Wesley. He makes inspiration to consist in the direct and intuitive perception of some truth either of thought or sentiment, and that this is the action of the Highest within the soul, the Divine presence imparting light. In this view Newton was as really inspired as Moses, for it was a more difficult thing to write the Principia than the Decalogue. (*Discourse of Matters Pertaining to Religion*, p. 205.)

As God speaks and acts in the material world by what we call the laws of nature, so His immanence in man gives to the legitimate and unperverted action of all the powers of the mind the dignity of a divine law, an interior and unwritten Decalogue. This is according to the prophetic announcement that the time would come when the Lord would put, or rather, as it is more literally translated, *give*, His laws in our minds and write them upon our hearts, or, as it is expressed by Jeremiah, the Lord would put his law in our *inward parts*. (Jer. xxxi: 31–34; Heb. viii: 9–11.) In accordance with the prevailing tendency to limit the action of God in man, there is only one faculty that has been accepted as His organ of communication with man. It has been so often asserted that conscience is the voice of God in man that it has become a religious axiom. This is undoubtedly true; but is God everywhere else silent in the human soul? Does He not speak and act through all our faculties? On the subject of conscience Reid, the Scotch metaphysician, says in the conclusion of his chapter on the sense of duty: "The sum of what has been said in this chapter is that by an original power of the mind which we call conscience, or the moral faculty, we have the conceptions of right and wrong in human conduct, of merit and demerit, of duty and moral obligation, and our other moral conceptions; and that by the same faculty we perceive some things in human conduct to be right and others to be wrong; that the first principles of morals are the dictates of this faculty, and that we have the same reason to rely upon those dictates as upon the determination of our senses, or of our other natural faculties."

On the subject of a Divine light within I have only space in this chapter to quote the language of Fénelon, Archbishop of Cambray, as one of the best representatives of the mystic theology. He says out of the depths of his own experience: "It is easy to perceive that our feeble reason is continually set to rights by another superior reason, which we consult within ourselves, and which corrects us. This reason we cannot change, because it is immutable; but it changes us because we have need of it. All consult this everywhere. It answers in China as in France and America. It does not divide itself in communicating itself. The light it gives me takes nothing from those who were before filled with it. It communicates itself at all times immeasurably, and is never exhausted. *It is the sun that enlightens mind as the outward sun does bodies.* This light is eternal and immense. It comprehends all time as well as all space. It is not myself; it reproves and corrects me against my will. It is then above me, and above all weak and imperfect men as I am. This supreme reason which is the rule of *mine*, this wisdom from which every wise man receives *his*, this supreme spring of light, is the God we seek."

The guiding principle of our lives is to be found not in a book, or in a whole library of works on theology, but is the voice of God in the depths of our own being. It is not a self-derived intelligence, but a constant revelation of a present and living God. He is our light and our salvation. (Ps. xxvii: 1.) In harmony with this view, Jesus the Christ says to all human souls: "Why judge ye not of your own selves what is right?" (Luke xii: 57.) This is a truth of not mere speculative interest, but of great practical value. It has its application to all the duties of life from the least to the greatest, and to the means of recovery to mental and bodily health and happiness. This inward oracle will not only teach us in regard to our moral and religious duties, but will give us the most unerring prescription for our mental and physical maladies.

CHAPTER XII.

ON DIVINE REVELATION AS A PAST EXPERIENCE OF MEN, AND AS A PRESENT NEED OF THE HUMAN MIND.

We have shown in what has been said in previous chapters that our relation to God is a vital one, in other words, that our life is a perpetual derivation from the Divine Being. But is it not equally true of our knowledge? Could we any more think without God than we could live without Him? A revelation of knowledge from Him is no more unreasonable in itself than a communication of life from Him, since mental action is the highest form of vital activity. All genuine knowledge, in philosophy, in science, and in religion, is, in a proper sense, a revelation from the Divine Mind. Here is its sempiternal source. The essential element in the idea of a revelation from God is that some truth is made known to us from Him. The word revelation (from *re* and *velo*, an unveiling and uncovering) has been defined the act of disclosing or discovering to others what was before unknown to them; and in its religious application it is the disclosure or communication of truth to men by God Himself. But is there any truth that does not come from Him? As the radii of a circle lead us back to the centre, so every ray of knowledge has an unbroken connection with the central Sun, the Divine Wisdom, and the revelation of it is only our coming to the perception, or conscious reception, of it.

Theologians speak of the Scriptures as containing a system of *divine* truth. All other knowledge is viewed by them as comparatively profane, and lacking the quality of sacredness. This is too narrow a view, and places an obstacle in the way of our spiritual growth. We ask the intuitive reason of every man, is such a distinction justifiable? Is there any truth that is not divine? Is not all truth sacred? The mischief of such a distinction lies in its immoral tendency, in causing in the public mind a too low estimate of the value of truth, and of an undeviating truthfulness in our every-day life. All truth should be viewed as a divinely sacred intellectual treasure, and all falsity as infernal. The one is the light of the angelic heavens; the other is the darkness and foul emanation of the abyss.

On this subject Morell, in his excellent work on the Philosophy of Religion, judiciously remarks: " The idea of a revelation always implies a process by which knowledge, in some form or other, is communicated to an intelligent being. For a revelation at all to exist there must be an intelligent being on the one hand to receive it, and there must be on the other hand a process by which this same intelligent being becomes cognizant of certain facts or ideas. Suppress either of these conditions and no revelation can exist. The preaching of an angel would be no revelation to an idiot; and a Bible in Chinese would offer none to a European. In the former case there is no intelligence capable of receiving the ideas conveyed; in the latter case the process of conveyance renders the whole thing practically a nonentity, by allowing no idea whatever to reach the mind. We may say, then, in few words, that a revelation always indicates *a mode of intelligence*. This point should be carefully noted, and we must not confound the idea of a revelation as a means of communicating truth from one mind to another with the object revealed."

" If a revelation, then, necessarily signifies *a mode of intelligence*, we have next to determine what mode of intelligence or what form of knowing which the term revelation implies. There are only two modes of intelligence possible to man. They are the only two methods of acquiring truth adapted to the present state of the powers of the human mind. To conceive a third mode is a psy-

chological impossibility. These are the *intuitional* and the *logical*
In the former we arrive at truth by a direct perception of it
Truth is seen in its own light.   It is thus self-evident or proves
itself.   In the logical mode of intelligence we arrive at truth
mediately, or as a necessary inference from other known and
acknowledged verities.   These two methods of knowing are the
only conceivable ones.   Sensation, which might be considered a
third, is found to be not knowledge, but only feeling.   Of itself it
can give no knowledge.   The senses of an idiot may be as perfect
as our own, and those of some animals are far more acute, yet
their knowledge is not in proportion."   (*Philosophy of Religion*,
p. 123–125.)

If a revelation from God must take place in harmony with the
laws of the human mind, and must be a direct *showing* of truth to
our intuitional faculty, the question arises, can it take place now
as well as at any former period of the world's history?   Is man
as capable of it today as some men were many centuries ago?
These are questions of great interest to every human soul.   Was
it once possible, but has now become impossible?   Does it not
rather arise as a practicable spiritual experience out of the necessary relations that man sustains to God,—that the finite mind
holds, and must forever hold, to the Infinite Mind?   Is it not
needed as much today as it ever was?   And, if so, will it not be
given if it is possible?   The soul cannot be satisfied with the dry,
mouldy, Gibeonitish crusts of the past experiences of others, even
though they were pious and semi-enlightened Jews, but requires
for its nutriment and spiritual growth the living bread that comes
down from heaven, and which, like the manna, is gathered fresh
every day.

The authors of all the separate tracts, poems, epistles, etc.,
which collectively constitute the book we call the Bible, are, at
least, thirty in number.   How many more there were we have no
means of knowing, as the names of the writers of many parts of
the volume are not given.   These are supposed to have received
a revelation from God.   We admit it to be a fact; but what does

the fact prove? Is it any evidence that no one else could? Do the writings of these men exhaust the supply of truth that could be made known from God, or do they fully satisfy the spiritual needs of all men everywhere? It is certain they do not. If thirty men received a revelation of truth from God, in harmony with the laws of mind, it would only prove that thirty, or even thirty thousand, more might enjoy the same experience. God is not far from every one of us, and He will respond to our sincere yearning for truth by sharing the infinite stores of the Divine Intelligence with the thirsty soul.

We would not undervalue that degree of truth which God made known in a way in perfect accordance with the laws of the human intelligence to thirty Jews in different ages of the world, and in sparsely scattered fragments along the stream of history. Place as high a value upon it as you please, or can possibly find in it; I admit it all. I would only enlarge the volume of Divine revelations so as to include all truth, as has been done by Jesus the Christ when he says: "Thy word is truth." All truth that ever came to man is a ray of the eternal Logos, the uncreated Word, the Divine Reason and Wisdom, made available to finite minds. It is the true light that lighteth every man that cometh into the world. The totality of truth is the Word of God in its fullness. But if it should be written the world itself would not contain the books. (John xxi: 25.) The real Word of the Lord is the God-Light within the soul, and not a book. It was the theory of Malebranche that in our vision of the objects of nature we do not perceive the objects themselves but the *ideas* of them which are in God. God is so united to our souls by His presence that He may be said to have that relation of place to the mind which space has to body. Wherever the human mind is there God is, and, consequently, all the ideas which are in God. (*Brown's Philosophy of the Mind*, Vol. II., p. 144.)

This theory of Malebranche seems to be only a modification of the doctrine of Augustine, which is the fundamental principle of his metaphysical philosophy, — that there is a supreme, eternal, and universal Truth which is ultimately present to every mind, and in which all minds alike perceive the truths, which all alike are, as it were, necessitated to believe, for example, the truths of arithmetic and geometry and the primary, essential truths of religion and morality.

"These truths we feel to be eternal, because we feel that they are not contingent on the existence of those who perceive them, but were, and are, and must forever be, the same; and we feel also that the truth is one, whatever be the number of individuals that perceive it, and is not converted into many truths merely by the multitude of believers."

"If, in discoursing of any truth, I perceive that to be true which you say, and you perceive that to be true which I say, where, I pray you, do we both see this at the same moment? I certainly see it not in you, nor you in me, but both see it in that unchangeable Truth which is beyond and above our individual minds." (*Brown's Philosophy of the Mind*, Vol. II., p. 144.)

This unchanging and everywhere-present light of truth is what is called in the Scriptures the Word of the Lord, the Divine Logos, and by Jesus the Christ, "the spirit of Truth," which was promised to guide into all truth. The human mind in all ages and climes has been in communication with the sphere of the Divine Intelligence. The light of the heavens has leaked down through the crystal dome and been caught by thirsty souls. The Jews and other ancient nations gathered and preserved some drops of the water of life (as Jesus symbolically calls the truth he preached) that fell from the eaves of the palace of God. But there is much more to be obtained and treasured up by coming ages. Those eminent Christian teachers, Origen and Augustine, looked upon Christianity as only a fuller development of truths that had before been made known in a degree to mankind, and the Gospel was viewed by them as directly connected with Divine revelations at all times and in all places. On this point Bunsen remarks: "The fact of a universal revelation, of a continuity of Divine influences, everywhere and at all times, remains as the anchor of the soul, as the Rock of Ages, on which Christ's Church will be built." (*The Angel-Messiah of Buddhists, Essenes, and Christians.* Introduction.)

Some of the best of the philosophical Greeks recognized the influential relation of the Infinite Mind and Life to the souls of men,— as high a view as that entertained by the Church, and even less narrow. Seneca distinctly declares: "Without God there is no great man. It is He who inspires us with great ideas and exalted designs. When you see a man superior to his passions, happy in adversity, calm amid surrounding storms, can you forbear to confess that those qualities are too exalted to have their origin in the little individual whom they ornament? A god inhabits every virtuous man, and without God there is no virtue." (*Epistles*, 41, 73.) Plato entertained a similar view. In Menon he makes Socrates teach that actual virtue comes untaught. It does not come by nature, but by the special inspiration of the gods." (*Grote's Plato and other Companions of Socrates*, Vol. II., p. 11.)

CHAPTER XIII.

THE NATURE AND EXTENT OF INSPIRATION.

Inspiration may be defined as the reception of a spiritual and Divine influence that augments the activity of our natural powers of mind, and exalts our mental faculties to a higher plane of thought and feeling. It is as if a new spirit was *breathed into* the subject of it, as the word itself (from *in* and *spiro*, to breathe) signifies. The word *inspirit*, which signifies to infuse new life and energy into another, expresses the exact idea of inspiration. It is to animate, to invigorate, to breathe into one a quickened action of the soul. It adds no new faculty to human nature, but stimulates to a higher range of action those we already possess.

Morell, in his profound work on the Philosophy of Religion, takes a very rational view of the nature of inspiration, and one that does not exclude it from the possibility of a present experience. He says: "Revelation and inspiration indicate one united process, the result of which upon the human mind is to produce a state of spiritual intuition, whose phenomena are so extraordinary that we at once separate the agency by which they are produced from any of the ordinary principles of human development. And yet this agency is applied in perfect consistency with the laws and natural operations of our spiritual nature. Inspiration does not imply anything generically new in the actual processes of the human mind; it does not involve any form of intelligence essentially different from what we already possess; it indicates rather the elevation of the religious consciousness, and with it, of course, the power of spiritual vision, to a degree of intensity peculiar to the individuals thus highly favored of God. We must regard the whole process of inspiration, accordingly, not as mechanical, but purely *dynamical:* involving not a novel and supernatural faculty, but a faculty already enjoyed, elevated supernaturally to an extraordinary power, and susceptibility; indicating, in fact, an inward nature so perfectly harmonized to the Divine, so freed from the distorting influences of prejudice, passion, and sin, so simply recipient of the Divine ideas circumambient around it, so responsive in all its strings to the breath of heaven, that truth leaves an impress upon it which answers perfectly to its objective reality." (*Philosophy of Religion*, pp. 150, 151.)

The doctrine was quite common among the theologians of past centuries that the inspiration of the writers of the Scriptures was verbal, and not merely a stimulus afforded to the intuitive faculty, — a theory entirely inconsistent with the difference of style among the writers of the Bible. This theory is maintained by Gaussen in his work entitled Theopneusty. Gerhard and the Buxtorfs even went so far as to affirm the Divine inspiration of the Hebrew vowel points. But all these theories would make the writings we call the Bible, or the Book, a matter of *dictation* rather than of inspiration. The prevalence of these extreme mechanical views has in recent times been pretty generally abandoned, and a more intelligent theory of inspiration, one that brings it more into harmony with the laws of mind, is taking its place. The following passage quoted from Akerman, in Hare's Mission of the Comforter, expresses the more advanced and rational view of the present day: "Theologians have not unfrequently been guilty of a gross error with regard to the Biblical idea of inspiration from looking upon it as mechanical instead of dynamical. From the passages cited (Gen. xii: 38; Job xxxii: 8; Isa. xi: 2; Mat. x: 20; Luke ii: 40: John xiv: 17, 26; John xvi: 13; Rom. viii: 16; 1 Cor. ii: 10; xii: 3; Gal. iv: 6; 2 Pet. i: 21) it is sufficiently evident that the Bible speaks of the working of the Spirit of God as dynamical. Hence theologi ans ought never to have encouraged the crude notion that persons under inspiration were like so many drawers, wherein the Holy Ghost put such and such things, which they then took out as something ready made, and laid before the world. So that their recipiency in reference to the Spirit inspiring them was like that of a letter box. Whereas inspiration, according to the Bible, is to be regarded as a vivifying and animating operation on the spiritual faculty in man, by which its energy and capacity are extraordinarily heightened, so that his powers of internal perception discerned things spread out before them clearly and distinctly, which at other times lay beyond his range of vision, and were dark and hidden." (*Hare's Mission of the Comforter*, p. 328. Note.)

Inspiration is a quickening, an awakening into conscious activity, of our spiritual perceptions or intuitions. The truths, thus discerned, can come to an external expression, so as to be conveyed to other minds, only through the words that are laid up in our memory. In a state of inspiration, the Divine element in man, which is usually latent or dormant, asserts its supremacy, and raises the intellect above the range of the senses and their fallacies into the clear light of truth. The mind is laid open to the reception of the living light of heaven, and comes into sympathetic conjunction with the general sphere of life and intelligence in the world above. The soul comes into vivifying contact with the Logos, the spiritual and living Word, which comes to the illuminated mind as it has to the prophets of all ages. All Scripture, that is, every sacred expression of truth above the ordinary level, is given by inspiration of God,—it is, as Paul affirms, a *Theopneusty*, a breathing into the receptive intellect of man the breath of life from God. It is a stirring of the Divinity within him, for holy men of God spake as they were *moved* by the Holy Spirit. (2 Pet. i: 21.) This may be affirmed not only of the Psalms of David, but of the hymns of the Vedas, and of all the higher forms of religious poetry and literature. Inspiration is promised as a permanent experience, and a perpetual privilege of the disciples of Christ. The Comforter, the Divine Paraclete, which was *to guide*

into all truth, was to abide with us forever. (John xiv: 16.)
Inspiration, so far as it is an intellectual illumination, is proffered
to all who seek it, in this passage of the Epistle of James: "If
any man lack wisdom, let him ask of God, who giveth to all men
liberally and upbraideth not, and it shall be given him." (James
i: 15.) No one can fail to notice the universality of the promise.
So far as we need an infallible guide to present duty, we have the
promise that when we turn to the right or the left we shall hear a
WORD saying: "This is the way, walk ye in it." (Isa. xxx: 21.) In
the Christian system, the Paraclete, the Holy Sprit, is as the carrier-
pigeon of heaven, to bear to men's souls messages from the realms
of Light and Love. It is a light, a guide, a warning, a presence,
ever near. It is a voice without a sound, a deep and calm revealing, which can only be heard by the inward ear in the profound
silence of the soul. In answer to the scholar, in "The Dialogue
on the Supersensual Life," Behmen answers the question, "How
may I *see* God and *hear* Him speak?" in these words: "When
thou canst for a moment throw thyself into that where no *creature*
dwelleth (that is, beyond all sensible images), then thou hearest
what God speaketh. If thou canst for awhile cease from *thy* own
thinking and willing, thou shalt hear unspeakable words of God."
This state was called by the devout Kempis "peaceful vacancy,"
— a state of mind entirely passive, a spiritual *inertia*, where the
soul acts only as it is acted upon, and is all rapt suspension, and
all the quivering, palpitating chords of its life are still. Then the
True Light, in its radiant splendor rains down from the opened
heavens, upon it, and gently lifts it to a higher plane of thought
and feeling. All genuine poets understand the relation of silence
of the soul to inspiration. Whittier in his poem of "The Vision
of Echard," says of him: —

> "He felt the heart of silence
> Throb with a soundless word;
> And by the inward ear alone
> A spirit's voice he heard.

> And the spoken word seemed written
> On air, and wave, and sod;
> And the bending walls of sapphire
> Blazed with the *thought* of God."

Longfellow, who seems to be penetrated with a feeling of the nearness and influence of the spiritual realm of life, says, in his "Sound of the Sea:"

> There comes to us at times from the unknown
> And inaccessible solitudes of being
> The rushing of the sea-tides of the soul;
> And inspirations that we deem our own
> Are some divine foreshadowing and foreseeing
> Of things beyond our reason or control."

The silence of the heart is always full of voiceless words from God and heaven.   If the soul would listen, and banish all other sounds, it could hear the inward WORD, and the spiritual ear would vibrate with a responsive echo of the Divine Thought.   The silence of the soul is a vacuum, and the life and light of the ever-present heavens comes in with spontaneous alacrity to fill the void.

> "Hearken, hearken!
> God speaketh to thy soul,
> Using the supreme voice which doth confound
> All Life with consciousness of Deity,
> All senses into one,—
> As the seer-saint of Patmos, loving John
> (For whom did backward roll
> The cloud-gate of the future), turned *to see*
> The voice that spake. It speaketh now
> Through the regular breath of the calm creation."

Inspiration is not, and cannot properly be, predicated of a volume, by whomsoever written.   It is not the quality of a *book*, but the state of a soul that is God-moved.   In what we call intuition, it is a sudden flash of the God-light within the mind.   This may be prolonged as a divine twilight while an author writes a poem or an essay.   But books, as the Vedas, the Zend-Avesta, the Koran, or the Bible, are not inspired, but only the minds of the authors.

Inspiration is the state of a soul that is first in a spiritual *inertia*, and then, moved by a divine impulsion, it mounts upward into God's sunning, and, in the great God-light of the heavens, sees truth in its reality, because it comes into sympathetic relations with the action of the One and Universal Mind. In this state we can say with the Christ: "The words I speak unto you I speak not of myself," or, as it is said in the second Epistle of Peter, when properly translated: "Prophecy [or the speaking from an inward, Divine impulse] came not at any time from the will of man [or from any purpose or volitional effort], but holy men of God spake as they were moved [that is, actuated or impelled] by the Holy Spirit." (2 Pet. i: 21.) A person in the exalted form of mental action which we call inspiration is conscious of *oeing in a state* rather than of making an effort.

In closing this chapter I wish to call the reader's thoughtful attention to two remarks. 1. God never designed to give to a few persons in the history of the world a monopoly of inspiration from Him, but it is the privilege of all. 2. Inspiration is not merely an illumination of the intellect, but a quickened activity of every department of our nature,— an impartation of life, health, and peace to the whole man. Life is One and Universal. Inspiration, in the sense of an influx of life from God, is seen everywhere throughout the three kingdoms of nature. As Paul expresses it: "There is one God who is above all, and through all, and in you all." (Eph. iv: 6.) Every atom of the globe is alive. Even decay and death are vital processes. There is no "inanimate matter," nor dead forces. In man we have the highest manifestation of life, but it is not confined to him nor limited to the animal kingdom. Life is exhibited everywhere, but not the same expression of it as in man and animals. "The life which works in your organized frame," said Leon, "is but an exalted condition of the power which occasions the accretion of particles into this crystalline mass. The quickening force of nature through every form of being is the same." (*Panthea: or, The Spirit of Nature*, by Robert Hunt, p. 51.) Says one of the most distinguished think ers of the present age, Herbert Spencer, in the Westminster Review: "The characteristic which, manifested in a high degree, we call Life, is a characteristic manifested in a lower degree by so-called inanimate objects." The celebrated Dr. C. G. Carus remarks: "The idea of Life is coëxtensive with Universal Nature. The individual or integral parts of nature are the members; universal nature is the total and complex organism. The relations of inorganic to organized bodies exist only by reason of this; hence, too, the universal connection, the combination, the never-ceasing action and re-action of all the powers of nature, producing the vast and magnificent whole of the world,—an action and re-action which would be impossible were not all pervaded by a single principle of life." (*The Kingdoms of Nature; their Life and Affinity.* Translated from the German in Taylor's Scientific Memoirs. Vol. I., p. 223.)

On this subject I cannot deny myself the pleasure of quoting the eloquent language of Prof. Grindon, a Swedenborgian scholar and philosopher. "We must never attempt to think of life in any of its manifestations apart from or independently of God. Life is uncreate, and wherever life is He is. The same grand principles which we find at the summit of creation, or in the intelligence of man, and which we acknowledge unhesitatingly to be by influx of the Divine Life, are embodied in every kingdom *below* man, in another and humbler manner,—animals, plants, and minerals, severally and in turn presenting them, after the likeness of descending octaves." (*Life: Its Nature, Varieties, and Phenomena,* p. 541.)

Life, and health, which is a mode or state of life, may come to us as an *inbreathing* or inspiration from God through the ever-present heavens, or it may come to us through the Universal Life of nature. The natural and the Divine are one and the same. To be in harmony and sympathy with nature is to be in union with God, which is life, health, and peace. Disease is what it has been instinctively called in common language, a *disorder,* or a want of harmony with the Universal Life. For this Intelligent and

Omnipresent Life of nature, from the first moment of our existence, is employed in building up organs, casting off worn out matter, repairing waste, and keeping the whole system in vigorous health, wholeness, and blissful harmony unless we obstruct its action by that mysterious power of the individual which we call free will. When we float in the current of the Universal Life, and make no effort to row against the stream, and our desires, aspirations, and volitions are in concord with the Divine operation in nature, then the heart beats time to the harmonious music of the heavens, and no longer, like a muffled drum, marks the measures of a funeral march to the grave. There may be an inspiration of health, as well as an exaltation of thought and feeling, for these are the whole of life, and their harmonized activity is spiritual health, which is translated with divine celerity into a physical expression in the bodily organism.

CHAPTER XIV.

THEOPNEUSTY, OR THE DIVINE AFFLATUS.

The word at the head of this chapter, at which I hope the reader will not be startled from its unusual appearance, is derived from a Greek term used by Paul in speaking of the inspiration of the Scriptures. It is a word that has been employed to some extent by German writers, but has not been much used in English. Paul declares that all scripture is *theopneustos,* or given by a Divine afflatus. In Schleusner the word is defined *afflatu divino actus, divino quodam spiritu afflatus,* that which is effected by a Divine afflatus, an influence from some Divine spirit. Robinson defines it as "God inspired, given from God." It is used by Plutarch in relation to dreams. Cicero, in the oration for Archias, speaks of the poet as one who was breathed upon or *into* by some Divine spirit,—*poetam quasi divino spiritu inflari.* Plato held the same view with regard to poetry. He believed that the poet was often so inspired that he said things that he did not himself fully understand.

> " Himself from God he could not free ;
> He builded better than he knew."

Josephus, who was a cotemporary of Paul, in his first book against Apion, speaks of the *twenty-two* sacred books of the Jews as having been written by an inspiration which came from God ($\varkappa\alpha\tau\alpha$ $\tau\eta\nu$ $\dot{\epsilon}\pi\iota\nu o\iota\alpha\nu$ $\tau\eta\nu$ $\dot{\alpha}\pi\dot{o}$ $\tau o\upsilon$ $\theta\epsilon o\tilde{\upsilon}$), or according to a breathing upon them of God. The mystic philosopher, the Alexandrian Jew, Philo, in his account of his mission to the Emperor Caligula, speaks of the Scriptures as *theochristic oracles* (θεόχρηστα λόγια), or oracles given from a Divine anointing, a symbolic expression for the reception of the Holy Spirit, the sphere of the Divine Life, and the Divine Intelligence. (1 John ii : 27.)

Though we may reach a different result in the end, yet we can say with Gaussen at the beginning of his work on the inspiration of the Scriptures: "Our design in this book, by the help of God, and the authority of his Word, is to expound, defend, and establish the *Christian* doctrine of inspiration."

If I have any comprehension of a true Christian philosophy and the spirit of the teaching of Jesus, it tends to make *general* what has been viewed as partial in its application, and the exclusive property of the few. Thus the Divine incarnation is not confined to one solitary person of history, but it can be predicated in a degree of all humanity. The whole of humanity embodies more of God than any one individual of the race. The principle of mediation, by a priestly aristocracy, is removed by Christianity, and every individual believer is brought face to face with God and made his own priest. According to Paul, or the author of the Epistle to the Hebrews, every Christian is a priest, and even a high priest, and has access to the holy of holies by a new and living way, that is, he has the privilege of the most intimate communion with God, without its coming through the intervening medium of an external priesthood. With regard to prophecy, or the speaking from an inward, Divine impulse, one of the highest functions and uses of the truly spiritual life, according to Paul, Moses prayed that all the Lord's people might become prophets, and that He would put His Spirit upon them all (Num. xi : 29), which was fulfilled on the day of Pentecost, in the outpouring of the Spirit upon all classes, when the Christian dispensation was opened, and when it emerged from its external, Judaistic shell. This has been illustrated in the whole course of the historical development of the true Christian life. So, with regard to inspira

tion, it is contrary to the whole spirit and genius of Christianity —
which, in all its essential principles, tends to make the gifts of
God universal — to confine it to the few Jews who penned the
books or tracts that, collectively, constitute the sacred canon of
Scripture.   The Divine *charismata*, or spiritual gifts, were not to
be the possession of the favored few, who were to have a monopoly
of them, but were to become the common property of all true
believers.   Paul affirms that all *scripture* is a theopneusty, or
given by a Divine afflatus.   This is true in its broadest sense.
The Word of God, as defined by Christ, is *truth*, and all truth is
from God, its primal fount.   No real truth in any department of
human knowledge can be sundered from the Divine Mind any
more than we can break the connection of a solar ray with the
central sun of our system.   The continuity is unbroken and indissoluble.   The Greek word for scripture, and the Latin-English
term which we have, signify an act of writing, and, by a figure of
speech, that which is written.   So far as the action is a recording
or external manifestation of truth, the writer must be in a receptive relation to God, for we can no more *create* a truth than we
can a world.   If the truth does not come to us immediately, but
through some intervening medium, it is none the less from God.
The water of the lake comes to our houses through various pipes,
but it is still the water of the lake.   If all power is of God, and
without Him we can do nothing, which are fundamental verities of
the Christian Creed, we can no more commit a truth to its external
expression in writing without God than we can live without Him.
If it were otherwise, the Divine Being would be unnecessary, and
man would become an independent existence.   But words sometimes
have a meaning different from their etymological or radical significance.   Thus the word Bible means simply a book.   Any book is,
according to the primary meaning of the term, a Bible, and it is
certainly a Divine revelation to us so far as it makes known any
truth that we did not before possess among our intellectual treasures.   So in Arabic Al Koran means the Book, the Bible.   But,
by a limitation of their proper and natural meaning, the Bible has

come to mean a particular book,— the Jewish and Christian sacred writings,— and the Koran the work of Mohammed. In this limited meaning of the word scripture, or writing, or Bible, it is still true that all the truth they contain is from a Divine afflatus. For it is a *maxima veritas*, a supreme verity, that all truth is from God, and can be traced back to Him as its primal source.

Inspiration is not a miraculous phenomenon, but an every-day occurrence, and arises naturally and necessarily from the relation that the human soul sustains to God, *the Father of Spirits*, as He is expressively called. Some of the profoundest Christian philosophers have taken this view. Among these we must place Schleiermacher, whose whole being was pervaded with a genuine Christian spirit acquired in early life among the Moravians. He rejects the idea of all miraculous inspiration, and attributes to the sacred writers only what Plato and Cicero attributed to the poets,— *afflatus spiritus divini*,— a breathing of the Divine spirit, "a divine action of nature, an interior power like the other forces of nature." With this view De Wette and many of the German writers agree. Inspiration, as I have shown in the previous chapter, being a quickening or vivifying of the intuitive faculty of the soul, may exist in different degrees of intensity. A writing can never long maintain its claim to being an inspired production unless it rises above the ordinary level of thought and expression to an unusual height. Hence, many of the books that were once accepted as a part of the sacred canon have been dropped out of it, and only those have been left that seem to bear this impress and seal of "high divinity," on the Darwinian principle of the survival of the fittest. Michælis rejected large portions of what we accept as the Bible. Luther threw out the Epistle of James. Swedenborg expurgated from the Old Testament several of its books, and all of the New Testament except the four Gospels and the Apocalypse, and yet held the highest possible view of the inspiration, and even absolute divinity, of the remaining portions of the volume. But would it not be better to accept the Pauline doctrine, that "*all* scripture (or writing) is given by inspiration of God," and that all holy men of God write as they are moved by an inward, Divine impulse and spiritual stimulus, but possess this in different degrees of intensity.   Even Gaussen, the most ultra-advocate of a mechanical, verbal inspiration, admits that the Divine influence was not felt in the same degree by all the writers of the Bible. (*Theopneusty*, p. 36.)   But the idea that the Book is inspired, and not the writers of it, is simply an impossibility.   Such a proposition, to use the language of Herbert Spencer, contains not only what is "unknowable" but even that which is "unthinkable." He asserts also "that every word of the Bible is as really from man as it is from God.   In a certain sense the Epistle to the Romans is entirely a letter of Paul; in a still higher sense, the Epistle to the Romans is entirely a letter of God."   (*Theopneusty*, p. 39.)   I am not certain that the same might not be predicated of one of the religious poems of Whittier, as that entitled, "My Psalm," and that most beautiful production, "The Eternal Goodness."   Here the divine idea is clothed in the choicest language, and so far as these poems contain any spiritual truth, that truth must be ultimately referred to the Divine Mind as its origin and emanating source. As I have before affirmed, we can no more think without God than we can exist without Him, and the same may be affirmed of the representation of our thoughts in writing or by vocal utterance.   I do not wish to deny the inspiration of what the Christian world calls the Bible.   I accept that doctrine, but protest in the name of humanity against confining it to such narrow limits, shutting it up within the contracted boundaries of Palestine, and confining it to a few individuals.   The land of the Jews is not the only place where the soul can come into fellowship with the life of God, or commune with the Divine Mind.   It is not the only point on the earth's surface where the heavens meet the earth, and commingle their life with ours.   An *inspired* apostle has said that "God is not far from every one of us," and that "in Him we live, and move, and have our being." (Acts xvii: 27, 28)   He is as near to us as our souls are to our bodies, and is our inmost life.   All the phenomena of our life have a closer connection with Him than most persons are conscious of, or ever come to believe. God's being and activity are coextensive. The one is as ubiquitous as the other. As no person can be outside the bounds of the Divine existence,—since God is everywhere and in all,—so no one can be *insulated* from Him and His ceaseless influence. Most persons are stone blind to this great truth, and the consciousness of it may exist in ten thousand different degrees, but in the highest degree ever realized in the history of the race it existed in the breast of Jesus the Christ. He could say: "The words that I speak unto you I speak not of myself, but the Father that dwelleth in me, He doeth the works." (John xiv: 10.) As the clay statue which God is represented as making had no life until it was breathed into it by the Divine Being, so all life is a ceaseless *inspiration*, an influx that has been continued to us through every moment of our existence. It is self-evident that what is the origin and perpetual support of life must be to us the fountain of health, both of mind and body. Health is as much the gift of God as is life itself, for it is only a state of life. To be made consciously a "partaker of the Divine nature" is to find in Him "the health of our countenance." As the Divine Being is the One and only Life, and our life is incessantly derived from Him, then it is certain that it did not have its beginning at our birth, nor will it end with what we call death. Thus, to know God is eternal life. There is no *future* life. We never go beyond the present. We reach that point but never pass it. Tomorrow never comes. Our existence is inclosed within *the divine moment*, the eternal *now*. Immortality is not something to be looked for in an impossible future that we never reach, but is, as both Jesus and Buddha taught, to be realized in the living present. All time and all space, as Kant and Swedenborg affirm, are *in* our-selves,—that is, within the enclosure of our spiritual being. As the body is a compound of all that the world contains, so the soul of man has in it the germ of all there is in the spiritual realm. In Buddhism it is taught that man, by meditation, and by coming to know the unreality and impermanency of the world of sense and the human body, can attain to a state of exemption from sickness, old age, and death. (*Hegel's Philosophy of History*, p. 177.) Does not Jesus teach essentially the same thing in his doctrine of the attainment of eternal life here and now?   As Shakyamuni Gautama became a Buddha (which signifies "one who knows") by the reception of a light from a higher realm, so Jesus became the Christ, the anointed or knowing one, in a similar way, and taught that through him our existence could become so linked to the Divine Being as to be exempt from death, and, by viewing the root of our individuality in the One and the All, to live everlasting life in the present.

CHAPTER XV.

INSPIRATION UNIVERSAL, OR THE PHILOSOPHY OF COMMON SENSE.

Sir William Hamilton very truly says that "our cognitions, it is evident, are not all second-hand." This is the key-note of his philosophy. It means, or ought to mean, when properly understood, that all our knowledge is not derived from other minds by instruction, but arises from within the mind itself, and is in reality a Divine inspiration and comes to us from the living Word, the eternal Logos, which is "the true light that lighteth every man that cometh into the world." Cicero, in his Tusculan Questions, which is a treatise on the immortality of the soul, long ago said: *Omnia autem in re consensio omnium gentium lex naturæ putanda est*, the agreement of all nations in anything must be viewed as a law of nature. On this ground he rests the proof of the existence of God and the reality of a future life. But this universal consent to a doctrine can be accounted for on no theory so well as to attribute it to an emanation from the Divine Mind.

Common sense, or the spontaneous action of the mind, is equivalent to an intuitive perception. It is an involuntary cognition. It is a knowledge that comes to us without any volitional or conscious effort of our own, and without any process of reasoning, and is really a Divine revelation. Much of our knowledge, especially that which relates to the practical uses and duties of life, comes to us in this way, and all that comes to us from without by instruction and from books, unless it can be made to rest on this basis

109

and be made one with the decisions of the *sensus communis*, or universal sense, is merely external, and has little value. These "cognitions at first hand," as Sir William Hamilton calls them,— these fundamental facts, feelings, and beliefs,— are seen in their own light and prove themselves. The number of self-evident truths is much greater than the limited number mentioned as such in works on Logic and Mental Science, and the Mathematics. As the essential conditions of all knowledge, the decisions of the common sense must be accepted as true. "To suppose their falsehood is to suppose that we are created capable of intelligence, in order to be made the victims of delusion; that God is a deceiver, and the root of our nature a lie." (*Wight's Philosophy of Sir William Hamilton*, p. 11.)

The voice of nature, when properly understood, is the voice of God. Hence, the maxim, *vox populi, vox Dei*. The phrase *common sense*, so much used in philosophy, and which was the foundation of the systems of Reid, and of Sir William Hamilton, means an intuitive perception of the mind. It has been denominated by a French author (*Chanet, Traite de l'Esprit*) as the universal reason, or natural logic. The truths thus acquired were called by Leibnitz instincts and *the light of nature*, which is only another way of affirming their Divine origin. They have been called intuitions, or an inward seeing and self-evident truths, or those which prove themselves. But they are really *impressions*, or a light from a higher sky, of which the mind is in a state of passive receptivity. They are a Divine revelation, an inspiration, or, as Swedenborg calls it, a state of perception or illustration, that is, a condition of mental lucidity occasioned by an interior, spiritual illumination. God is our Light as well as our Life.

This seems to have been acknowledged in all ages. Hesiod closes his poem entitled, Works and Days, with these remarkable words :—

"The word proclaimed by the concordant voice
Of mankind fails not: for in man speaks God,"

There is a remarkable passage in Aristotle's Ethics which gave rise to much discussion. "The problem is this: What is the beginning or principle of motion in the soul? Now, it is evident that as God is in the universe and the universe in God, that the Divinity in us is also, in a certain sort, the universal mover of the mind. For the principle of reason is not reason, but something better. Now what can we say is better than even science, except God?" (*Ethics.* Liber VII., c. 14.) According to this, all intellectual action is originated by the Divine Life within us.

The principle of *common sense,* or the natural light which all men possess, is from the Divine Logos, or Word, the emanative sphere of the Divine Intellect. It has been variously denominated by different philosophers as instinct, intuition, feeling, belief, faith, inspiration, and revelation. Jacobi, who has been justly called the German Plato, and who is to be classed among the profoundest of Christian philosophers, makes the foundation of all knowledge to be faith, by which he means *a feeling of the truth.* In the mental economy belief takes the place of knowledge. When it rises from probability, its lowest form, to certainty, by which is meant an undoubting assurance, it comes next to knowledge. But faith is more than an intellectual belief. It is a mode of knowing. In its highest degree it is an intuition, an interior perception. It is that which affords a knowledge of supersensible things, and gives us the assurance of their reality and truth. Whatever we *feel* to be true, we are compelled to believe. In this way we gain a knowledge of what is unattainable by sense. Thus, faith becomes the highest mode of knowledge. It is the "substance of things hoped for, the evidence of things not seen." (Heb. xi: 1.) It is, also, as Paul affirms, the gift of God, and, consequently, an inspiration. (Eph. ii: 8.) Fichte says: "All my conviction is only belief, and it proceeds from feeling or sentiment, and not from the discursive understanding." When we wish to express the highest possible certainty of anything, we say we *feel* it to be true, and no logical demonstration can add force to this inward persuasion. Ancillon, whose system is in harmony with that of Jacobi, says that, "Belief, in the philosophical sense, means the apprehension without proof, reasoning, or deduction of any kind, of those higher truths which belong to the supersensible world, and not to the world of appearances. This internal, universal sense, this highest power of mental vision in man, seems to have much in it of the *instinctive*, and may, therefore, be appropriately styled *intellectual instinct*. For on the one hand it manifests itself through sudden, rapid, uniform, resistless promptings, and on the other hand these promptings relate to objects which lie, not within the domain of the senses, but belong to the supersensible world." (*Wight's Philosophy of Sir William Hamilton*, p. 152.)

Luther must have had some such idea of belief as an inward feeling or intuition of the truth when he affirmed "that all things have their root in *belief*, which we can neither perceive nor comprehend. He who would make this belief visible, manifest, and conceivable has sorrow for his pains."

Anselm, one of the deepest thinkers of the mediæval age of the Church, adopted the maxim, *crede ut intelligas*, believe, that you may understand, where faith is taken to be one of the highest forms of knowing. Algazel, of Bagdad, in the Latin translation of his works, makes it a fundamental principle that faith is the root of knowledge,— *radix cognitionis fides*. But by faith, we must always bear in mind, is not meant a cold, intellectual apprehension of the truth, but a *feeling* of the truth. This interior light, call it what you will,— common sense, the light of nature, instinct, intuition, impression, faith, the Divine Word that *came to* the prophets, a revelation, an inspiration, or even the Holy Spirit, — is the highest authority within us, and the divinest light for human guidance. It should always be consulted in the cure of disease. The physician should be influenced by it in the selection of his therapeutic devices. In the mind of the patient, when left free to act without obstruction or interference, it will give a more unerring prescription than the science of medicine can furnish. For what the patient *feels* ought to be done is the best thing to do. It is oftentimes, if we understood it aright, a prescription written by the finger of the Deity within us. By whatever name we call it, it is a Divine oracle within us, whose utterances are less ambiguous and more unerring than those of Dodona or Delphi.

With some slight modification of the language, which does not affect the idea, I can say with S. Baring-Gould: The question of the truth of what the Church calls inspiration is one I do not discuss. We have a revelation in our own nature. An historical revelation, an apocalypse to others in the past, is that which we can never satisfactorily prove to ourselves. The revelation which we have in the depths of our own nature — the light and life of the eternal Word there — never grows old, and it is always there to be questioned according to our spiritual needs, and to be sought unto for guidance, as the Jew went to the Urim and Thummim, and the Greek to the oracle of Apollo at Delphi. On the authority of this revelation, and not on tradition, oral or written, will the Church of the future be founded. (*Preface to Origin and Development of Religious Thought.*) There is in the penetralia, or inmost recesses, of all souls a region where a Divine Word will respond to our sincere craving for truth, and where Divine secrets hidden from the senses will be revealed to us.

CHAPTER XVI.

THE THERAPEUTIC VALUE OF PRAYER.

Prayer may be defined to be the outward expression of an inward desire,—the reaching out of the mind to grasp that which will satisfy a conscious need. It is the Divine method of opening the soul upward to receive what God is more than willing to give.

Prayer is one of the chief elements of a religious life. It is inseparable from religion, and a valuable specific for the mental and spiritual disturbances that underlie all diseases. It is the vehicle, the medium, through which spiritual medicine is given. It is a natural instinct of the soul. It is as natural for us, under certain circumstances, to look to some supreme power above us, or within us, for help as it is for birds of passage, at certain seasons of the year, to go South. And God never impressed an instinctive tendency upon any living thing, from the least to the greatest, without furnishing the means for its satisfactory gratification. If, in distress of body or unhappiness of mind, we are drawn by a spiritual instinct to God in prayer, it is because it is a part of the Divine plan that we should thus find relief. I am aware that it is unusual to class the exercise of prayer among hygienic agencies; and medical science has not given it a place among their therapeutic devices. But this is owing to the incomprehensive and superficial philosophy of life and health that prevails among medical men. Prayer is a conscious recognition of our dependent condition and subjection to powers unseen, but superior to our own. There are certain flowers that, from a vital impulse implanted in them, constantly turn towards the sun to receive his vivifying light and heat. So a humble consciousness of dependence that causes the soul to look to God fits us to receive what we most need. Thus, there is at the same time a moral and hygienic efficacy in prayer. The influence of a calm trust and faith expressing itself in prayer, uttered or unexpressed, over the functions of organic life, cannot be over-estimated. It is a spiritual and potential influence and force brought to bear upon the hidden spring of disease. It is one of the most potent prophylactic agencies against the inception and cause of all morbid conditions.

The proposal of Prof. Tyndall, some years ago, to subject the efficacy of prayer for the sick to what he considered a scientific test, somewhat shocked the religious world, and yet seems in itself a reasonable one. To divide a hospital into two departments, one of which is to be subjected to the prayer-cure, and the other to the ordinary system of medication, is a test of the therapeutic value of the two methods of cure that no real Christian or believer in the sanative efficacy of spiritual forces need fear to accept. But the patients should be expected to pray for themselves as well as to be subjected to the intercession of others. The believer in the curative efficacy of prayer would have the advantage in one respect, —that his remedy was not a *poison*, which cannot be said of many of the drugs that are employed in medicine. It should be borne in mind that it is only one kind of prayer that will save the sick, —the prayer of *faith*. (James v: 15.) This we venture to affirm will be found more efficacious than any system of drug medication. But it must include the combined prayer and faith of both the patient and physician. It is as much an established principle in the science of medicine that faith will make us whole as it is that quinine is a specific for intermittent fever, or iodine for scrofulous swellings.

The efficacy of prayer upon ourselves can be defended upon philosophical grounds. In certain conditions prayer is as natural as our respiration.   A man in distress *spontaneously* cries for help when he believes it possible that succor is in hailing distance; and the true religious spirit always feels that God is thus near to it, and is "a present help in time of trouble."   The spiritual man is in speaking, and even whispering, nearness to the Divine Being, the Central Life.   Such a one does not, in time of need, stop to ask whether prayer is logical or scientific.   He does not even pray from a sense of *duty*, but because he cannot very well help it. It is a spontaneous movement of the religious spirit within him, and is the outward manifestation of an instinctive spiritual impulse, and is as natural a movement of the soul as certain reflex muscular movements are in the body under the influence of the proper sensational stimulus.   It is no more natural for a merry heart to laugh or to sing than it is for a troubled soul to pray. (James v : 13.)   All emotional *excess* of either bliss or pain in the soul must find an outlet, or disease is the result.   An overstrained boiler without a safety-valve will burst.   Prayer is the valve that opens of itself when the painful ebullition of our feelings reaches a certain degree of pressure, and thus life and health are preserved.   In times of strong emotion we instinctively feel that we must *do* something to relieve ourselves, for such states of mind cannot long continue without creating great disturbance in the physiological functions.   There are various modes of relieving the over-excited feelings, and liberating the pent up suffering within us, such us walking the room, climbing the mountain, or visiting foreign lands; but none of them are so efficacious as prayer.   A truly religious man, in times of great mental disturbance, turns to God in prayer as instinctively as the hungry infant seeks the maternal breast, or the young fowl, in time of danger, runs to the shelter of the protecting wing of its parent.   Thus, he finds rest, and health, and peace.

It is manifestly impossible to construct a theory of prayer that would perfectly satisfy the so-called man of science.   And what goes under the name of science, much of which is a mere surface knowledge, does not meet the deeper needs of the religious nature of mankind. The one is as the body, the other as the soul of things. Much that is pompously called science is to the spiritual nature of man like the husks on which the prodigal son fed, but came near dying of hunger.

The theory of prayer that satisfies the profoundest thinkers of the religious world is that which views it as a spiritual *instinct* and a necessity of man's inner nature. "The instinct of prayer is the most manifest of all the religious instincts, and is more nearly self-directive than any other of them; and it is so strong that, at times, it breaks through every philosophical theory of necessity, or pantheism, or atheism itself." (*Instinct, Lowell Lectures*, 1871; by P. A. Chadbourne, LL.D., p. 283.) All our instincts are given us by the Creator for our preservation, our guidance, and our good. Hence, the instinct of prayer, when we follow its promptings, must lead to blessedness. This is the philosophical view of it. Instinct is designed of God to be a pillar of cloud by day and a pillar of fire by night to go before us, to conduct our march to the realization of our supreme good. As S. Baring-Gould has said: "We have absolutely no instance in the whole world of animated nature of an instinctive *penchant* without a corresponding object to which it tends, and which can satisfy that *penchant*." Thus, the spiritual instinct of prayer leads to an inter-communion of the soul with God, and finds its satisfaction in union with the only Life, and the reception of good from that supreme source. He who would live tranquilly, wisely, and healthfully will find somewhere in his own soul the guiding light of his course. To follow anything outside of this, only so far as it meets a response within, is to be led blindly by an *ignis fatuus*, a specious, but bewildering and fallible, guide. It is grasping at a shadow and missing the substance.

The true spirit of prayer cannot be shut up within the limits of any stereotyped formulas, but will find vent in a liturgy of its own creation. By a creative force inherent in its own essence it will find an ultimate expression in forms that it calls into existence at the time. We are speaking of prayer in its reality, and not the

semblance of it so common in the outward worship of the religious
world.   It is only real prayer — the crying out of the soul unto
the living God — that can have any therapeutic value to either
mind or body.   An ill prayer, as Mrs. Browning says, God uses
as a foolishness, to which He gives no answer.   The mere reading or saying a prayer over a sick man or a sinner will not restore
the one to health or convert the other any more than the repetition of the burial service at the grave will raise the dead to life.
It must be the spontaneous and almost irrepressible out-pouring of
the thoughts and feelings of the soul into the listening ear of a
present God.   It is only a certain degree of mental pressure, or
intensity of feeling, that can generate the real spirit of prayer, and
give efficacy to it.   All else is a worthless formalism.

The longer a man practices medicine, the less confidence he has
in material and external remedies.   Their value is a perpetually-
diminishing and vanishing quantity, until he ceases to take them
himself or administer them to his own family, and to others only
from the force of habit, and in the smallest doses.   The more profoundly a man studies the science of medicine, the more he sees the
comparative worthlessness of all chemical preparations and combinations, whether taken into the stomach or applied to the external
surface of the body, and the more highly he will estimate the
value of spiritual remedies, or those that act from within outward,
or from the center to the circumference of our being.   He will
become a convert, in spite of all his medical books, to one of the
principles of the system of Hahnemann, — that the smaller the
quantity of the drug the higher the potency; and the dilution or
trituration that brings the drug down to the dividing line between
something and nothing, so that you cannot tell which it is, has the
greatest sanative efficiency.   This is the nearest possible approach,
on a material plane of thought, to the adoption of a science of
spiritual medicine.

CHAPTER XVII.

CHRIST AND DISEASE; OR, THE POWER OF THE SPIRITUAL LIFE OVER THE BODY.

The highest form of existence is that of a true religious life, which, in its essence, is a harmonious union of goodness and truth, love and wisdom, benevolence and faith, in the character and activity of the individual. Where intellect and love are harmoniously united and blended, and act in perfect concordance, the resulting product is spiritual power. The omnipotence of God is the union of infinite wisdom and infinite love, or the knowing how to do what His goodness inclines Him to do. He who is, in this respect, an image of God, partakes of His spiritual almightiness. When a true philosophy is taken into the mount of transfiguration, and transformed into a divinely human religion, its face shines from the radiance of a higher sun, and possesses a power over ourselves and others that it could not otherwise have. When philosophy and religion are combined into a harmonious unity, each adds power and influence to the other. All religion should be made scientific, and all science religious. There is no inharmony between them when both are properly understood. The attempt to demonstrate the perfect agreement and concordance of the two, which is being made by many at the present time, is a laudable one, and promotive of the best interests of the race, though to accomplish this the current religious creeds must part company with some of their irrational dogmas, and science give up many of its unproved assump-

119

tions. But this will be no loss to either, as it is only eliminating an element of weakness from each.

All the most influential thinkers of the past — men who have mingled their thoughts with the current of the world's life, and given shape and direction to its historic development — have been profoundly religious men. As an example of these " world-historical " persons, as Neander would call them, we may mention Socrates. He was a man of a great and, in that age, unusual religious fervor, and subject to those temporary exaltations of the mind which he made no great mistake in looking upon as Divine visits, for the higher religious activities, and the intellectual illumination that accompanies them, bring the soul into a nearness to God. In this state, all Divine and spiritual things lose in us their feeling of remoteness.

Among the ancients, Anaxagoras, Pythagoras, and Plato were men in whom the religious element in their nature gave elevation to their intellectual range. In more modern times, we may mention Schelling, who has been called the German Plato, and Fichte, who might with equal propriety be denominated the German Socrates; and, in addition, we might name Schleirermacher and Neander; and even Hegel was a member of the church. In Emanuel Swedenborg we see a man in whom science and religion were so wedded as to render even a temporary divorce an impossibility. His intellect was always and everywhere religious, and his religion was at all times intellectual. He deserves above all men of modern history the appellation of the spiritual philosopher. The system of spiritual science which is unfolded in his voluminous writings, and exemplified in his remarkable experiences, is having a silent but powerful influence in moulding and modifying the religious beliefs and changing the thoughts of men, throughout Christendom, on spiritual things. This influence, though it falls upon the world as noiseless as the dews of night, will increase in the future.

The founders of the great religions of the world were men in whom the intellect and the religious nature were blended more or less harmoniously. This is what gives their systems of doctrine such an almost unyielding grasp upon the minds of men, and such influence over so great masses of the world's population. Such men were Confucius, Buddha, Zoroaster, and we may add Mohammed. In all these examples which we have given of spiritual power there is some common principle. Can we discover what it is? It is that they were men of strong intellect, and were profoundly religious men. They were religious, not superficially, not in momentary and transient moods, but all through their being. Their religious fervor transported them into the third heavens, but also carried the intellect with it into a Divine realm of life and thought. Hence their thoughts, when given to others in their writings, have a Divine warmth and spiritual vitality in them, and are not mere cold and logical intellectual conceptions, like moonbeams reflected from polar ice. The religious nature exalted the intellect to a Divine realm of thought, where they became inspired, and recipient of the living Word, the indwelling Logos, of which they became in a true sense the incarnations. In all such men, in a mitigated sense, the Word is made flesh and dwells among us. It is impossible to be spiritual in our intellectual conceptions without being religious. To reach the higher degrees of inspiration, or quickened intuition, without a fervor of religious feeling is as impossible as to fly without wings.

The highest example in human history of the perfect union of the intellect with the religious nature, and the resultant spiritual power, is seen in Jesus the Christ. In him there was the most intimate blending of the purely human and the truly Divine, so that in his personality where the human nature ended and the Divinity commenced no one can perceive. The boundary line between the Godhead and manhood is not clearly drawn. There is in him a deification of humanity and a humanization of God, and somehow in him God comes very near to the souls of men. In him we witness the spectacle of a human nature and soul filled with God,— with all the fullness of God. But he expected, and expressed the wish, that all his disciples in every age should be,

in this respect, a copy of the Master,— that they should be one
with God as he and the Father were one.   (John xvii : 20–23.)
As the highest representation of God in human history, there is
in his life, as unfolded in the Gospels, a revelation of the thoughts
and feelings of God.   No man can be actuated by a Divine influence and afflatus without in some way, and to some extent, mani-
festing the feelings of the Deity.   But Paul affirms that God gave
the Spirit to the Christ without measure, and the Divine love was
the motive power of all his activity.   He spent a large fraction of
his public life in the cure of "all manner of sickness and disease"
among the people.   His activity seemed naturally to take that
beneficent direction.   So far as the Christ-principle is in us, we
shall have power to do the same.   The drift and current of our
inner life will exhibit itself as a spontaneous impulse to do good
to the souls and bodies of men.   Jesus seemed to have a divinely
clear conception of the spiritual origin of disease, and of the efficacy of spiritual remedies in its cure.   He did not look upon sickness of the flesh as the real disease, but as the effect of an *a priori*
spiritual malady ; and when this antecedent cause ceases to oper-
ate, the morbid effect comes to an end.   As Jesus the Christ was
perpetually moved by a Divine influence and impulse in his career
as the great Physician, it shows that in God there is a prepetual
conatus, an irrepressible endeavor, an unchangeable willingness to
heal our diseases of mind and body.   In all our struggles against
every morbid condition, within and without, we can, with unerring certainty, count upon God and his omnipotent love as our
unfailing ally in the battle with evil and suffering.   If God be for
us, what can prevail against us?   Here is the standing-ground of
an assured and unyielding faith in Him for the cure of our own
sicknesses and those of others through us.   If I have any understanding of the system of the Christ in the cure of disease, he
found the cause of it in some prior disturbance of the spiritual
principle in man, and he applied his healing power to the mental
root of the malady.   All his *mighty works* had a redemptive aim,
that is, they were designed primarily to deliver men from spiritual

evil. Matter was viewed by him as an unsubstantial *appearance*, and mind was the only reality. Through the restored and redeemed soul he healed the body of its diseases, both functional and organic. To illustrate his Divine method of cure, and to make it an available, practical system, will be the aim of all I have to say in the subsequent chapters of this volume.

CHAPTER XVIII.

By the Christ-principle, or that by which Jesus became the Christ, I mean a *spiritual intelligence.* It is not science or knowledge on the plane of sense; it is not a knowledge imparted by instruction from without, and imported into the mind, but arises from within,— the God-light in the soul, the living Word. Nor is it knowledge *alone*, a coldly luminous intellectual state, like moonbeams reflected from the snow fields on a winter's night, but it is an interior light that has in it the warmth of a Divine love.

That Jesus, after the age of thirty years, exhibited a marvelous power of healing the sick without medicine, and which so far surpassed the power of his contemporaries as to be deemed miraculous, is a well-established fact, and as well certified as the principal facts in the life of Alexander or Cæsar. It is not improbable in itself; and many marvelous cures have been effected in every subsequent age, and even in the century in which we live, that render it entirely credible. On this subject I cannot do better than to use the language of Dr. Hase, with some additions of my own. These so-called miracles cannot contradict the laws of the world, which are the constant expression of the Divine will, and the established Divine order. Therefore, amid all apparent contradictions, we must seek for an accordance with law.

According to the Gospel narratives, his acts of healing were not

124

always unconnected with bodily contact, the imposition of the hands
or other outward means. (Mark vii: 33; viii: 23. John ix: 6.
Mat. viii: 16; xvii: 21.) In this way they may have some
relation to Rabbinical or Essene methods of cure, and in some
measure communicable by instruction. This is rendered probable
by its continuance in the apostolic church. (1 Cor. xii: 10, 28.)
It has been supposed by some that Jesus spent his early life
among the Essenes, who were called in Egypt Therapeutæ, or
healers. This may or may not be true. We have no historic
evidence of it, and it is, in itself, a matter of little importance.
But whatever means he used, *the power of the Word and the Spirit
was always predominant.* He demanded as an indispensable condition a *trustful submission*, or an act of faith. From the lack of
a state of receptivity, as a consequence of the absence of this need-
ful mental state, his power of healing was not always exercised
(Mark vi: 5), nor did all the sick who sought a cure find it
(Mark i: 32, 34). On one occasion, he healed only one out of a
multitude of sick people. (John v: 3.) *Perhaps all cures, by
every method, are confined to the region where the power of the
will and of faith over the body exists.* These cures, therefore, are
not without analogies in all ages and countries, and may hence be
reduced to the action of some spiritual law. A resemblance is
afforded us in the cures effected by animal magnetism, but only so
far as it contains a mysterious power over disease, arising out of
the great life of nature; and perhaps, moreover, the means which
Jesus used may have stood in some relation to magnetic or psychological phenomena. *But the marvelous power of Jesus appears
far more like an intelligent mastery of nature by the soul.* The
mind of man, originally endowed with dominion over the earth,
recovered its old rights by the holy innocence of Jesus, conquering the unnatural power of disease and death. Here, therefore,
there was no violation of the laws of nature, but, on the contrary,
the disturbed order of the world here recovered its original harmony and truth. Even the wonderful power exercised over external nature may be reduced under the same law, and may be under

stood according to an accelerated process of nature. (*Hase's Life of Jesus*, pp. 96–99.)

Jesus lived in harmony with the perfect order of nature, that is, the will of God, which is expressed in nature, was his supreme law. What a person who thus comes into the true order of his life can do, the history of the world furnishes us but an imperfect means of knowing, from the paucity of examples of that state. A knowledge of nature's laws, and a life in harmony with the will of God, as expressed in what we call nature, invests the soul of man with a fraction of God's omnipotence. God is immanent in all natural law. To be perfectly natural is to attain to the blessedness and power of a life in God. When a divinely-illuminated intellect is wedded to an exalted state of the religious affections, such a man will be a Divine power in the world, a Divine fact in human history. But his activity will assume a beneficent direction, and probably in the cure of disease, and the removal of the mental unhappiness that underlies it, as naturally and spontaneously as the needle points to the pole. There is a *natural* antagonism between the Christ-principle and disease,— a spontaneous resistance to the abnormal spiritual state which is the root of every morbid condition of the body. The human body does not contain room enough for both to occupy it in harmony. The Christ-principle, as the most potent and positive force, will bind the "strong man" and cast him out. As soon as a man comes into possession of it, he is at once turned into a good Samaritan, and goes forth to heal the wounds and hurts of humanity by wine and oil, the symbolic representatives of good and truth.

There are many things done today from an advanced knowledge of nature's laws, and her hidden forces, that would have been deemed eighteen centuries ago as the greatest of miracles. But as common events and every-day occurrences they have lost the element of *wonder*, and are, consequently, no longer miraculous. They are not *surprises*, as the word miracle means, but ordinary things, like the germination of grain, the rising and setting of the sun, and the still mysterious ebb and flow of the tides. The cures wrought by Jesus the Christ are as much in harmony with nature, when properly understood, as the operation of the electric telegraph and the telephone, or the taking of photographs. The law by which they were effected is not an incommunicable Divine secret and impenetrable mystery, but will some day be as well understood as any of the processes of nature, and better than the action of medicines in the cure of disease. Then will be fulfilled the words of the Christ: "The works that I do shall ye do also; and greater works than these shall ye do, because I go to my Father." As spiritual knowledge increases, and Divine light penetrates the solid darkness of the world, the boundaries of the seemingly impossible will become an increasingly narrow area. When the hitherto mysterious relations of God and man, spirit and matter, and soul and body, are better understood, what are called miraculous cures will be the every-day occurrences in the life of the true physician. The supernatural will disappear from science and history, and miracles will cease to be miraculous. The phenomena of the electric telegraph eighteen hundred years ago would have been more wonderful than anything accredited to Jesus in the Gospel narratives. The grand secret of all his cures is found in an intuitive knowledge of the relation of mind and body, of spirit and matter, and the absolute dominion of the one over the other. There has always been a yearning in the human soul to penetrate the darkness on this subject, and to lift the veil from its mystery. It shows itself in the history of magic, which is almost coëval with the authentic annals of the race. But the fullness of time — the Divine, auspicious moment — for the revelation of the great secret had not come. There is in men's minds a deep, prophetic intimation that the day-spring from on high is about to visit us, to give light to them that sit in darkness and in the region and shadow of death, to guide our feet into the way of peace. (Luke i: 78, 79.) Then sickness, disease, and death, with a *quantum* of suffering that attends them, at which the benevolent heart stands appalled, will not be viewed as the infliction of a relentless fate, for which there is no remedy but passive submission.   Science with its higher knowledge of the mental causes of disease, and of the efficacy of unfailing spiritual remedies, will no longer stand in powerless and dumb amazement before it, but will become the power of God and the wisdom of God unto salvation.

Of the thirty-three so-called miracles of the Christ, recorded in the Gospels, twenty-four were the cure of the sick.   So far as Jesus was a representative of God, and a manifestation in the flesh of the Divine Being, this shows that God is more interested in healing the sick than in anything else.   It is the favorite work of the Divine Love, the recreation of the Infinite Goodness, the pastime of the Infinite Spirit-Presence and Life.   But the healing of the sick by Jesus was no violation of the laws of nature. As one has said : " The miracle is thus not unnatural, nor can it be, since the unnatural, the contrary to order, is of itself the ungodly, and can in no way, therefore, be affirmed of a Divine work, such as those with which we have to do.   The very idea of the world, as more than one name which it bears testifies, is that of an order ; that which comes in then to enable it to realize this idea which it has lost will scarcely itself be a disorder.   So far from this, the true miracle is a higher and purer nature, coming down out of the world of untroubled harmonies into this world of ours, which so many discords have jarred and disturbed, and bringing this back again, though it be but for one prophetic moment, into harmony with the higher.   The healing of the sick can in no way be termed against nature, seeing that the sickness which was healed was against the true nature of man,—that it is sickness which is abnormal and not health.   The healing is the restoration of the primitive order."   (*Trench's Notes on the Miracles of our Lord*, p. 20.)

God has managed, and perpetually manages, to insert into our nature a tendency toward health, and against the unnatural condition which we call disease.   When our flesh receives a wound, a strange nursing and healing process is immediately commenced to repair the injury.   So in all diseases, organic or functional.

This mysterious healing power, the *vis medicatrix naturæ* of the older physiologists, sets itself to work at once to triumph over the morbid condition. The results of its action bear all the marks of the highest intelligence, and thus exclude the idea of all chance. According to I. H. Fichte, these results are effected by an unconscious, or rather preconscious, action of the mind, which is the only living force of the body. But the only question with which we wish to deal at persent is, cannot this healing process be greatly accelerated by a voluntary and conscious action of the mind, assisted, if need be, by some other person? I unhesitatingly affirm, from experience and observation, that it can. By some volitional, mental effort and process of thought,— call it, if you will, *fancy, imagination*, or *faith*, or all combined into an unnamed power,—this sanative *conatus*, or healing power which God has given to our physiological organism, may be greatly quickened and intensified in its action upon the body. Here is the secret philosophy of the cures effected by Jesus the Christ. Understanding the law and the mental process by which they were accomplished, they may be repeated upon ourselves or others under like conditions. In reference to one of the most seemingly impossible of the cures effected by Jesus,— the case of the leper of Capernaum,—Furness very justly remarks: "That it ought not to be hard to account for the cure, and to conceive how a mental and moral influence could have wrought to overcome the disease, if we hold to the philosophy of many of the wisest of men, which teaches that the mind, instead of being an accident of the body, is its creating, organizing life." (*Jesus*, by W. H. Furness, p. 92.) This is the law that is illustrated by all the so-called miracles of the Christ, so far as they relate to the healing of the sick; and all the others, if they are not mythical, are of minor importance. There is a law of the action of the mind on the body that is no more an impenetrable mystery than the law of gravitation. It can be understood and acted upon in the cure of disease as well as any other law of nature. Here knowledge, and especially *spiritual intelligence*, is power, and, in the eyes of the multitude, the results of its operation in the healing power of Jesus were deemed a miraculous potentiality. As a law of nature expresses the uniform mode in which the Divine force manifests itself, a conformity to law is to us the only source of power. It is thus alone that we can make the Divine power available for the cure of disease. Every method of cure, in order to its success, must conform its therapeutic devices to the Divine operation in nature, and these can only accelerate and intensify the natural process of healing. He who best understands how to do this will be the physician whose cures will be the most frequent, and, to the world at large, the most marvelous.

CHAPTER XIX.

JESUS AS A SAVIOUR, OR HEALTH-GIVER, *MINUS* THE ENCHANTMENT THAT DISTANCE LENDS TO THE VIEW.

To save and to heal, according to the highest authority in etymology, are the same word at the root. Jesus as a Saviour was the Health-Giver in the fullest sense of the term. He did not heal the hurts of humanity slightly but fully. In his system, salvation was not the superficial thing that it came to mean in the Church. It was not the mere forgiveness of the sins of men; it was much more. It was not a part of man's nature, but the entire man that was the subject of it. The invalid was made whole — that is, *hale* — in every department of his being. In the character of a Saviour or Healer let us briefly look at him, subtracting from the view all theological and mythical additions.

The inspired sentiment of the poet Campbell, that "distance lends enchantment to the view," finds frequent illustrations. Things distant either in time or space often seem larger and of more importance than every-day occurrences around us. This added magnitude, which distance lends to them through the imagination, must be subtracted in forming a rational estimate of them. In the days of my childhood, in reading of the thirty-one kingdoms overrun by Joshua and his Jewish followers, those petty tribes swelled into dominions like those of Russia, or England, or France. But they all existed, without crowding each other, in a territory not much larger than New Hampshire. When we read

131

of the *sea* of Galilee and the *ships* upon it, the average religious man or woman fancies a large body of water with vessels upon it but little less in capacity than the Great Eastern ; whereas the sober fact is the whole lake of Gennesaret, which is only eighteen miles in length and six miles wide, and shallow in depth, might be emptied into our lake Superior without perceptibly raising its waters; and the *ships* were only small boats, many of which might be taken on board an ordinary man-of-war without discommoding the crew.   So from the miracles of Jesus the Christ we are to eliminate the apparent magnitude which distance gives them, and bring them into a sober philosophical reality.   Seen through the intervening atmosphere of eighteen centuries, they are viewed as a sort of *mirage*, and greatly magnified, and assume unnatural, if not impossible, proportions.   Eliminating all this "enchantment" which distance lends them, they are brought into the compass of events that are today possible, if not of frequent occurrence.   Yet they are still what they were called, "mighty works" (δύναμεις, an exhibition of *spiritual power*), and they were, and still are, as they were sometimes denominated in the New Testament, "signs" (σημεῖα), that is, "they were indications or tokens of the near presence and working of God.   They were signs and pledges of something more and beyond themselves, and indicate the connection in which the doer of them stood with a higher power."   (*Trench's Notes on the Miracles of our Lord*, p. 11.)

It is a truth of the intuitive reason, and one that is self-evident, that the same cause, other things being equal, will produce the same effects.   Hence the spiritual agencies and forces employed by Jesus the Christ in the cure of disease will effect today the same results.   If he who understands them and uses them with this end or aim does not possess them or cannot control them in equal intensity and power, only *similar* effects will be produced, — the same in kind, but less in degree.   That his "mighty works," or, as the word has been inaccurately translated, his miracles, which were mostly those of healing, could never be repeated in subsequent ages, by his disciples or the learners in his school, is contrary to his express declarations. (Mark xvi: 17, 18; John xiv: 12.) In the first passage, the laying the hands upon the sick so that they should recover was to be the "sign" or outward manifestation of a genuine faith, and was always to follow its exercise in that direction. In the other passage the possibility and the practicability of these curative results being reproduced is based upon an implied promise of aid from him out of the heavens into which he was to ascend; and these always touch the earth at the point where the believing soul stands, and are never removed from us by spatial distance, but are as near to us as our souls are to our bodies. For the spiritual world is the universal and everywhere present realm of *mind*. Our minds are already in it and constitute a part of it. The power to do these works was not to proceed from a crucified body and dead Jesus, but from an ascended and living Christ, whose eternal life and spiritual power were to be imparted to his disciples or scholars, and incorporated into their being. Peter declared to the lame man, who was healed at the gate of the temple, that it was in the name of Jesus Christ of Nazareth, or by a power derived from him, that he was made whole and able to walk. (Acts iii: 1–16.) To attempt such things, unless our natural powers are augmented and reinforced by a power from on high, is like a totally disabled man trying to walk without crutches, or a bird with broken wings attempting to fly.

As to the historical fact of the actual existence of such a person as Jesus eighteen centuries ago there can be no rational doubt. We have the same evidence of it that we have of the existence of Alexander, Cæsar, Charlemagne, Napoleon, or even George Washington, and far more than we have of the existence of Confucius, Zoroaster, or Buddha. Yet I am constrained to believe that the Christ-principle, the living Word, the Divine Logos, the reception of which in full measure made the son of Mary the Anointed One, or the Christ, is of far more importance than the mere historical personal Jesus. The Word, the light that lighteth every man that cometh into the world, and the unsealed fountain of all inspiration, was personified and incarnated in him, and this light is still the life of men.   This Word — this illuminating and vivifying power — is represented by John in the Gospel that is most emphatically Christian, and which my friend Rev. E. H. Sears calls the heart of Christ, as the primal, creative energy.   "All things were made by it, and without it was not anything made that was made." (John i: 3.)   Whoever will open his soul upward to receive it from a sympathetic conjunction with the Christ can do the works that he did, and have power from on high to heal the souls and bodies of men.   This "light of life," this uncreated and creative Word, is seeking to diffuse itself through all human souls as their highest mental energy and power.   It is striving for admission through the sensuous envelope in which we are enclosed, like the pressure of the atmosphere upon a vacuum. This Word of God is not a *book* to which men are to resort for instruction, but is the every-where-present light of truth that *came* to the souls of men; and it will come to us, as it has to the prophets and inspired messengers of all ages, if we will hold the soul as a recipient vessel open and upward to receive it.   Jesus did this as no one before had ever done, and thence came his spiritual power.   That which is itself the creative energy must have the highest and divinest sanative virtue.   If we will consent, it will arise in us "with healing on its wings," and can, under the proper conditions, be transmitted to others as God's "saving health."   In a mitigated but true sense we can become Messiahs and Saviours to others, — imperfect copies at least of the original Christ.   Then will be fulfilled the words of Jesus: "As the Father has sent me into the world, so I send you into the world," to multiply and perpetuate my "mighty works" in saving (or healing) men.

As Jesus, the son of Mary and the "son of man," became the Christ, or Knowing One, by his receptivity of the Logos, or the Word, the Divine Source of all intellectual and spiritual illumination, so as the Christ he was an embodiment or incarnation of the Word, the emanative sphere of the Divine Intellect.   The entrance of the Word gave him light. (Ps. cxix: 130.) It was a perpetual light unto his feet, and a lantern to his path. (Ps. cxix: 105.) In him the Word was made flesh and dwelt among us, full of grace and truth. (John i: 14.) During his fleshly manifestation he was a *living teacher* to his disciples. He left behind him no written instruction, or formulated expression of his doctrines, but promised that after his graduation to a higher realm of life he would ever be present with his disciples in spirit, and continue to be their living teacher and guide. It was an idea of many of the early Christian Fathers that the Christ and the Word are identical. So the real Word of God is not an inanimate book, but a living and ascended Christ, who is accessible to the soul of the sincere believer at all times and in all places. This illuminating influence of the Christ, as the Word, is referred to by John: "But the anointing which ye have received of him abideth in you, and ye need not that any man teach you: but as the same anointing teacheth you of all things, and is truth, and is no falsity, and even as it hath taught you, ye shall abide in it." (1 John ii: 27.) In the Cabalistic symbolism of the East the anointing with oil signified the reception of spiritual truth, and the consequent power for the successful discharge of the duties of an office. Hence, by the reception of the Word, God anointed Jesus with the Holy Spirit, and with power, and he went about doing good and healing all that were oppressed with evil. (Acts x: 38.) He in turn promised the same Divine Word and Spirit to his disciples and scholars, to qualify them to proclaim the Gospel of truth, and to heal all manner of sickness and disease among the people. (Mat. x: 1.) The promise has his present indorsement and is negotiable today, as will be shown in the following chapter.

CHAPTER XX.

Jesus foretold to his disciples that after his apparent départure from them by death he would manifest himself to them in the Spirit, and as a Spirit. The Paraclete, or Comforter, the name this spiritual presence and influence was to bear, was promised as a substitute for his personal and material presence. This higher form of manifestation was to be a permanent and perpetual arrangement in the kingdom of God. It was to abide with his disciples forever. (John xiv: 16–18.) "Lo, I am with you always, even unto the end of the world." (Mat. xxviii: 20.) He declared it expedient for them that he should go away, or be removed from the recognition of their external senses, in order that, when freed from the limitations of time and space, by his ascent in the scale of life to the spiritual world, he might be more intimately present to their inward being. His going away only expresses his removal from their outward vision, and this bodily absence was necessary as a preparation for his more perfect manifestation in the Spirit and as a Spirit. His material absence was preparatory to his second advent, or his coming again in an invisible but divinely real and all-pervading spiritual efficacy to perfect their inward life. Christ as the Spirit could act from within, and consequently with much greater power in all those offices in which we most need him. The religious world makes a great mistake when they separate, in their conception of him, the Holy Spirit from the Christ,

136

and make it anything but the Christ influencing the soul. It is his *second* and higher coming to the world, his advent to us not in the flesh, in which manifestation we know him no more (2 Cor. v: 16), but as Christ the Spirit. It is important that we keep in mind the distinction between Jesus and the Christ. Jesus was the son of Joseph and Mary. The Christ is Jesus *plus* the Divine illuminating Word, or a mere human personality with the immense addition of an open communication with the Divine Intellect and Life. In this latter character he was to reappear to his followers. He says: "If I go away, I will come to you;" and this going away, or elevation above all material and fleshly conditions, was necessary to his nearer and perpetual presence. Let it be borne in mind that his coming as the Paraclete, or the Comforter, was to be more than a substitute for his personal and material presence and external manifestation. If he could instruct his disciples in the truths of the kingdom of God, he can do it far better now. If he could heal disease, when he was in the flesh, by removing the unseen mental cause, he can do it now with greater spiritual facility. Christ as the Spirit is more to us than the mere son of Mary ever could have been. This is a truth we are in great danger of overlooking. As the Paraclete, he was to be the infallible guide to all truth and present duty. (John xvi: 13.) He was to be a principle of life abiding in the soul, raising the intuitive faculty to the clear perception of spritual truth, swaying the desires of the soul, exalting its affections, and strengthening all its faculties.

According to the Johannean Gospel, the second coming of the Christ was to be in the character and office of the Paraclete. This word is one of deep significance. By the early Greek Fathers, as Origen, Epiphanius, Chrysostom, Theophylact, and Cyril, the term was interpreted so as to present the Spirit of Jesus, which was to come to his disciples, as the Comforter or Consoler, which has been followed in our English translation. In the early Latin Church the word was taken to mean an Advocate. In the first Epistle of John (1 John ii: 1), the only place where the word occurs in the New Testament out of the Johannean Gospel, it is rendered Advocate, and applied to the Christ. But the Latin *Advocatus* and the English term Advocate refer to the pleading of causes, and do not express the meaning of the word Paraclete as applied to the Holy Spirit, or to the office and work of Christ as the Spirit. The English word *Counsel*, if we are to use a legal term, would come much nearer the meaning of the Greek, as signifying one whose function it was to advise, to direct, to support, rather than to plead.   Campbell, following Ernesti, gives to the word the meaning of Doctor or Teacher, or an inward Monitor. This comes nearer to its true significance. Hare prefers the word Comforter to express the meaning of the Greek term Paraclete, using it in its etymological sense, as the strengthener and supporter. But it means more than can be expressed by any one word in our language. It may include all the different significations given above, and no one of them alone exhausts its full force. It is one of those untranslatable words, with a depth of spiritual meaning that cannot be expressed by any single term, with which we so often meet in the profound utterances of the Christ. To my mind it is used to represent the idea of a perfect substitute for the personal and bodily presence of Jesus with his disciples. It is Jesus the Spirit, and still in the character and office of the Christ, imparting to men the Logos, the living and illuminating Word, the interior light and life of all souls. Whatever he could do for his disciples or scholars during his fleshly and more material manifestation, he can do for them now. The inspiration of the Paraclete, or spiritual teacher, is a higher source of instruction, and a more unerring guide than were the verbal communications of Jesus with his early followers, or than the written Scriptures ever can be. It is the *spirit of truth*, and addresses the soul in the language of ideas. The disciples made far more progress in spiritual knowledge after his outward removal from them than before this. After the descent upon them of the Pentacostal influences, when they came under the tuition of the Paraclete, or the influx of the life of the Christ as a Spirit, they were changed into other men. The gross Jewish carnality of their thoughts respecting the kingdom of God disappeared before their awakened spiritual perceptions. Christianity, by establishing the kingdom of God in the souls of men, lays little stress upon the written Word, or any external things. The infallible guide is the Spirit. Jesus left behind him no written creed, no stereotyped and changeless system of doctrines, and no established ceremonies of worship. And he was reported, with the possible exception of John, by those who had an imperfect comprehension of the profound depth of meaning in his utterances. He bequeathed to his followers instead of these his spiritual presence and influence as the Paraclete. All was left to be unfolded by the Spirit to meet the wants of the souls of men in all ages. Christianity is an inward life springing from Jesus the Christ that was deposited in humanity, and left free to work itself out in its appropriate forms of external manifestation. An inspiration from the Spirit of God he bequeathed to his followers as their perpetual inheritance. He came to connect in the consciousness of men the sundered tie between us and the Divine Being. All religion arises from the natural and necessary connection of man with God, the finite with the Infinite, the purely human with the Divine. The peculiar essence of Christianity consists in the vivid and intense consciousness of God within, which it generates in the soul. It springs from the immediate intuition of the Paraclete or the Spirit of Jesus. Through this he is still present with his followers. God is incarnated in the center of our being, and comes to self-limitation in all men. This was taught by Schelling, the Christian pantheist. The Holy Spirit, or an influx of life and light from God, is as necessary to the life and growth of the human soul as the light and heat of the sun are to the growth and health of plants, and the Paraclete is the divinely appointed medium through which it comes to us.

The Paraclete, in the fully developed Christian system, was to come to men not merely as the "spirit of truth" to kindle within us the light of a spiritual intelligence, and as a vivifying stimulus to our intuitive perceptions, but he was to be present with us as the "light of life," and a quickener of all the vital activities of the soul and body.   It was to be not only an inspiration of light in the intellect, but its influence was to affect all the springs of our being.   Christ in coming to us the second time, and as the Spirit, was to be manifested not as the light-bringer only, but as the life-giver and healer of men's souls and bodies.   He came in the flesh, and still comes as the Paraclete, that men might have life, and that they might have it more abundantly.   (John x: 10.) Says John: "The Life was manifested, and we have seen it, and bear witness and show unto you that Eternal Life which was with the Father, and was manifested unto us." (1 John i: 2.)   His life-giving power, during his fleshly manifestation, was seen in his healing "all manner of sickness and disease among the people." But his manifestation as the Paraclete was, according to his own words, designed to be more than a substitute for his material and personal presence.   The relation of the genuine believer to him is represented by him as a vital one like the connection of the branch with the vine.   The branch has no independent and separate existence, but only a perpetually-derived one.   He could say to his disciples: "Because I live, ye shall live also, and without me ye can do nothing."   Paul's bliss-giving faith recognized the ascended Christ as sustaining this vital relation to him, so that he could no more die or be diseased while consciously and sympathetically united to him than a stream can dry up while connected with an inexhaustible fountain.   He almost lost the idea of his individual existence, just as Jesus himself often seemed to feel that his personal existence as the son of man was merged in the Divine Being, and he spake and acted from Him.   So Paul could say: "It is not I that live, but Christ liveth in me" (Gal. ii: 20); and that when Christ, who is our life, shall appear, then shall we also appear with him in glory.

    It seems to have been the aim of Jesus the Christ, and the design of Christianity, that springs from him as its living root, to accustom men to forget the body, and to live above it, so that they can live forever without it, and thus attain to a state of everlasting life, in which death should be an impossibility, and disease a nonentity, an absolute nihility. Thus Jesus says,— and there is a profounder meaning in his words than the shallow faith of the Church recognizes,— "Verily, verily, I say unto you, he that heareth my words, and believeth on Him that sent me, hath everlasting life, and shall not come into condemnation, but is passed from death unto life." And in another place: "He that liveth in me, and believeth in me, shall never die." (John v: 24; xi: 26.) In his representation of himself as the good shepherd he declares that he lays down his life for the sheep, where the Greek word which is rendered "lay down" means also to put into, to impart. He communicates his own everlasting life to his followers.

He who has attained to this higher faith in the risen Christ is so taken possession of by him, so pervaded by his spiritual presence, that his individual being becomes altogether secondary, and "is hid with Christ in God." (Col. iii: 3.) If we could suppose a small rill to come to a confluence with the grand Mississippi, the Father of Waters, and retain its distinct existence, and yet ceased to flow onward of itself, but was borne along by a mightier current, it would be an expressive symbol of the union of our life with the Divine Life in Christ. An idea like this is at the bottom of that profound little work of Madame Guyon, entitled Spiritual Torrents. The connection of the believing soul with God in Christ is not the destruction of our individuality, for if that were lost there would be nothing left to be united to him. It is the conjunction of two distinct lives in a higher unity. It is not an annihilation of our personal existence, but an infinite addition to it. It is a truth that commends itself at once to our intuitive reason that no man has life in himself. Our being is not self-originated and self-supporting, but is continually communicated from the One Life. Our existence is perpetually imparted from God, and our preservation is a momentary creation,— consequently an inspiration of life and health can be as reasonably expected, and is as available to our faith, as an impartation of light to our intellect. This doctrine is intuitively true, and perfectly harmonizes with the teaching of the Jewish and Christian Scriptures and the Sacred Writings of all nations.   The idea of the nearness of God to man, and his immanence in human nature, is coming to the recognition of the souls of men everywhere, and in the future will enter more fully into the life of humanity.

PART II.

THE

RELATION OF SPIRIT TO MATTER,

AND OF THE

SOUL TO THE BODY IN MAN.

"Judge not according to the appearance, but judge righteous judgment" (δικαίαν κρίσιν, according to the real nature of things). John vii: 24.

"My sensations are in myself, not in the object, for I am myself, and not the object; I am conscious only of myself and of my own state, not of the state of the object. If there is a consciousness of the object, that consciousness is, certainly, neither sensation nor perception,—thus much is clear." *Fichte's Vocation of Man, Popular Works,* p. 271.

CHAPTER I.

The doctrine of Bishop Berkeley, contained in his "Treatise Concerning the Principles of Human Knowledge," published in the year 1710, that all we know of matter is its power of making certain impressions upon our minds through the senses, and that what we call the properties of matter, as color, hardness, extension, form, taste, smell, etc., are ideas in the mind alone, and without a mind to perceive them could have no existence, has never been successfully combated. It has been met with ridicule, and "coxcombs have vanquished Berkeley with a grin," but have never refuted him. When Berkeley denied the existence of matter and an external world independent of a perceiving mind, he meant by matter that unknown *substratum* the existence of which Locke and the sensualist philosophers of his school had declared to be a necessary *inference* from our knowledge of qualities, but the nature of which must forever remain unknown to us. Philosophers had assumed the existence of a material substance,—a *noumenon*, as it was called, which underlies all *phenomena*, or sensible appearances, a *substratum* supporting all qualities, an unknown something in which all accidents inhere, like plants in the soil. Berkeley very properly and logically rejected the idea of this unknown substance, this "incomprehensible somewhat," as a thing not provable by our senses, and he replaced it by a known cause, a spiritual substance. The existence of this substratum in which

145

all the properties of matter were supposed to inhere, and from which they arise, is confessedly unknown and unknowable, and hence is a fiction, a baseless hypothesis. Said Berkeley: "If by matter you understand that which is seen, felt, tasted, and touched, then I say matter exists. I am as firm a believer in its existence as anyone can be, and *herein I agree with the vulgar.* If, on the contrary, you understand by matter that occult substratum which is *not* felt, *not* tasted, and *not* touched,— that of which the senses do not and cannot inform you,— then I say I believe not in the existence of matter, and *herein I differ from the philosophers and agree with the vulgar."* (*Lewes' History of Philosophy,* Vol. 2, p. 298.)

Take from any material object all its sensible properties, or what the mind alone perceives in itself, and what have you left ? The thing to you has no existence, and is annihilated. There is nothing left that can be an object of knowledge, or of which we can form an idea. Matter has the root of its being in mind, and without this it has no existence. That which is not perceived is all the same as that which has no existence, and the mind can perceive nothing but *ideas* in itself. Thus, for example, a certain sensation or idea of color, taste, smell, figure, and consistence being observed together in the mind constitutes a distinct thing which we call an *apple* or an *orange.* Another combination of ideas we name a stone, a tree, or a house. But all that we have any knowledge of is in ourselves. "In all perception," says Fichte, "thou perceivest only thine own condition." (*Popular Works,* p. 269.)

All the properties of matter are now viewed by scientific men as only so many forms of force; as, for instance, color is a modification of light, and light is taken to be a vibratory movement of the ether. This may be true, but color is certainly a sensation or an idea in the mind, and where there is no mind there is no color. Hardness or solidity is only a sensation of resistance ; and when we touch an object and say it is hot, we mean that we feel a *sensation* of heat. If, as modern science affirms, all the properties of matter are forms of force, and we go one step further, as we inevitably must, and show that all force is spiritual, and all causation mental, then matter itself becomes only the manifestation of spirit, and mind the only real substance. Berkeley affirmed that "there is not any other *substance* than spirit." (*Principles of Human Knowledge*. Sec. vii.)

Leibnitz taught that all force is spirit. It belongs to the essence of the soul. He declared that the material universe is derived from, and owes its continued existence to, spiritual forces. He viewed matter as the *externality of mind*, the manifestation of force, the phenomenon of spirit. External nature, in his view, was an "unconscious soul." (*Lewes' History of Philosophy*, Vol. 2, pp. 274–276.)

In the transcendental philosophy of Kant it is demonstrated that space and time, which are the essential conditions under which matter is viewed, have their origin in the mind, and are only modes of thought, or "subjective forms of sensation." According to Schelling, "Nature is spirit visible, and spirit is invisible nature." Oersted very truly remarks: "All matter is more nearly related to spirit than we generally imagine." (*Soul in Nature*, p. 4.) Swedenborg viewed the external world as the *ultimation* of the spiritual universe. The natural world, with all its objects of beauty and grandeur, is the outside boundary of an interior spiritual realm, — the point where the wave of creative influx proceeding from the Central Life terminates, or is staid. Accordingly, every object in nature corresponds or answers to something in the spiritual world, and to which it sustains the perpetual relation of an effect to a cause. Matter in all its forms is only spirit made visible to the sensuous range of the mind, or the space-creating power of the soul. All material things are the counterparts of spiritual entities, and together they constitute an undivided and indivisible whole. This doctrine was applied by the great spiritual philosopher to the human body, which was viewed by him as the form or outside boundary of the mind, the counterpart of the spirit, and having no independent existence of its own. It was the constant creation of the soul, and was an outward response to its internal states.

Spirit, or mind, is the only *substance*, or is that, as the word signifies, which is the underlying reality of all material things. Mind and matter sustain the necessary relation of substance and form. These are always connected in thought. Every substance must be manifested and conceived of as a form. A substance without a form would have no real existence, but would be an *ens rationis*, an ideal entity. Matter is the form of spirit, or that which gives it a definite limitation in space. The mind or spirit is the substance or underlying reality of the body; and as every change in a substance necessitates a modification of its form, or external manifestation, so a change of mental state is followed by a corresponding alteration of the bodily condition, either in the direction of health or disease.

Swedenborg makes a distinction between substance and matter, and this is of great importance in philosophy. He, like Spinoza, uses words with almost mathematical exactness of meaning. He employs the term substance in its etymological sense (from *sub*, under, and *sto*, to stand), as that which is the spiritual basis, the underlying reality of things. Substantial things, he affirms, are the primitives of material things, and differ from them as the spiritual from the natural, the prior from the posterior, or, in other words, as a cause from an effect. (*True Christian Religion*, 79.) Aristotle introduced into his philosophy the same distinction, or, at least, one quite similar to it. He represented every thing as having in itself both substance ($\mathring{v}\lambda\eta$) and form ($\mathring{\epsilon}\iota\delta o\varsigma$). The latter, as the Greek word signifies, is that which is seen. It is that which makes the former visible. Thus, form is the manifestation, the boundary, the limitation of substance, or, in the language of the Scandinavian Seer, the ultimation of spirit. Matter is spirit made visible and tangible, or the externalization of mind. Ideas, as was taught by Plato, are the only *real* things. When projected outward by the mind, and viewed by the mind as external to itself, and upon the plane of sense, they become mate rial things. Ideas are not mere mental conceptions, but real, spiritual entities. These are the realities that underlie all material and sensible objects. They are spiritual creations, and go forth from the Infinite Mind, and in their ultimate expression they are material forms. These are permanent so far as the material universe represents and expresses the fixed ideas of the Infinite Soul and of the spiritual world, and established and unchanging truths in the realm of mind. It is this that gives to nature its stability.

With regard to the relation of matter to spirit one thing is certain,—that all we *know* of matter is in our own minds. All that is ever seen of what we call the *visible* world is not and cannot be external. Its externeity or outness is only apparent, and not real. This truth was demonstrated with great acuteness of reasoning by Berkeley and his contemporary, the Rev. Arthur Collier. *What I see is not external.* Vision is in myself,—in my mind. We may see things beside ourselves, or other than ourselves, but we certainly see them *in* ourselves. This distinction is well made by Litchtenburg in 1799. He says: "To perceive things *outside* ourselves is a contradiction; we perceive only *within* us; that which we perceive is merely a modification of ourselves, therefore *within* us. Because these modifications are independent of ourselves, we seek their cause in *other* things that are outside, and say there are *things beyond us.* We ought to say *preter nos* (besides ourselves); but for *preter* we substitute the preposition *extra* (without), which is something quite different, that is, we *imagine* these things in the space *outside* ourselves. This, evidently, is not perception, but it seems to be something firmly interwoven with the nature of our perceptive powers; it is the form under which that conception of the *preter nos* is given to us,—the form of the sensual." (*Zöllner's Transcendental Physics*, p. 36.) The same is true of feeling. When I touch an object, it feels cold or hot, smooth or rough, hard or yielding. But all these so-called qualities of matter are only sensations in me. Beyond those sensations it is not possible for me to know anything of it. Even Sir William Hamilton admits that we do not see the sun, but only an image of it, and that no two persons see the same sun. He also affirms that we perceive extension only in our own organs, and not in the objects we see or touch. He also admits that all the secondary properties of matter are only sensations in the mind. (*Mill's Examination of Sir William Hamilton's Philosophy.* Vol. I., p. 199.) I do not mean by this to deny the reality of what we call the material world, but only to affirm that it has no separate existence, but is bound up in an eternal unity with mind; and if the realm of spirit should cease to be, the material world would instantly perish with it and in it.

What has been said above may throw some light upon the remarkable assertion of Swedenborg, that *God creates the world through man;* by which we are to understand that what we call the creation is a purely gerundive matter,—God's perpetual act,—and that He holds the work *to man*, at every stage, so as to represent him always at his present point, and act upon him fitly to his present state. In this way the world is linked to man, and constantly made to represent him to himself. (*Bushnell's Nature and the Supernatural*, p. 188.) This may be the meaning of the saying of Protagoras, that "Man is the measure of all things." Akenside speaks of —

> "The charm
> That searchless Nature o'er the sense
> Diffuses,— to behold in lifeless things
> The inexpressive semblance of himself,
> Of thought, and passion."

The objects of nature represent the things of the mind,— our ideas and feelings. The *appearance* of what we call the outward world to us is always, to some extent, a reflection of our inward states. This may be seen in its seeming changes from our varying moods of joy and sorrow. In the one case outward nature seems to smile and wear a cheerful aspect; in the other everything assumes a sombre hue, and a pall of gloom is spread over the landscape. The music of nature and all its harmonious sounds are changed to dirge-like strains. Thus, God holds the world up to man as a mirror to reflect his inward states, and we continually, as it were, create the world in which we live, and mould it in harmony with our interior condition. This will be more fully realized in the world to come.

It is very generally admitted that we do not directly perceive an external world, but only *infer* its existence from our sensations which are in our own minds. Dr. Thomas Brown, in his "Lectures on the Philosophy of the Mind," admits that the mind *is conscious or immediately cognizant of nothing beyond its subjective states;* but he assumes the existence of an external world beyond the sphere of consciousness on the ground of our universal belief in its unknown reality. Independent of this *belief,* there is no reasoning on which the existence of matter can be vindicated; the logic of the idealist he admits to be unassailable. (*Sir W. Hamilton's Discussions on Philosophy and Literature*, p. 62.) Prof. Ferrier, in his Institutes of Metaphysics, affirms that matter *per se*, and the whole material universe *by itself*, is absolutely unknowable. This is the fundamental idea of his philosophy. Matter in itself, or without, that is, outside of mind, cannot be known. We can, he says, only know ourselves as knowing it, which is only another form of expressing Berkeley's doctrine, that we only know an external world in ourselves. (*Institutes of Metaphysics*, p. 121.)

An external world has no existence independent of mind. All the objects of creation are in their inmost reality, as Hegel affirms, the thoughts of God, or, as Jung-Stilling expresses it, essential, realized ideas of God, or, as it were, pronounced words of the Creative Mind. These ideas, which are the inmost reality of things, are in the Divine Mind as His creative thoughts, and are not perceived only as our thought of them is a repetition of the Divine thought; or, as Malebranche has it, we see all things in God, or because of our union with Him. Time and space are in ourselves, as Kant and Swedenborg both teach. "We are so organized that when we *think* of things, they appear to us *separately*, that is, in space, and in succession, that is, in time. Time and space have their origin in our own souls; out of us in the being of nature neither of them has any existence. Now, as every movement in the whole creation occurs in time and space, without both of which no motion can possibly take place, therefore all movements in the whole creation are merely forms of ideas in our souls, which do not take place in nature." (*Jung-Stilling's Pneumatology*, p. 19.)

All the objects of nature are *phenomena* or appearances, as Hegel, Fichte, Berkeley, Swedenborg, and all the idealists affirm. By this we do not mean that they are an empty show, but that the appearance does not stand on its own feet, and has its being not in itself but in something else of which it is a form of manifestation. God, who is the Universal Life, when he lends existence to the " passing stages of the show in himself," may be described as the goodness that creates the world. He is the all-pervading Being or Life, of whom the world is the phenomenon or manifestation. The same is true of the human body. It is the phenomenon of spirit, an appearance of which the soul is the underlying reality.

With regard to the immediate consciousness of external things, taught by Descartes, Jacobi, Sir William Hamilton, and some others, Hegel truly says, " that nothing more can be meant by it than the consciousness of certain *sensations*. To have such a thing is the slightest of all cognitions; and the only thing worth knowing about it is that such an immediate consciousness of external things is an error and a delusion, the sensible world being altogether void of truth: that the being of these external things is accidental and passes away as a show; and they are characterized by having an existence which is separable from their essence and notion." (*Hegel's Logic*, pp. 119, 120.)

On this subject J. S. Mill remarks, " Matter may be defined a *permanent possibility of sensation*. If I am asked whether I believe in matter, I ask whether the questioner accepts this definition of it. If he does, I believe in matter: and so do all Berkeleians. In any other sense than this I do not. But I affirm with confidence that this conception of matter includes the whole mean ing attached to it by the common world, apart from philosophical, and sometimes theological, theories." (*Examination of Sir William Hamilton's Philosophy*, Vol. I, p. 243.)

Says Rev. Arthur Collier, in the introduction of the *Clavis Universalis:* "That in affirming that there is no external world, I make no doubt or question of the *existence* of bodies, or whether the bodies which are seen exist or not. It is with me a first principle that *whatever is seen is.* To deny or doubt of this is arrant scepticism, and at once unqualifies a man for any part or office of a disputant, or philosopher, so that it will be remembered from this time that my inquiry is not concerning the existence but altogether concerning the *extra*-existence of certain things or objects, or, in other words, what I affirm and contend for is not that bodies do not exist, or that the external world does not exist, but that such and such bodies, which are supposed to exist, do not exist externally, or, in universal terms, that there is no such thing as an external world."

The above well-guarded language, which I adopt as my own, is equally applicable to the human body. It does not exist independently of mind, but is included in the being of spirit.

It was the doctrine of Fichte, Schelling, Hegel, and Cousin that matter and mind in their underlying reality, or substance, are one and the same. Matter is only a phenomenal manifestation of mind or spirit. That the so-called properties of matter are only so many affections or modifications of mind, take as an illustration beauty and sublimity, which we attribute to various objects. "Beauty is not anything that exists in objects independently of the mind which perceives them, and permanent therefore as the objects in which it is falsely supposed to exist. It is an emotion of the mind, varying therefore, like all our other emotions, with the varying tendencies of the mind in different circumstances."

So of sublimity. "The sublimity which we *feel*, like the beauty which we feel, is an affection of our mind, not a quality of anything external." (*Brown's Philosophy of the Mind*, Vol. III, pp 148, 151.)

But the same may be said of all the so-called properties and qualities of matter.   There is in us a tendency to reflect our mental states upon outward things, or, in other words, to external-ize them.   We make things outward which are only so in *appear-ance*, and not in reality.   We hold our hand near the fire, and say that the fire feels warm,— that there is heat in the fire.   Yet this is not strictly true.   The heat is not in the fire, but is a sen-sation or feeling in our mind.   As we hold our hand nearer to the fire, this sensation becomes more and more vivid, until at length it becomes painful.   This is only the same sensation of heat inten-sified.   No one would think of saying that the pain was in the fire, yet the pain is only a higher degree of heat.   The same is true of the sweetness of sugar, and the bitterness of wormwood.   All the varieties of color are admitted by all philosophers to be only affections or modifications of the mind.   It is not a quality of external things any more than heat or beauty is.   None of the properties of matter, either primary or secondary, have any exist-ence independent of a perceiving mind.   Kant, admitting with-out question the previous doctrine of philosophers, that the mind has no immediate knowledge of any existence external to itself, adopted it without hesitation as a principle — *that the mind is cognizant of nothing beyond its own modifications*, and that what our natural consciousness mistakes for an external world is only an internal phenomenon, a mental representation of the unknown and inconceivable.   After admitting this, his attempt to demon-strate the existence of an unknown external world is universally admitted to have been a signal failure.   (*Hamilton's Lectures on Metaphysics*, p. 643.)   Every attempt to prove the existence of anything in matter that does not exist in mind, or that does not coëxist with it, or that can have an existence independent of a perceiving mind, must forever be a failure.   Reid's attempt to refute Berkeley made me a convert to idealism more than two score years ago.   In all my reading and study of mental philoso-phy I have never found anything that could weaken the force of Berkeley's reasoning.   His position is logically impregnable.   I fail to see the truth of Sir William Hamilton's theory of the duality of consciousness, or that in every state of perception by the senses we are conscious of two things, the *ego* and the *non-ego*, or that which is myself and that which is not myself. I know not how it may be with others, but for myself I can affirm that in every act of sensation I am conscious only of the sensation itself, and of an idea, both of which are in myself, that is, in my mind. *I may believe* that something exists besides myself, but I am *conscious* only of my own mental states and acts, for consciousness is the cognition of what transpires within my own mind. I may believe that there is such a place as London, or Paris, or Calcutta, but am not conscious of the existence of either one of them. The same is true of an external world, of which those cities are a part.

All the properties of matter — and beside those properties we know nothing of it — are as certainly modifications or phenomena of mind as are memory and imagination. With regard to all the objects of nature, Berkeley affirms that their *esse* is *percipi*, or that their being consists in being perceived. He says: "Some truths there are so near and obvious to the mind that a man need only open his eyes to see them. Such I take this important one to be, viz.: that all the choir of heaven and furniture of the earth, in a word, all those bodies which compose the mighty frame of the world, have not any subsistence without a mind, that their *being* is to be perceived or known; that consequently so long as they are not actually perceived by me, or do not exist in my mind, or that of any other created spirit, they must either have no existence at all, or else subsist in the mind of some Eternal Spirit,— it being perfectly unintelligible, and involving all the absurdity of abstraction, to attribute to any single part of them an existence independent of a spirit. To be convinced of which the reader need only reflect and try to separate in his thoughts the *being* of a sensible thing from its being perceived." (*Berkeley's Works*, Fraser's edition, Vol. I., p. 158.)

The force of Berkeley's reasoning, to prove that all the qualities and properties that we attribute to matter are phenomena of mind alone, and without a mind to perceive them could have no existence, even Prof. Huxley, one of the best representatives of modern materialistic science, cannot avoid feeling and admitting. I cannot perhaps better close this chapter than in his words, taken from the Critique of Prof. Fraser's edition of Berkeley's Works, entitled "Metaphysics of Sensation."

"Suppose that I accidentally prick my finger with a pin. I immediately become aware of a condition of my consciousness,— a feeling which I term pain. I have no doubt whatever that the feeling is in myself alone; and if any one were to say that the pain is something that inheres in the needle, as one of the qualities of the substance of the needle, we should all laugh at the absurdity of the phraseology. In fact, it is utterly impossible to conceive pain except as a state of consciousness."

"Hence, so far as pain is concerned, it is sufficiently obvious that Berkeley's phraseology is strictly applicable to our power of conceiving its existence,—'its being is to be perceived or known,' and, 'so long as it is not actually perceived by me or does not exist in my mind, or that of any other created spirit, it must either have no existence at all, or else subsist in the mind of some Eternal Spirit.'"

"So much for pain. Now let us consider an ordinary sensation. Let the point of the pin be gently rested upon the skin, and I become aware of a feeling or condition of consciousness quite different from the former,— the sensation of what I call touch. Nevertheless, this touch is plainly just as much in myself as the pain was. I cannot for a moment conceive this something which I call touch as existing apart from myself, or a being capable of the same feelings as myself. And the same reasoning applies to all the other simple sensations. A moment's reflection is sufficient to convince one that the smell, and the taste, and the yellowness, of which we become aware when an orange is smelt, tasted, and seen, are as completely states of our consciousness as is the pain which arises if the orange happens to be too sour. Nor is it less clear that every sound is a state of the consciousness of him who hears it.   If the universe contained only blind and deaf beings, it is impossible for us to imagine but that darkness and silence should reign everywhere."

"It is undoubtedly true, then, of all simple sensations that, as Berkeley says, their *esse* is *percipi*,— their being is to be perceived or known.   But that which perceives or knows is mind or spirit; and, therefore, that knowledge which the senses give us is, after all, a knowledge of spiritual phenomena."   (*Critiques and Addresses*, pp. 326, 327.)

In another work Prof. Huxley admits that matter may properly be considered as *a mode of thought*.   (*The Physics and Philosophy of the Senses*, by R. S. Wyld, p. 45.)   Prof. Faraday, in a paper published in the Philosophical Magazine in 1844, avows the belief in *the immateriality of physical objects*.   But if they are not material, in the popular acceptation of the term, what are they but modifications of the mind, or phenomena of spirit?   If, on this admission, they have any existence, any reality at all, they must be ideas or sensations in a perceiving mind.

CHAPTER II.

In the first chapter of the Johannean Gospel all things are said to have been created by the Logos, or Word, which, in its highest significance, means the Divine Intellect or Thought. This pregnant utterance of the friend of Jesus has a profounder import than is generally recognized by commentators. It implies that the objects of nature are the externalization of the thoughts of God, the ultimation of the Divine ideas. Hence external things, as we call them, are the visible words of a spiritual language,—that is, they are the representation of ideas to the mind by visible signs. Spoken language represents ideas by audible and articulate sounds; written language does the same by visible characters. When we see the word *tree*, it suggests to our minds a certain idea, or combination of ideas, and this is the only thing that we really perceive. But the word and the idea are very unlike each other. The connection is an arbitrary one, and the visible form only suggests the thought. So, when one pronounces the word *house*, the sound has no resemblance to the idea, and a person wholly unacquainted with the English language would get no conception of the object represented. It would have to him no meaning. The objects of the visible world are a sort of optic language. They excite ideas in the mind, and these are the only direct objects of perception, and in this way God speaks every day and in every place to the *eyes* of all men. Language, we are to bear in mind, is the representation of ideas by visible signs. But the objects of what we call the external world excite ideas in the mind, and hence may properly be called a Divine language. The objects of nature are God's mysterious manuscript, in which his thoughts are written, and by Swedenborg's science of correspondence the soul can learn to read this arcane, Divine language. Nature is a book, and we have as much reason to think that the Universal Mind, or He whom we denominate God, speaks to our eyes, as we have for believing that our intimate friend is speaking to our ears. This view is taken by David in the expressive language of one of his psalms. (Ps. xix : 1–4.) In the first chapter of Genesis God is represented as *speaking* into existence the objects of creation, where the *Deus dixit*, God said, as Augustine observed, signifies only the exercise of the Divine volition and thought.

The power of interpreting the visual signs of the Divine language of creation, and translating them into their ideas, is a spiritual instinct, an intuitive perception, or an inspiration. It is partly acquired, or at least improved, by experience. As it was remarked in the previous chapter, all that we know of an external world is our own sensations. Hence J. S. Mill calls the outward world "a permanent possibility of sensation." Ideas are the only objects of perception and of knowledge, and these are continually presented to the mind by the sensible world which perpetually goes forth from God, and represents the thoughts of the Divine Mind. Our perception of these ideas, which we project into space and give to them an apparent externeity, is equivalent to a constant act of creation by the Divine Being. There may be a far-reaching and profound truth in the theory of Malebranche, that we see all things in God, or by virtue of the union of the human soul with the Infinite Mind. We do not perceive an external world ; what the mind sees — and the body is cognizant of nothing — is within itself, that is, we have perception only of ideas that are present to the soul. Persons have been known to medical science who have come into the world with congenital cataract, and who

in after life have been restored to sight.   At first, they have not
the least conception of the distance or externality of objects.
Everything seems to *touch* the eyes, or in reality to be in the
mind.   This may not be so far from the truth.   In the spiritual
philosophy of Swedenborg it is taught that, in the other life, the
scenery in the midst of which we live and move is a constant creation from ourselves, and corresponds to our inward states.   It is
a projecting outward of what is really within ourselves, and which
is made to represent it.   Its outness is only apparent.   Nearness
and remoteness are only feelings of sympathy or antipathy.   Locomotion through space, or what appears to be such, is effected by a
change of state, or, as it is called in the Scriptures, being carried
away in the spirit.   In that realm of life all outward things are
the counterpart, the visible exhibition, of things in ourselves, and
have life only so far as they are correspondences.   In this world
there is an inherent tendency, a spontaneous impulse, to express
by some outward manifestation our internal states; there the
expression is more complete, and we live in a world and in the
midst of scenery created from our interior states of thought and
feeling.

   But this law of correspondence extends through the whole universe, and is seen here as well as in the life above.   It is only
another way of expressing the necessary relation of cause and
effect.   Every object of the material world derives its existence
from a spiritual idea, or entity, of which it is the manifestation
upon the plane of sense.   The two are connected as an indissoluble unity, for an effect cannot exist without a cause, nor a cause
without an effect.   Spiritual things, which belong to the realm
of causation, are the *real* things, and material things are their
shadow or outward manifestation.   The whole outward world is the
ex-istence of the spiritual world, or the realm of mind.   The one is
as the body and the other as the soul in man.   I believe without
a hesitating doubt that the whole visible universe, including our
own corporeal organism, is only spirit manifested and made visible
and tangible.   If we could suppose the world of *spiritual* realities

to be withdrawn or annihilated, the whole visible universe would disappear as instantaneously as you can snuff out a candle. The external universe is inclosed in the being of the world of mind, and is the permanent effect of an ever-operating spiritual cause. The seeming or *quasi* externality of a visible object is no unquestionable evidence of its real externality. An amputated limb is not missed from the consciousness. The person who has suffered this mutilation *feels* it as much as he ever did, and it has the same apparent externality. He has even a sensation of pain in it. But is it external? By pressing one eye a little out of its natural position, and then looking at a statue,— for instance, the Greek slave,— you will see two of them, and both seem equally external; and yet it has never been claimed that only one of them is external. Perhaps in neither case is that which is seen external, but the object of perception is only an idea, and, for aught we *know*, the externality of both may be only apparent and equally unreal. For if the reader of this has not lived long enough to learn that things in their deepest reality are not always what they seem to be, it is to be hoped that he will live to be as old as Methusaleh, if it be necessary, in order to incorporate into his mode of thinking and feeling the lesson taught in that profound utterance of Jesus the Christ: " Judge not according to *appearance*, but judge righteous judgment." (John vii: 24.) Within the compass of this brief sentence lies enclosed the unexpanded germ of the doctrine of Berkeley with regard to the external world. From that doctrine, when once established, there hang many important practical conclusions in relation to the connection of soul and body, and the dominion of mind over matter. If all outward things are created by the Logos, then by the power of the Word and the Spirit matter may be controlled, and a diseased body made whole.

CHAPTER III.

THE BODY IS INCLUDED IN THE BEING OF THE MIND.

The proposition at the head of this chapter will seem to many as startling and incredible, perhaps absurd and ridiculous. I will try in as brief a compass as possible to explain what is meant by it. There is such a thing as apparent truth and *real truth*, and these are often quite different, as Swedenborg long ago demonstrated. It has been affirmed by philosophers, and has been so often reiterated by others who receive their scientific and religious creed second-hand, that the mind is *in* the body, that by the world at large it has come to be accepted as an unquestionable truth,—a fundamental verity. The body has been called the clothing of the spirit, and its habitation sometimes its prison. Descartes located the soul in the pineal gland, others have made the whole brain its seat, and some of the older philosophers located it in the stomach, or in the region of the epigastrium. Others still have generously given it more room by extending it through the whole body. It was the opinion of Aristotle that the soul as an *indivisible whole* is in every part of the body. (*Bowen's Metaphysics of Sir William Hamilton*, p. 267.) This expresses a degree of truth, but is not the highest truth in regard to it. As there is not a point in the universe where the whole Deity is not present, so the soul is everywhere in its own world, which is the corporeal organism. While it is true that God is *in* the world that perpetually goes forth from Him, Paul expresses a higher truth, that the world and all things are in God, that is, included in his Being. (Acts xvii: 28.) So it was the opinion of Berkeley that the human body, including of course the brain, exists in the mind, and not the mind in the body. (*Berkeley's Works*, Fraser's edition, Vol. I., p. 301. Note.) The mind is more than the body; its action is not bounded and limited by the corporeal organism. It may, and often does, act independently.

One thing is certain,—*there is not one single quality, attribute, or property of the body of which we can form any conception that is not in the mind.* What we call sensation is admitted by all to belong to the spiritual nature or organism and not to the body, though the latter may be according to the appearance. The eye does not see, the ear does not hear, and the sensory nerves do not feel. This is acknowledged even by Locke. Strength is not a bodily condition, but a mental force, as the body is only a passive and unconscious instrument of the soul. As we have seen in a previous chapter, all the so-called properties of matter are sensations or ideas in the mind. The same is true of the body. The soul, the mind, the spirit, is what constitutes *myself*. I affirm with Bishop Berkeley, the English Plato, and with Swedenborg, the Scandinavian Seer and spiritual philosopher, that mind is the only *substance*. Without it nothing material could exist. The body has no independent being or life in itself. The soul is the real *man*, and the body is its *ex*-istence, or outward manifestation, to itself and to others. We are so constituted that when the soul takes a view of itself the idea, or image, is projected outward so as to appear distinct from itself,—this state of perception becoming permanent is what constitutes the body. It is the soul viewing itself as something outside of itself, analogous to the way in which we see the image of ourselves in a mirror. In either case the externality is more apparent than real. The body is the representation of the soul, which the latter sees of itself, as in a glass. It has only a *quasi* outwardness, which is a necessary condition of the mind's becoming visible to itself. This will be true of the soul forever. In the other and higher life it will create for

itself a spiritual body which will possess an apparent externality to
the soul, but which will be only the reflected image of itself

I do not deny the real existence of the body, but only that it
has an independent being   It perpetually lives in and from the
mind   We are so formed by the Creator that what we call matter
must be viewed as in space; but Kant has clearly proved that
space and time are not real entities, but subjective states, and the
necessary conditions under which we conceive the existence of
things external to ourselves. (*Critic of Pure Reason,* pp. 23–47.)
The body is formed by the image-making faculty of the soul, or
what we call in mental philosophy the imagination, acting, as we
shall have occasion to show hereafter, unconsciously to ourselves,
though its voluntary and conscious activity may modify the bodily
condition.   This image, or reflection of the soul, according to a
necessary law of thought, must be viewed as external to itself, in
the same way as the objects of fancy or imagination are seen as
out of the mind, and having an appearance of externeity, although
they are really in the mind.   The things we see in the imagination differ from the objects of our sensations only in the degree of
intensity in which we perceive them.   The one may have as real
an existence as the other.   "Thus, from a view of the two powers
taken together, we may call sense (if we please) a kind of transient imagination, and imagination, on the contrary, a kind of permanent sense." (*Hermes;* by James Harris; London, 1736; p.
357.)   It has long been taught in mental philosophy that, as to
the objects of the external world, we do not see the things themselves, but only their images, which are supposed to be formed
upon the retina.   This image, or idea, is all the evidence we have
of their existence, and this, it must be confessed, is in the mind.
The existence of anything beyond this is only an *inference,* a
belief, and I simply deny the logical and necessary connection of
the conclusion with the premises.   The same reasoning applies
with equal force to our own bodies.   The body is the externalization of the idea, or image, which the soul forms of itself, and is
thus the perpetual creation of the mind, just as our soul is thus

continually formed of God. The Divine Being projects Himself outward in thought, and the universe is the result. We do the same, and the body, which has been called a microcosm, or little universe, is the product. Thus, the soul perpetually creates its body out of itself just as God creates His universe, not from nothing, but from Himself. The body is not something superadded to the mind, but a representation of the mind to itself, and also, when interpreted aright, to others. It is a *word* of which the soul is the meaning. It is not a mere appendage of the soul, but is a manifestation of the soul itself under the limitations of time and space. This destroys the dualistic conception of man as a being made up of soul *and* body, and reduces the two departments of his nature to an indivisible and inseparable unity. He is not a living personality divisible into two distinct and separate halves, but they are one, and the soul is that one. The soul has taken, and ever will take, the body as its own creation into a personal union with itself,—" a union the most consummate and absolute of which we know, or of which we can conceive, infinitely transcending the completeness of the most perfect mechanical and chemical unions, and they are as completely one to us as if they were one substance." This assertion of Prof. Krauth, in his edition of the great work of Berkeley, is true; for the spirit is the one and only substance, and the body has no existence except in and from that. The body is the shadow, and the mind is that to which it belongs, and to which it is attached, and the two are vitally linked together.

When one affirms that the mind is *in* the body, what does he mean? Do his words imply the same as when he says the bird is in the cage? or the man is in the house? He surely cannot mean this. So, when I invert the principal terms of the proposition, and assert that the body is in the mind, I do not mean the same as when I say that one material object is inclosed within another, as, for instance, a gem in a casket. I only affirm two things,—that the body does not, and cannot, limit the action of mind, and that the mind neither lives in it nor from it. As Sir

Thomas Brown expresses it: "That mass of flesh that circumscribes me limits not my mind." (*Religio Medici*, Part II., Sec. 11.) The body is that which gives to the soul the property of visibility, both to ourselves and others; but it does not manifest the whole of the soul. As long as the soul lives it will create for itself a body, or an outward expression of itself,—a something that represents it and corresponds to it. This will be true of it forever. What the world calls death, which is only transition to a higher degree of life, and an ascent in the scale of existence, does not disrobe the soul of a bodily manifestation, and leave it a "formless puff of empty air." This is taught by Paul in that remarkable passage in his second epistle to the Church at Corinth, where he uses both the Pythagorean and the Platonic form of expression for the body as the garment and the habitation of the soul: "For we know that if our earthly house of this tabernacle were dissolved, we have a building of God, a house not made with hands, eternal in the heavens. For in this we groan, earnestly desiring to be clothed upon with our house which is from heaven: if so be that being clothed we shall not be found naked." (2 Cor. v: 1–3.) The soul could no more have an *ex*-istence without a body than God could *ex*-ist without a universe that He perpetually creates out of Himself, and which manifests Him. Paul declares that "there is a natural body, and there is a spiritual body" (1 Cor. xv: 44), which, in connection with the context, means that as we have a body here in this rudimentary stage of existence fitted to the uses of the soul, so when we graduate to the next higher plane of life we shall there have a body adapted to the external activity and manifestation of the spirit. But in both worlds the body is the outgrowth of the soul, and its visible representative, and is bound up in an indissoluble unity with it. If destitute of a bodily expression, souls or spirits could never become visible to others, even if they could to themselves. The body, by a necessary law of creation, corresponds to the soul, that is, it is an effect of which the soul is the cause; and an effect is always included in its cause, and is its outward manifestation.

It will be asked, if the body derives its existence from the soul and is only its external manifestation, why must we *eat* in order to live? To this question the answer is at hand. It is not the object of eating our daily bread to give us life. Digestion does not generate the vital force, but is itself a vital action. We were *born* alive, and consequently lived before we ever took any nutriment into the stomach. Our ante-natal existence was a dependent and derived mode of being through the umbilical cord. When this was cut, we entered upon an existence independent of the maternal organism. But that spiritual something that answers to the umbilical attachment, and forever binds us to God, the Primal and Central Life, has never been severed. In Him we live, and move, and have our being. Our existence is, and ever will be, inclosed within the womb of Infinite Being. We can never be so born, or born again, as to be independent of Him. Because He lives, we live also. He is the true vine, we are the branches; but the immortal sap of a Divine Life circulates through the minutest twig and leaf of our tree of life. If we look to food, or medicine, or anything else, for *life*, we are searching for it where we shall never find it. Life in its highest sense is conscious or unconscious union with God.

In an age which exhibits a tendency to *idolatrize* the tangible and material, it is to be hoped that it will not be deemed mentally unhealthful to call the attention of men, even if only for a passing moment, to the *possible* reality of something that lies beyond the range of the external senses, even if the reader does not see and feel the full force of my conclusions. If it be thought that I go to an extreme of *idealism*, let the reader take it as a spiritual medicine, on the principle of the *antipathic* method of cure, for our equally extreme sensualism both in religion and philosophy. I believe with the full force of an interior *conviction* that there is something beside matter in the universe, even though matter be reduced to the bathybius, or deep-sea mud of Häckel (the vital stuff of which things are made), or to the protoplasm of Huxley, or the bioplasm of Beale. The mind is more real than the body, though its existence cannot be detected by the microscope. Man is more soul than body. The mind is the reality, and the body its phenomenon, or appearance. The body is the spirit formulated. It is a symbol addressed to sense of our inner soul-life. It is our fixed mode of thought and feeling organized into structure. It is the *interpreter* of the mind, and translates its invisible states and acts into sight. It is like a thin, transparent, gauzy dress, worn upon the stage of this life, which partly conceals, but more fully reveals, the form or inward quality of the spirit; for what the body is as to strength or weakness, health or disease, will ever depend upon the state of the soul. If with some we call the body the clothing of the spirit, it is a garment that fits so closely to it that it cannot be distinguished from the spiritual personality it encloses, but exhibits its form and character. If we say with others that the body is the habitation of the soul, then I affirm it is a crystal palace that does not hide its occupant, but discloses all his movements.

The idealists do not deny the *reality* of external things. They only deny that they have any reality independent of mind, as all the so-called properties of matter are modifications or sensations of mind. They correspond or answer to something in the mind, and without the mind they could not exist. When men attribute to objects a real existence, they do not err; they only err when they suppose that those objects can or do exist independent of a perceiving mind. There can be no external world without a world of spirit in which it exists. The world of matter with all it contains is bound up in an indissoluble unity with the world of mind, and in fact exists in it. So it is with regard to the body. All the properties of our bodies are only modifications of our minds. They are reducible to feelings or sensations in the soul. It is a well-known fact that the conscious *feeling* of a limb remains after amputation. The same is true of every part of the body and the whole of it at death. All that constitutes the essence of our material organism, the *feeling or sensation* of a body, is not buried, but survives and is transferred with the soul to a spiritual realm of life. This is the spiritual body of which Paul and Swedenborg speak. (1 Cor. xv: 44.) All that is most real and substantial and enduring in the human body the soul takes with it and in it when it graduates to a higher realm of being.

This view of the human body was held by Jonathan Edwards, the greatest of American metaphysicians, who embraced the philosophy of Berkeley with regard to the external world. He says: "When I say the material universe exists only in the mind, I mean that it is absolutely dependent on the conception of the mind for its existence. The human body and the brain itself exist only mentally, in the same sense that other things do." (*Memoirs of Jonathan Edwards*, by Sereno E. Dwight, Appendix, Remarks in Mental Philosophy.)

CHAPTER IV.

MATTER AN UNSUBSTANTIAL APPEARANCE, AND IS CREATED AND GOVERNED BY THOUGHT.

Matter offers no resistance to the movements of spirit, for Jesus appeared in the midst of his disciples when the doors were closed. It is penetrable by spirit, and the two can occupy the same space. We must bear in mind that phenomena, or sensible *appearances*, are quite different from the *reality* of things. The senses never give us anything but seeming truth. The sense of vision, which is supposed to be one of the most perfect and reliable of our senses, is an imperfect and illusory one, and gives us ideas that reason and intuition must correct. The picture from a magic lantern projected upon a screen seems to be a *solid* reality, as much so as a granite boulder, but it is only a combination of light and shade. When it tells us that the image reflected from a mirror is a solid substance, it gives us only an apparent truth that requires to be rectified by some higher power of perception. When it tells us that a straight stick immersed in water obliquely is bent, its testimony is fallacious and must be corrected in order to arrive at the real truth. When it tells us as plainly as it can inform us of any thing that the sun rises and sets, that the moon is about the size of a cart wheel, that the dome of heaven is a solid arch, our reason has to rectify the mistake, and introduce a counter and more reliable testimony. So when it tells us that matter is *solid* and composed of indivisible atoms and molecules, no two of which can occupy the same space, it deceives us again, and its testimony must be ruled out. The solidity of matter is an illusion of the senses. All that we know, or can know, of matter is that it is a manifestation or externalization of spirit in the form of force. The attraction of gravitation, which in its intensest form is what we call cohesion, gives to matter its appearance of solidity. Faraday admits that the common doctrine of the impenetrability of matter, or that no two kinds of matter can occupy the same space, is untenable, and contrary to some of the most obvious chemical facts. However this may be, one thing is certain, that matter is penetrable by spiritual substance or force. The mind permeates the bodily organism, and fills it with its own life, though the body does not contain the mind, and limit its action.

Galilæo, in the preface of his works, expresses the opinion that matter is not impenetrable. Mitchel, Boscovich, and perhaps Dr. Priestly, entertained the same opinion. Dr. Darwin declares that the impossibility of two bodies existing together in the same space cannot be deduced from our idea of solidity, or of figure, which we acquire by the sensation of touch. He says: "The uninterrupted passage of light through transparent bodies, of the electric ether through metallic and aqueous bodies, and the magnetic effluvia through all bodies, would seem to give some probability to this opinion. Hence, it appears that beings may exist without possessing the property of solidity as well as they can exist without possessing the properties which excite our smell or taste, and can thence occupy space without detruding other bodies from it." (*Zoonomia*, Sec. xiv., 2, 3.)

The doctrine broached by Boscovich many years ago, and which Faraday declared he could demonstrate to be true, may come nearer the proper conception of matter than we are aware of, viz., that the old notion of ultimate and indivisible atoms is a mere fiction, and that what we call matter, in its last analysis, is resolvable into *points* of dynamic force. This doctrine of Boscovich makes an approach to the true conception of matter as being only an external manifestation of spirit. It brings it next to nothing, for in geometry a point is defined to be that which has position without magnitude.   But force is spiritual, as mind is the only causal agent in the universe.   All the properties of matter are only *affections* or *feelings* in ourselves, and their transference to something outside of our own minds, so far as their *reality* is concerned, is only an apparent truth.   I must be pardoned in again affirming that all we know, or *can* know, of matter is in ourselves, *our own sensations and feelings*.   It is only by an externalization of our own inward affections that we come to project them outward, and conceive of them as something outside our own being. Leibnitz taught that *sensation* was not an impression upon the body coming from without, and affecting the mind, but it arose from within.   As before stated, all that we know of the properties of matter are affections of ourselves.   When I say that an orange is sweet, the sweetness is a sensation in myself.   It is the same with other so-called properties of material things,—as redness, hardness, roughness, smoothness.   These are only affections of myself, my own mind, and thought, and feeling; and, by the operation of a law that we do not fully understand, they are transposed out of ourselves into space, and regarded as the qualities of things existing independently of ourselves.   So with regard to the human body, all its apparent changes, conditions, and qualities are within the mind, *and are only modes of thinking and feeling*.   The body, with all its varying states of health and disease, pleasure and pain, strength and weakness, is only the externalization, or ultimation, or projecting outward in appearance to ourselves, of our inward condition.   I find this view clearly stated by Fichte.   He says: "I am compelled to admit that this body, with all its organs, is nothing but a sensible manifestation, in a determinate portion of space, of myself,— the inward thinking being,—that *I*, the spiritual entity, and *I*, the bodily frame in the physical world, are one and the same, merely viewed from two different sides, and conceived of by two different faculties, the first by pure thought, the second by external intuition.   And this thinking, spiritual entity, this intelligence, which, by intuition [or sensation] is transformed

into a material body, what can it be, according to these principles, but a product of my own thought, something merely conceived of by me, because I am compelled to imagine its existence
by virtue of a law to me wholly inconceivable?" (*Vocation of
Man, Popular Works*, p. 306.)

In the system of Fichte the sphere of existence was supposed
to be exactly synonymous with the sphere of thought, and that all
the *reality* there was to the human body was in our thoughts and
feelings, and that to live truly means to *think* truly. There is a
mental force, a spiritual power, and a sanative value in our thoughts
that are but poorly understood by the world. There are many well
authenticated facts given in medical works illustrating the power
of that form of thinking which we call imagination in the cause
and cure of disease. These I am not disposed to doubt nor deny,
but only refer them to a general law of our being,—that the condition of the body is an effect of which the state of the mind is the
cause. Underneath and back of the disease there is a fixed and
chronic mode or habit of thinking and feeling that must be changed,
and when this is effected, by whatever means we employ, the
abnormal condition is remedied at the root, and the body adjusts
itself to the new order of things in the spiritual organism as surely
as an effect is connected with its producing cause.

There is a mysterious power in our thoughts. I proved some
years ago by a series of experiments that to direct our thoughts
to another person affects him through any distance of space. The
more intensely this mental influence is concentrated upon another
the more marked the effects. If we properly understood this spiritual power and the laws that govern it, our thoughts, directed to the
sick and unhappy, would do more for their recovery than all the
chemical remedies in the whole Materia Medica. When a patient
is in a passive and consequently receptive condition, his mind is a
carte blanche, or white paper, on which, by this wonderful spiritual
force, you can write any impression you please, and through the
mind inaugurate a new physiological movement, and effect a radical change in the direction of health and harmony. La can

thoughts are equally and perhaps more influential in changing our own mental and bodily condition. There is a creative power in them. The universe is the thought of God, and owes its origin and continued existence to the *imagination* or image-making faculty of the Divine Mind. "According to the Targum called after Onkelos, it was the Thought or Word of God which created man in his own image, in an image which was before God." (*Bunsen's Angel-Messiah of Buddhists, Essenes, and Christians,* p. 101.) So our bodily condition is the result of our way of *thinking.* If we would change it for the better,— as from weakness to strength, from disease to health, from pain to ease,— let us *imagine* or *fancy,* or *think* and *believe,* that the desired change is being effected, and it will do more than all other remedial agencies to bring about the wished-for result. Thought is one of the most prominent of the phenomena and manifestations of life. Descartes went so far as to make the very existence of the soul to consist in actual thought, under which he included the desires and feelings, as he defined thought to be all that of which we are conscious. (*Metaphysics of Sir William Hamilton,* p. 217.) There is a profound truth in the celebrated proposition of Descartes, by which he attempted to prove to himself his own existence, as the starting point in his philosophy, — *cogito, ergo sum,* I think, therefore I am. I might modify the statement, and with equal truth say, what I am is always according to my way of thinking. My inward thoughts and feeling give shaping to my outward form and condition, so that I am what I really *think* I am.

If we accept the conclusions of modern science, that matter is evolved from force, and go a step further, as we must from a logical necessity, and make all force but an operation or energy of spirit, then mind and body are not two independent existences, or distinct entities and substances, separated by the whole diameter of being, but are one substance under two forms of manifestation. If there is any one point on which scientists are agreed, it is that all we know of matter is from its properties, and these are forms of force. As Morell has said: "Matter, after all, may perhaps be reduced to force, and force *to spirit* as its source and spring." (*Mental Philosophy on the Inductive Method*, p. 66.)

We have an illustration of the spiritual origin of force in the relation of feeling and motion in the human body. A sensation, that is, a feeling, generates a muscular movement, as when we involuntarily jerk the hand back when it comes in contact with hot water. This is what is called a reflex movement. The feeling which is confessedly in the mind is transmuted into a motion in the body. All the involuntary movements of the muscles and action of the organs are caused by something in the mind that may be expressed by the term sensation, of which we may or may not be conscious. A feeling in the mind is translated into a muscular action in the body, which is the material equivalent of a spiritual movement or *emotion*, as we expressively name it. Dr. Laycock, though he takes a too material view of human nature, yet affirms that "Matter is fundamentally nothing more than that which is the seat of motion to ends, of which mind is the source and cause." (*Mind and Brain*, Vol. II, p. 4.)

He seems also to approve the doctrine of Anaxagoras, one of the most spiritually enlightened of the Greek philosophers, that mind is the cause or first principle of motion,— νουν μεν αρχην κινησεως. (*Mind and Brain*, Vol. I, p. 329.) Mind has been defined to be that which has the power of beginning motion. Power, force, energy — words so much used in modern science — are not properties of matter, but belong only to mind or spirit. Force in action is motion. Wherever this is seen in the universe, from the trembling of a leaf in the breeze to the upheaval of a mountain, there is mind back of it as its cause. It is but the pulsation of an ever-present Divine Life in nature, the all-pervading, ever-acting Welt-Geist, or World-Spirit. So the body of man is only "matter's passive heap." It is the soul that gives to the corporeal mass all its life, and sense, and motion. It is possible for mind, through volition and intelligent thought, to hold supreme and exclusive control over every part of it. The mysterious psychological energies that are slumbering in it may be aroused to action for the cure of all its diseases.

The materialistic philosopher will affirm that matter is the only *substance*, and that mind and thought are its higher properties and activities.   I affirm from the stand-point of the idealistic philosophy that mind or spirit is the only real substance, and matter is its external form or manifestation, and in our physical organism the mind is the cause, and the condition of the body the effect. There is a law of preëstablished harmony between them, somewhat like that taught by Leibnitz.   The body is the correspondent or answering echo of the mind.   God created the soul and its body in such a way, and so adjusted them to each other, that the soul *represents* and contains within itself all the simultaneous movements of the body, and nothing can take place in the latter that does not preëxist in the former.   He so made and fashioned the body that it must do *as of itself* all that the mind thinks and wills.   The motions and conditions of the body are coincident with the thoughts and volitions of the soul, acting consciously or unconsciously, and follow them as an effect a cause.   The body is like the hands of a clock, a simple indicator; the thoughts and feelings are the internal and invisible machinery and force that give movement to the hands.

There is a practical importance attached to these principles that takes them out of the class of mere idle speculations.   The sensualistic and materialistic philosophy, or what Hegel expressively characterizes as the "dirt philosophy," has been applied to medicine.   I only wish to show that idealism is capable of furnishing a more efficient means of the cure of disease.   Its principles were employed by Jesus the Christ, and put to a practical and beneficent use.   In concluding the discussion of the subject in this chapter, I can do no better than to borrow his language and feebly echo his words: "If ye know these things, happy are ye if ye do them."   (John xiii: 17.)

If the reader, unaccustomed to the discussions of speculative philosophy, does not at first see the full force of the principles unfolded in this and the three preceding chapters of the volume, he would do well to carefully read and study them again.   He may find in them a mine of golden, practical truth relating to health and happiness that had better not be abandoned without sinking the shaft deeper. A mere surface working may not put him in possession of the full extent of their treasure. If he fully masters the principles they contain, and mentally appropriates them as his own, he has won the key that unlocks the spiritual mystery of health and disease, and has found the reason why he is in the one or the other of those states. He may find in those principles, when clearly apprehended, something to which the language of Paul is not wholly inapplicable: "Howbeit, we speak wisdom among them that are perfect [or fully instructed], yet not the wisdom of this world, nor of the princes of this world, that come to naught: but we speak the wisdom of God in a mystery, even the hidden wisdom which God ordained before the world unto our glorification." (1 Cor. ii: 6, 7.) If he does not find in them what answers to this, there is surely a spiritual value in them that will well reward his search.

CHAPTER V.

Few men are ever brought to feel the full worth of their own minds, and physicians practically, if not theoretically, undervalue the importance of the mental aspect of disease. The mind is the only principle of motion in the body, and its only life. It is our inward being. All that a man really *is* belongs to the mental organism. It is the theatre of the Divine energy, the home of immortal thought, the spring of the aspiration of the infinite. It is the real location of hell and disease, and of heaven and health. "All essential interests center in the soul; all that do not center there are circumstantial, transitory, and evanescent: they belong to things that perish." (*Dewey's Discourses on the Nature of Religion*, p. 9.)

The introduction into mental philosophy of the doctrine of the unconscious, or, as it is usually called, preconscious, mental action is a most important advance in the science of the mind. The notion which has usually been entertained by psychologists is that the acts of the mind are precisely co-extensive with the consciousness, and that whatever is done unconsciously, though apparently intelligently, yet springs from some objective source, and not from the mind itself. This doctrine, that the regions of intelligence and of consciousness are coëxtensive, has of late years been abandoned and come into deserved discredit. Sir William Hamilton many years ago reproduced that most fruitful idea of Leibnitz, the doctrine of *unconscious thought*, and pointed out the fact that there is always going forward more or less energetically in the soul a process of latent thinking. He adopts the doctrine, so prevalent among German psychologists, "*that the mind exerts energies and is the subject of modifications of neither of which it is conscious*, and distinguishes three degrees of mental latency. (*Bowen's Metaphysics of Sir William Hamilton*, pp. 235–253.) Dr. Carpenter, taking a more material view, designated the same phenomena under the term *unconscious cerebration*. Dr. Laycock has brought them under the general category of the reflex action of the cerebro-spinal nerves. But this reflex action takes place with undeviating certainty, and with unerring intelligence. When a sensation generates a muscular contraction, and expends itself in a given movement, it is still the mind that is the occult cause, for the reason that sensation is not a *bodily* affection, but a mental phenomenon. The doctrine of the unconscious, or, as it is more properly called, *preconscious*, mental action has been fully developed in the German systems of psychology, particularly those of Carus, and the followers of Herbart, and especially by Immanuel Hermann Fichte in his Anthropology, and his smaller work entitled Philosophical Confessions. So that the idea of the preconscious life of the soul, and of an intelligent mental action beyond the range of the external consciousness, may be considered as fully established in philosophy, and is one that will be fruitful in results.

This unconscious mental action, or latent thought and intelligence, is a doctrine of great importance in physiology and mental science. We affirm that the soul has an *a priori* existence,—that it precedes the bodily organism, and forms the body according to its nature and for its use in the external world. What is the nature of this preëxistence we do not attempt to decide. It may lie beyond the limits of the human understanding for the present if it is not to be classed among things *unknowable*. If we affirm with Swedenborg that life is uncreated and uncreatable, then our individual life must perpetually spring from the Divine Being, and though never absolutely disconnected from its Source, yet we come to a distinct individuality in our conception.   In this God comes to self-limitation, and the soul enters into time and space, and thus becomes an individual.   If it is once admitted that the soul-principle has an existence prior to that of the body, then it follows that it may exist after the dissolution of the body.   The fact of its preëxistence thus becomes the strongest evidence of its immortality.   The soul is the architect of the body, and forms it by an unerring intelligence, by a process of unconscious thinking.' "The whole of the preconscious state of the soul is essentially and specially a process of *thinking*, without, however, its thought as yet touching the threshold of consciousness.   In this simple idea there lies nothing less than a new future for psychology, as also for the question respecting the relation of the soul and body.   My philosophy has chiefly aimed at giving a concrete and experimental development to this same idea.   When, therefore, in the plastic and physical processes it recognizes an *intelligence* which develops organic forms in space, and which stands in manifest analogy with the art-instincts of animals, and the creative æsthetic faculty in man, we cannot but think that we are only giving back again, truly and pointedly, the actual characteristics which experience presents us." (*Immanuel Hermann Fichte's Philosophical Confessions*, translated by Morrell, p. 16.)

The doctrine of Fichte is that the body is formed, and afterwards all its physiological processes carried on, by an unconscious mental action,—an instinctive and intelligent *thinking*. He expressly affirms that "no organic activity is possible without the co-operation of thought, which thought can unquestionably exist only in the soul: inasmuch, however, as it precedes sensation, the principle by which consciousness is awakened, it must necessarily remain unconscious. The acts of the morphological and physical impulses are not conceivable without the constant operation of this same instinctive power and unconscious thinking." (*Philosophical Confessions*, p. 19.)

All movements of the bodily organism, all changes in our physical condition, are manifestations of mind. Mind is the only causal agent, the only active principle, in the universe, and especially in the body. Morrell, in his valuable work on Mental Philosophy on the Inductive Method, has clearly shown that the so-called vital force, nerve-force, and mind-force, are correlated, or mutually influence each other, and are interchangeable, the one into the other. This conclusively proves that they are one at their root, and are probably only different forms of mental force. We can adopt the expressive language of Schelling, "that all physical motion, activity, and life-effort are only an unconscious *thinking*," or in the clearer, inspired declaration of Fortlage, "that the external functions of the nervous system are only mind becoming visible." On this subject I. H. Fichte has said: "The structure of the nervous system presents us with a perfect reflex of psychical relations; and that consequently there must be various mental processes corresponding with the different functions which we find to exist in connection with nervous activity."

There are two widely different modes of viewing the relation of the cerebro-nervous system to the mind. The one, the materialistic view, teaches that mental action is the result of cerebral activity. This theory is adopted more or less fully by Carpenter, Laycock, Maudsley, and Lewes. This materialistic view attained its culmination in Moleschott, who affirms that thought is a secretion of the brain, as the bile is that of the liver. The other, the spiritualistic view, is that the mind has priority of existence, and by its plastic power forms the body and the nervous system as an instrument adapted to its own use; that it can act independently of the brain and of all organic conditions; and can, and does in fact, survive the dissolution of the body. After a patient study of the nature and laws of the human mind, and of its relation to the body, for more than forty years, I am compelled to adopt the latter hypothesis as explaining more clearly all the mental phenomena. The first theory would greatly shake, if not overturn from their foundation, our comforting assurance and blissful hope of immortality. The religious instinct and consciousness intuitively and spontaneously grasp the latter theory as the only one in harmony with its nature.   It is the property of a genuine religious life in the soul that it spontaneously accepts all truth that is fitted to afford it the proper nutriment, and rejects with an involuntary repulsion whatever is not thus adapted to its nature.   This it does by a Divine instinct, acting independently of the logical reason.   The mind is not the result of organization, and, consequently, dependent upon the body for its existence, but is itself the organizing principle.

This unconscious mental action in our bodily organism may be the result of the connection of the individual soul with the Universal Mind, or the general sphere of life and intelligence in the universe, or something like that which Swedenborg denominates the *maximus homo*, or grand man.   We are parts of this stupendous whole.   All individual thought and knowledge spring from an Intellect that is common to all, and in which our power of knowing has the ground of its existence.   In other words, as there is but One Life in the universe, and all the various forms of existence are but manifestations of it, the same is true of thought and knowledge.   The theory of a *common intellect* was earnestly maintained by the Arabian philosopher Averroes, also by Alexander, Themistius, Cagetanus, and Zabarella.   The *vision in the Deity* of Malebranche is only a modification of it.

Preconscious mental activity in the body is an unconscious or latent thinking, as Leibnitz denominated it.   In the philosophy of Fichte life and thought are one and the same.   To think is to live, or, more properly, to exist.   He says: "It is obvious that the phrases thought and life, thoughtlessness and death, mean precisely one and the same thing.   Thought is the element of life, and, consequently, the absence of thought must be the source of death." (*The Way towards the Blessed Life, Popular Works*, p. 419.)

The power to think in all men is derived by influx from the Lord.   (*Swedenborg's Arcana Celestia*, 2004; 2 Cor. iii: 5.) Hence, as Fichte affirms, thought is something of the Divine Life in man.   "Pure thought is itself the Divine Existence (*Daseyn*);

and, on the other hand, the Divine Existence is nothing else than pure thought." (*Popular Works*, p. 406.) It is this that gives to thought a spiritual potency and creative agency, and invests it with such influence over our own condition and that of others, a subject we shall more fully discuss in what follows.

Our individual vitality is never disconnected from the Universal Life. "The knowledge of the lowest expression of life constitutes physics; that of the organic, physiology; that of the highest, or spiritual, psychology. The latter may be defined as the science of the Life of God in man's soul, physiology as that of the Life of God in his body. And as that Life is essentially One, psychology and physiology, in their high philosophical idea, are connected as soul and body, and each is an exponent of the other." (*Life: Its Nature, Varieties, and Phenomena,* by Leo H. Grindon, p. 208.)

CHAPTER VI.

There are two things in regard to the relation of mind and body that are self-evident to the intuitive reason. First, that the mind is the only life of the body,— that there is no indefinable and mysterious something in our bodily organism distinct and separate from the soul which is the cause of all vital action. Life is a force, a spiritual principle of motion. Secondly, every movement of the body, physiological, or muscular, or functional, and every conceiv. able bodily state as to health or disease, strength or weakness, are effects of which some action of mind, conscious or unconscious, is the efficient and only cause. As Immanuel Hermann Fichte has said: "An individual soul must be at the basis of these physical facts for this reason, that all the processes of life are at the same time *instinctive actions*,— that is, an unconscious kind of thought, which it would be absurd to locate anywhere but in the soul itself." (*Philosophical Confessions*, p. 32.)

One thing we know,— that certain changes of the body always follow certain determinate mental alterations. The soul is the plastic principle, that is, it gives arrangement and form to the matter of which the body is composed. It builds up the organism and forms the body so as to adapt it to the wants and uses of its own nature. In this constructive effort, this *geometric activity*, it acts unconsciously to us, but with the highest intelligence originally impressed upon it, something like the artistic effort of the bee in forming its cell in the most exact mathematical proportions, so as to contain the largest quantity in the smallest compass. The mind is thus the organizing principle. It has priority of existence; it precedes all bodily organization, and accompanies it as a cause in the process of all its changes. It alters the condition of the body to harmonize it with its own states. It works silently, instinctively, and with an unconscious but unerring intelligence, and by an invariable law, to effect this result. For it is a law of God that *spirit* should control and govern matter, and the body outwardly express the mind.

The whole bodily structure is changed in a brief period. It is an old opinion, formerly current in physiology, that the body is renewed once in seven years, so that no particle of matter now enters into the different tissues that was there seven years ago. But this change takes place much more rapidly, and in a far shorter period, than was formerly supposed to be requisite. It is now thought to be accomplished in one year. It is not unreasonable to suppose that this renewal of the body is effected in one month, or, at the farthest, once in three months. The amount of waste, worn out material which passes off through the various excreting channels is, in a very limited time, equal to the weight of the whole body. But all this renewal and disintegration of cells and tissues is effected by the plastic influence of the mind. The soul is in this case the intelligent but unconscious agent in the change, exercising a sort of providence over the world of its creation. All these morphological changes, and organic activities, are effected by the mind through an *intelligent instinct*, but acting beyond the range of our ordinary sense-consciousness. If the mind and its spiritual forces and influences are the plastic or formative principle of the body, then it follows that to change our mental states must of necessity modify our bodily condition. This is demonstrably true as a fact of experience. If, then, we make to ourselves a new heart and a new spirit (Ezek. xviii: 31), or change our affectional and intellectual states, the unconscious instinctive action of the changed and renewed mind will form to itself a body in harmony with itself.

Fichte supposes that the mind, as the plastic or organizing prin-ciple, effects these changes in the body, in renewing and building up the physical structure, by a power which he calls *fancy*. By this he does not mean what is usually called imagination, but *intelligence in its instinctive and spontaneous operation*. But this creative power sometimes rises from the preconscious range of mental action and exhibits itself in the highest efforts of artistic genius, which are only the outward expression, in a permanent form, of internal and preëxisting ideas or mental creations. But if this mental power effects such changes in the body, when acting as an unconscious and intelligent instinct, why may it not be pos-sible for us to direct it to the changing of our bodily organism in disease by a conscious volitional effort? Is not imagination a mode of force, that is, a spiritually creative power? and if so, ought it not to be taken into account in all our remedial devices? If a condemned criminal, from the trickling of warm water over the arm, and supposing, or imagining, or fancying, it to be blood from a divided artery, actually died, without the loss of a drop of blood, why may it not act with the same efficiency in prolonging life, and in effecting those organic and functional changes that constitute the cure of what we call bodily disease? Imagination, or fancy, may create disease, as physiologists admit; and why may it not be intel-ligently employed to cure it? There have been collected and pre-served in the science of medicine many well-authenticated facts showing the manifold and positive effects of the *fancy* upon the bodily organism, so that there is no room to call in question its vast formative power and influence in modifying our physical con-dition both in the direction of disease and health. What no one doubts we need not waste time in formally proving by an array of cases. This is as well established as any principle in what goes under the name of medical science. The morbific effects of the imagination upon the bodily condition are as fully proved as the action of arsenic or prussic acid; but it seems to me self-evident that such a power can be made to produce the highest therapeutic results just as well. It is manifest that we have here an almost unused and undeveloped principle of great practical value in the cure of disease. All the great discoveries of modern times, as the expansive power of steam, the electric telegraph, and the telephone, have left in the public mind a suspicion that there are yet many latent and unused powers of nature that await discovery, and that may be turned to a useful employment. It is possible that in what we have said in this chapter there may be a principle of great practical value in its application to the cure of diseases of both mind and body. It is possible that we have made some approach towards the discovery of the natural, and consequently the *Divine*, method of cure. Let anyone intelligently bring this creative and plastic power of the mind to the cure of his malady, and he will find it a most potential spiritual remedy. Let him, by a conscious volitional effort, employ this artistic instinct, this plastic influence of the mind, upon a diseased organ, and fancy, or intelligently imagine, that it is becoming changed for the better, and that within a given time it will be well, and he will be astonished at the therapeutic result. The more fully he can *make himself believe* that the necessary change is being effected, or will be accomplished in an hour, a day, or a week, the more marked will be the result; for faith is the most intense form of voluntary mental action. Why should we not be able to believe this? For it is only the same power at work that, in the preconscious region of mental activity, carries on all the organic and physiological movements in building up the body from the cradle to the grave, only in the supposed case it is combined with, and aided by, a voluntary and conscious mental effort. This is calling to our aid, in a time of need, the only power in nature that can change the bodily tissues, and excite the various organs to their proper functional movements. The soul possesses a most marvelous plastic power, and this formative element in the body can be made to accomplish far more than could be effected by any general physical or chemical laws. If, as an unconscious but intelligent instinct and impulse. it presides over all the involuntary processes of life, may not its action be intensified and accelerated by a voluntary effort of thought working in harmony with it and in the same direction? The science of medicine will never be able successfully to combat disease until it takes as its foundation principle the words of Jesus the Christ: "It is the spirit that maketh alive; the flesh profiteth nothing." (John vi : 63.)

The individual mind as an image of God, and standing at the summit of creation, is God's vicegerent, and, by virtue of a power perpetually derived from Him, is, in a secondary sense, a *creator*, or, if that be deemed too strong an expression, it is a modifier of the condition of its own body, the world of its formation. It can generate a new *status* of the corporeal organism where its reign is supreme. If, when we are sad, we can make our face to smile; or, when inwardly disturbed, can cause the body to wear the outward appearance of tranquility; or, when in danger, can check the too rapid pulsations of the heart, and be self-possessed and self-poised; or, if under an otherwise painful surgical operation, as has often been done, the brave soul can triumph over pain so as to lessen its intensity, if not to become wholly insensible to it,— then, by an intelligent use of this divinely ordained dominion of the mind over the body, a diseased organ can be controlled, and its morbid condition changed. If we were properly instructed in the use of the power inherent in the very nature of the mind, in nearly all cases of disease, especially in their incipient stage, the services of a physician would become unnecessary, the common practice of running to a physician in every ailment would be far less frequent, and the sale and use of drugs would be largely diminished.

CHAPTER VII.

FAITH MAKES US WHOLE; OR, THE CHRISTIAN METHOD OF CURE.

The Christian method of cure, or that practiced by Jesus, was through faith. The expressions, so often occurring in the Gospels, "Thy faith hath saved thee," "Be it unto thee according to thy faith," and "Thy faith hath made thee whole," express the fundamental idea in the system of healing disease by Jesus and his disciples. It was the cure of the body through the influence of the plastic and sovereign mind upon it. In an act of faith the mind rises out of the preconscious range of its action, and from an intelligent impulse it becomes a conscious, voluntary effort, but loses none of its creative efficiency, for faith combines into a concentrated form, and into a unity, all those mental states — as thought, imagination, belief, and feeling — which influence the condition of the physical organism.

There is an interesting fact showing the power of the mind over the most inveterate diseases, first mentioned by F. V. Mye in his "De Morbis et Symptomatibus," and which has been often quoted as being well authenticated. We simply give it as representing hundreds of analogous cases that might be given. At the siege of Buda, in 1625, when the garrison was on the point of surrendering, in consequence of the prevalence of scurvy in an aggravated form, the Prince of Orange caused to be introduced a few bottles of sham medicine, as a sovereign remedy and infallible specific for the disease. This given in drops as such produced the most aston

189

ishing effects. Such as had not moved their limbs for months before were seen walking in the streets sound, straight, and whole; and many who declared that they had been rendered worse by all former remedies recovered in a few days. (*Gorton's Principles of Mental Hygiene*, p. 166; *Combe's Principles of Physiology*, p. 272.)

In the explanation of this interesting fact the inquiry arises, what was the principle or medium of cure in this case? Every one will answer at once that it was the influence of the mind on the body. It was certainly not the effect of medicine, for there was no medicinal value or virtue in what was given. But what particular mental state, or what form of mental action, was it that possessed such therapeutic efficiency? It would commonly be attributed to what is called *imagination*. I can discover here but little that answers to the idea expressed commonly by that term. It was *faith* that made them whole. It was their confidence in the remedial virtue of the prescription that effected the astonishing results; and this was no miracle, but the expression of a general law in regard to the action of mental forces upon the bodily organism. But would it not be better, rather than to resort to the device of sham medicines, to instruct the patient in the use of this spiritual principle of cure, and educate him to make an intelligent exercise of faith and imagination for the cure of his mental and bodily diseases, and to teach him how to believe unto salvation? He should be informed how to exercise a saving or healing faith in his own God,— the Divinity that dwells within him. It becomes then an intelligent method of cure, and far more reliable than the administration of drugs in allopathic or homeopathic doses. A genuine act of faith in God is a movement of the whole being towards Him, and brings the soul into a vital contact and vivifying conjunction with the Central Life.

In what has been said in the preceding chapters, the influence of the mind on the body has been shown; but faith is the most intense form of mental action. When the mind rises from the preconscious to the conscious range of action, its activity separates itself into two distinct phases, the intellectual and the emotional; but at the summit of our being, in a genuine act of faith, they unite in one intense focus. "Faith," says Morell, "we regard as the highest intellectual sensibility. It is not possible to say whether it resembles most an intellectual or an emotional state of consciousness; the two seem to be perfectly blended in that pure spiritual elevation where our intellectual gaze upon truth is not separable from the love and ecstasy we feel in the contemplation of it. 'He that loveth not,' says the apostle John, 'knoweth not God,' his consciousness has not reached that high elevation where knowledge and love are inseparable, and in the light of which alone we can know God aright."

"Faith, then, when perfected, is the state of consciousness which links our present to our future life. The denizens of heaven are termed indifferently Cherubim and Seraphim, spirits that are replete with knowledge or burn with love; and, as we have just seen, it is the cherubic and the seraphic life *united* which expresses the perfect state of man's consciousness on earth,—a state in which we have equally a perception and a love of the beautiful, the good, and the eternally true." (*Philosophy of Religion*, pp. 24, 25.)

When I recommend faith as an efficient remedy for the cure of disease, or an intelligent exercise of belief by a volitional effort, combined with an act of the fancy or imagination, I shall be met with the question, Can anyone believe without evidence? To this I answer that belief or faith is a form of *knowing*. It takes the place of knowledge. It is a mode of cognition that acts beyond the limited circle of perception by the senses. In its highest form it is an intuition of the love, an inward seeing, a clear perception of truth, without any objective or external evidence. Hence, in the Hebrew language we have the same word (*amuna*) to express the idea of faith and that of truth. Much that goes under the name of knowledge, when closely analyzed, is found to be nothing but a *belief* in varying degrees of certitude.

On the subject of the nature and essence of faith and its relation to knowledge, Coleridge very truly says that "it consists in a synthesis (or uniting together) of the reason and the individual will. By virtue of the latter, therefore, it must be an energy; and, inasmuch as it relates to the whole man, it must be exerted in each and all his constituents or incidents, faculties, and tendencies; it must be a total, not a partial, a continuous, not a desultory or occasional, energy. And, by virtue of the former (that is, reason), faith must be a light, a form of knowing, a beholding of truth."

Faith and knowledge cannot be separated. On this subject Cousin remarks that "to believe is, in a certain degree, to comprehend. Faith, whatever be its form, whatever be its object, whether vulgar or sublime,— faith cannot but be the consent of reason to what reason comprehends as true. This is the foundation of all faith. Take away the possibility of knowing, and there remains nothing to believe, for the root of faith is removed." (*Introduction to the History of Philosophy*, p. 133.) In all faith there is knowledge, and in all knowing there is much that is only believing. Subtract from the sum total of all that we call knowledge what is only an *undoubting belief*, and what is left would be capable of being expressed in a small compass. Faith, or belief, has been greatly undervalued by scientific men. I only aim, in the brief limits of this chapter, to restore it to its proper place in religion, in philosophy, and in medicine, or the science and art of healing. But this was done in the philosophical system of Jacobi, a condensed and comprehensive view of whose doctrine will be given in what follows.

There is a higher source of knowledge than that which we derive from the senses or from reason. Jacobi affirmed that all knowledge, communicated through the medium of the understanding, by which he meant the logical faculty, must be of a contingent character, or depend upon the truth of things that precede it, and consequently can never be considered as absolute knowledge. To demonstrate any truth by the logical method, we must infer it from another that lies beyond it; this again from another still more remote, and so on to an endless extent. The logical method, or the mere reason, can never free itself from these trammels, and can never reach a position where truth is seen in its own light by a direct intuition. Faith, which in its highest form is an *inward seeing*, is the divinely-appointed method of attaining to *real* knowledge. Our knowledge of an external world is only a *belief.* We do not directly and immediately perceive it, but are cognizant only of our sensations and ideas that are really in our own minds. From these we *infer* the existence of external things. But all outward things, including our own bodies, are only an inference, a belief. The existence of the body, and all of its conditions of health and disease, are only a belief, as we know nothing of it except in our minds. It is in the enclosure of our inner being. A change of our *belief* in regard to it, if it be real, is all the same as an alteration of the bodily state.

Jacobi taught as the central idea of his philosophy "that all human knowledge of every description must rest upon faith or *intuition.* As it regards sensible things, the understanding finds the impressions from which all our knowledge of the external world flows ready formed. The process of sensation itself is a mystery; we know nothing of it till itself is passed and the feeling it produces is present. Sensation is never knowledge, but only feeling. Our knowledge of matter must rest upon faith, or intuition. There is, however, another and higher species of faith than this. Just as sensation gives (or is supposed to give) us an immediate knowledge of the world, so there is an inward sense — rational intuition or a spiritual faculty of perception — by which we have a direct and immediate revelation of supersensual things. We gaze upon them with the inward eye, and have just as firm a conviction of their reality as we have of those material objects upon which we look with the bodily eye. It is by this two-fold faith, or revelation, that man has access to the whole material of truth,—material which his understanding afterwards moulds into various shapes, and employs on the one hand for the purposes of this life, and on the other for the preparation for the life to come. Leave out, however, this direct inlet to our knowledge, and all demonstration, all definition, in short, all philosophy, are but a sport with words, a superstructure sometimes complete enough in itself, but baseless as the most airy visions of the imagination." (*Morell's History of Speculative Philosophy*, pp. 598, 600.)

Belief and imagination, which are combined in faith, are a source of knowledge far more reliable than sensation or an objective demonstration, and, in fact, the former usually precedes the latter. Faith is an inward seeing, and nearly all the great discoveries in science and the arts are made by the intuitive faculty, and are a revelation to faith, which explores the ground, and external demonstration follows after. They are first seen by the mind, and subsequently confirmed by experiment and mathematical calculation. But the discovery is not the result of these subsequent investigations, but almost always precedes them. Take as familiar illustrations the discovery of the identity of electricity and lightning by Franklin, of a Western Continent by Columbus, the law of gravitation by Newton; also the invention of the air balloon, the voltaic battery, and the discovery of the metalic bases of the earths. The idea of all these first existed in the mind of the discoverers. As to the last named, it had long been prophesied by Lavoisier. I may also add that all these discoveries have again given a spur to intuitive anticipations which have afterwards been justified by experience. So that here we find an application of the profound remark of Schiller, that what the spirit promises, nature performs. (*Oersted's Soul in Nature*, p. 12.) Every philosopher first *imagines* his theory, and then goes to work to collect facts to illustrate and confirm it. But it first comes to the mind as an intuitive perception, a vision of faith, which does not wait for the slow and laborious induction of facts. It has its origin in an inspirational flash of a higher light than either reason or the senses can give.

The sum of all that has been taught in this chapter is this: Faith is the Christian means and method of cure, and is based upon a correct philosophy of human nature and of the relation of the soul to the body. All belief implies some degree of knowledge, and faith, which is always united to imagination, is an inward seeing, and is the highest form of cognition and degree of knowing. The mind, as all admit, affects the body; and I affirm that its varying states are the body's health or malady. The soul creates for itself a body in harmony with it, and is the operating cause of its conditions of health and disease. But faith and imagination are the most intense and influential forms of mental action that can be brought to bear upon the physical organism. The very existence of the body, as something outside of the being of the mind, is only an *inference or belief*, an apparent rather than a real truth. Therefore to change our belief with regard to the body, either involuntarily or by a conscious volitional effort, modifies its condition. If we believe and imagine that a change is being effected in ourselves, or in others who are in *contact* with us, it will be so; for whatever in this way the soul predicts will find its fulfillment in the altered condition of the body. Fear in its varying forms of doubt, anxiety, foreboding, and melancholy, is the spiritual root of disease, and a prophecy of it, and faith sustains the same radical relation to health; and their previsions and predictions will be realized in the corresponding modifications of the physical condition.

Belief being the foundation of all knowledge, as was taught by Jacobi, and also by Sir William Hamilton, so it is the ground of all *reality*. To believe that we have a thing and to *have* it are one and the same so far as our mental possession of it is concerned. They are inseparable states of consciousness. Hamilton truly observes: " The ultimate facts of consciousness are given less in the form of cognitions than of beliefs. Consciousness, in its last analysis, in other words, our primary experience, is a faith." Belief in its higher form is a *complete conviction* that a thing is true, or that it really exists. In this sense, to believe that we have a thing is a mental appropriation of it, and it becomes to us a reality. Its reality to us is in exact proportion to the strength of our faith. To believe that we are well, or are becoming so, makes it a reality to the extent of our inward conviction of it. This principle was

taught by Jesus the Christ when he said : " Be it unto thee according to thy faith," which expresses a law as uniform in its operation in the realm of mind as gravitation is in the region of nature.
(Mat. ix : 29.)   Also in that remarkable saying : " What things
soever ye desire when ye pray, believe that ye receive, and ye
shall have."   (Mark xi : 24.)   This is based upon a correct philosophy of the mind, that to have, and to believe that we have, are
a single and inseparable act of the soul.   Take away our *belief*
in the possession of anything, even though we may hold it in our
hands, it is to us as good as annihilated.   The testimony of our
senses to the existence of an object, if we have no faith in its
reality, brings no evidence or conviction with it.   To believe that
we have a disease is to have it, while the full persuasion of it
remains.   On this subject James Mill truly observes : " To have
a sensation and to believe that we have it are not distinguishable
things.   When I say ' I have a sensation,' and say ' I believe I have
it,' I do not express two states of consciousness, but one and the
same state.   Sensation is a feeling ; but a feeling and the belief of
it are the same thing."   (*Phenomena of the Human Mind*, Vol.
I, p. 255.)

It is in accordance with one of the deepest laws of the spiritual
universe that salvation, in the sense attached to it by the Christ,
as including the restoration of both body and soul to health and
harmony, is, and must ever be, through faith.   This is not an
arbitrary condition of it, that might as well have been something
else, as the making of a pilgrimage, or the offering of a sacrifice,
but is a necessary prerequisite and concomitant of it.   It can
enter into us as an actual mental possession, and become a living
reality in no other way.   But it is important to remark that
belief is not a mere passive state of the intellect, but is also a
voluntary act.   Hence we should not wait for a saving faith to
come to us, but by a volitional effort use the power we already
possess.   In the Gospels men are blamed for not believing, which
could not in justice be done if belief and unbelief were wholly
beyond the control of our volitions.   On this point Bain says :

"In its esential character, belief is a phase of our active nature, otherwise called will." (*Note to Mill's Phenomena of the Human Mind*, Vol. I. p. 394.)

In conclusion, let me say in the words of another, who in his theology is intensely orthodox: "It is the want of *faith* in our age which is the greatest hindrance to the stronger and more marked appearance of that miraculous power which is working here and there in quiet concealment. Unbelief is the final and most important reason for the retrogression of miracles." (*Christlieb's Modern Doubt and Christian Belief*, p. 366.)

If the doctrine of Jesus is true, that in the cure of disease it is unto us according to our *faith*, the only object of a *Christian* physician in giving medicine, and the only ground on which he could justify it to himself, is to furnish the patient a πôυ στῶ, or standing ground, for faith and imagination, on which they may rest their Archimedean lever. A bread-pill, or colored water, or the antiquated bones of a reputed saint, are as good as anything else for accomplishing this. But perhaps the best device for giving to faith a material foothold is found in the dilutions and triturations of homeopathy. A sugar-of-milk globule, medicated or unmedicated, answers every rational purpose of medicine.

CHAPTER VIII.

VOLUNTARY AND INVOLUNTARY ACTION OF THE MIND ON THE BODY.

Nearly all the physiological processes and functional movements of the various organs are carried on by an unconscious and involuntary or automatic mental action. They take place in accordance with the highest intelligence, and, consequently, must be the resultant of some form of mental action. But it is an interesting fact, and one that has its practical importance, that all these so-called automatic movements may be modified, and even controlled by the voluntary action of the mind. Take as a familiar illustration of this the act of respiration. Breathing is usually automatic, and accomplished without any conscious, volitional effort. All the muscles concerned in the respiratory movement, as the intercostal, the diaphragm, and those of the abdomen act when we sleep and when we wake, and without any expenditure of will-force on our part. Yet at any moment we can, by our will, take those muscles under our control, and the breathing passes from an involuntary, automatic movement to a conscious and voluntary act.

The action of the heart is almost always an involuntary movement, and effected by an unconscious action of the mind. Yet there have been persons who could influence and even control its systolic and diastolic motions. The distinguished physiologist, E. F. Weber, of Leipzig, found that he could completely check the beating of his heart. By suspending his breathing, and violently

198

contracting his chest, he could retard the pulsations; but there was danger of carrying it too far and falling into a syncope.

The contraction of the iris, the colored circle that surrounds the pupil of the eye, under the influence of light is a purely reflex or involuntary action, and to close the iris would seem to be an impossibility. Yet there are men who have learned how to do this. The celebrated Fontana had this power, and Dr. Paxton, a medical man now living at Kilmarnock, is said to have the ability to contract or expand the iris at will.

To move the ears is impossible to most men, yet some have learned to do it with ease, and all could, by practice, acquire the power to do it. Certain movements of the toes are impossible to us now, or are effected with great difficulty, and yet there are cases where, from the loss of the fingers, persons have acquired the ability to use them in writing, sewing, drawing, and painting. These facts go to prove that all the muscles of the body are made to obey the sovereign will, and that there is no real and essential distinction between what we call voluntary and involuntary organs. The motor influence in both is the mind, in the one case acting preconsciously, in the other consciously, and by a volitional effort. We can use our toes with as much facility and skill as the newly-born infant can his fingers, only we have not educated them.

All the involuntary, physiological movements and vital processes, which are ordinarily carried on by an unconscious action of the soul, can be influenced and controlled by a volitional effort of the fancy, or imagination, when intelligently directed to the production of a desired result. This is true of the action of the liver, the kidneys, the skin, and the processes of digestion, circulation, excretion, and secretion. The body is the passive instrument of the mind, and it is in harmony with an established Divine order that it should obey its supreme behests. It is not unreasonable to suppose that the time will come when the relation of the mind to the body will be so fully comprehended that what are called the involuntary functions will be as certainly influenced by an intelligent volitional effort as are now the muscles of our arms.

All that is necessary is that the now partially-sundered links between the organs that act automatically, or by a preconscious mental influence, and the will should be restored. When this connection is established, what is now deemed impossible will become practically easy, and all the organic actions and physiological movements will be under our control, and will be influenced in any desired direction by the fancy or imagination, by the power of thought and of our faith and volitions. "Thus, it appears that even the actions which most distinctly bear the character recognized as involuntary, uncontrollable, are only so because the ordinary processes of life furnish no necessity for their control. We do not learn to control them, though we could do so, to some extent, in the same way that we do not learn to control the motions of our ears, although we could do so." (*The Physical Basis of the Mind*, by G. H. Lewes, p. 371.)

All the movements of the body are classed as voluntary or involuntary, as they are performed by a conscious effort or an unconscious mental influence; but in either case the moving principle, the motor power, is the mind. There are certain physiological processes and muscular movements that are supposed to be automatic and fixed by an iron necessity, and wholly beyond our control. Yet there is no part of the body that is not under the dominion of the mind, and that cannot be influenced by an intelligent voluntary action. It is an error to affirm or believe that these movements and functions of an organ *cannot* be affected, and that they are altogether beyond the interference of mind with their action, and cannot, by any volitional effort, be modified. Darwin, in Zoonomia, mentions the case of a person who could suspend the pulsations of the heart at pleasure, and of another who could at will move his bowels by accelerating their peristaltic action. Lord Brougham speaks of these cases as almost monstrous. But, why so? They were done in harmony with some *law* of the voluntary action of the mind on the body, which being known would empower us to repeat them. The action of the perspiratory glands would seem to be as far beyond voluntary control

as any part or function of the human organism, yet Mayer mentions that some persons have the power of perspiring at will. Prof.
Beer, of Bonn, has the rare power of contracting or dilating the
pupil of his eye at any moment.   In his case *thought* seems to be
the motor power.   When he thinks of a very dark space, the pupil
dilates; when of a very bright spot, the pupil contracts.   Here is
a principle in reference to the influence of thought on the human
organism of great importance.   (*Noble: The Human Mind*, p.
124.)   In the same way, when we think of something sour, as
lemon juice, it affects the salivary glands, and causes the mouth to
water.   Thus the *thought* of an object, as of some medicinal
preparation, has an effect similar, even if less in degree, to that
of the thing itself.   Through the medium of thought we come into
contact with the spiritual principle or essence of the drug.   It is
an experiment anyone can try upon himself.   Thus, an idea, a
thought, an imagination, may act as a medicine, or as a poison.
There is a potential virtue in thought that is not fully understood
and appreciated.   "As a man thinketh in his heart, so is he."
This is one of the wisest things that Solomon ever said.   In the soul
reside all the active vital powers.   Given a certain psychical state,
and a correspondent bodily condition follows with all the unerring
certainty of the relation of cause and effect.   There is a power in
thought over our bodily condition that is not recognized in the science of medicine.   No person ever dies of disease but from *thinking* and *believing* that he is diseased.   Here is the root of the
malady.   As Fichte has truly said: "In the mind — in the self-
supporting life of thought — life itself subsists, for beyond the
mind there is no true existence.   To live truly means to think
truly, and to discern the truth." (*The Way Towards the Blessed
Life*, p. 12.)

On the influence of thought upon the body Sir William Hamilton says: "I can in imagination represent the action of speech,
the play of the muscles of the countenance, or the movement of
the limbs; and when I do this, I feel clearly that I awaken a kind
of tension in the same nerves through which, by an act of will, I

can determine an overt and voluntary motion of the muscles; nay, when the imagination is very lively, this external movement is actually determined. Thus we frequently see the countenance of persons under the influence of imagination undergo various changes; they gesticulate with their hands, they talk to themselves, and all this is in consequence of an imagined activity going out into a real activity." (*Bowen's Metaphysics of Sir William Hamilton*, p. 455.)

We are to bear in mind that imagination is only a mode of thought, and every idea in the mind tends, by its inherent nature, to an actuality in the body. The effects of imagination are as clearly felt, when it acts upon the involuntary and so-called automatic organs,—as the stomach, the liver, or the intestinal canal, — as when it acts upon the muscles that are under the more immediate dominion of the will. When its force is exerted upon these organs, by *thinking* and *believing*, the activity we wish to induce in them, an imagined action goes forth into an actual one, for the only living force of the body is the mind. What physiologists call the *vis vitæ* is a mental energy. Matter, whether in the human body or in the world at large, is always passive and inert, but activity and freedom belong to the essence of spirit.

CHAPTER IX.

THE MORBIFIC AND SANATIVE INFLUENCE OF THOUGHT.

Mind is the only active power in the universe, and to most people its influence is unintelligible and incomprehensible. It is only because it acts unseen and unobserved that it has come to be under-valued. Its power is hidden from the view of the senses; but the most potent forces of nature act silently and with no noise or show. The kingdom of the heavens cometh not with observation, or under the cognizance of the senses. Mind is the only causal agent in the realm of matter, and certainly in the human body. A simple thought, which is a mental act or state, has a marvelous power over the body. It may in its influence be morbific, or that which generates disease, or it may be sanative and promotive of health. In many diseases, especially those of a so-called nervous character, there is too much *thinking*, or rather too much thought in one direction, and in a wrong direction. This state of thinking and feeling is the cause of the bodily condition. As the body is the creation of the mind, and is always its ultimation or outward ex-pression, a chronic disease is the fixedness of a thought, the petri-faction of a morbid idea. Thoughts or ideas are the most *real* things in the universe. They are the interior soul of things, and the underlying reality of all outward and visible objects. The things we behold in the natural world are the thoughts of God, and by studying them we come into communication with his thoughts, as we do with the ideas of an author by reading the words of his book. The mind is the real man, and its thoughts act on the body as a spiritual poison, or as a mental medicine; for health and disease, in their spiritual essence, may be resolved into modes of thinking. A man is well so long as he *thinks, feels, and believes* himself so, for to be sick and not know it is all the same as not to be sick; and for a physician to tell a patient that he has a disease is oftentimes to create it; and to assure him that he has it not, except in his own thought, and cause him to *believe* it, is a short and easy method of curing him. What is all this but a change of thought? It is the substitution of one way of thinking for another.

Let us look for a moment at the power of thought. Whatever a man consciously makes or invents is always first a thought, an idea, before it is shaped into an objective or external thing. The house in which we live, or the ship in which we sail, first exists as a spiritual reality in the mind of the architect and builder; the picture in the soul of the painter, and the statue in the idea of the sculptor. This was the doctrine of Plato four centuries before Christ. Everything exists in idea before it can have an external and material realization. A visible thing, whether it be a granite boulder or a physical disease, is the *outness* of a thought, the externalization of an idea; and an idea is the inward existence, the spiritual reality, of a sensible object. But there are false ideas and true ones, a right and a wrong way of thinking. A false or fallacious idea is ultimated or externally manifested in the body by disease; and then truth is the best medicine. Thought is a *creative* power, and it always forms something in its own image, a likeness and correspondence of itself. A bad thought, a false and fallacious idea, a wrong conception and belief ultimate themselves in the body in disease,—acute, if it be a temporary mental state, and chronic, if it be a confirmed mode of thinking. Preëxistent ideas and feelings are the patterns after which the body shapes itself by a necessary law of spiritual cause and material effect. The sincerity and deepness of our belief, or recognition of those ideas as realities, is always the measure of the extent and permanency of their effects upon the body. The condition of the body is only the interior becoming the outward, and the excellence or defect of the idea is the body's health or malady. The disease is preceded by an *a priori* wrong way of thinking, and the cure is the result, in every case, of an antecedent change of thought and idea. This is the philosophy of the system of cure practiced by Jesus the Christ, and forever consecrated by him as the Divine method of healing both soul and body. Everything resolves itself back into an idea. The solid frame work of the world, with all its objects of beauty and use, are but the crystalization of God's thoughts. Fulton's idea became solidified into a steamboat, Stephenson's into a railroad, and Morse's into a telegraph. A factory is only somebody's thought condensed into a material manifestation; and any faulty way of thinking, any defect in the original idea, makes the machinery go wrong, and causes an imperfect manufacture. Here is the whole spiritual theory of disease; for what is true of a mill is more certainly true of the body and its relation to the mind. Men have only begun to realize the power of thought over the external organism,— the influence of ideas, of imagination, of faith, and feeling over the corporeal condition and the physiological functions. This is, as I have just said, the Divine method of cure, because the relation of soul and body is analogous to that which God sustains to the visible world. Jesus the Christ, who exhibited the highest type of humanity, and was, consequently, the divinest manifestation of God, found the remedy for disease in *truth*. He came to make known the truth, and thereby save the lost, or those who, in their bewilderment, had wandered away from it. Truth is that which *is*. Error, which is the soul of disease, is that which is not. The one is the reality of things; the other has no being. If, then, we supplant in the mind of another an error by substituting for it a positive truth, we put something where before there was in reality nothing. Disease is often but an error, a fallacious idea, a falsity, a wrong way of *thinking*, and, consequently, in itself a nihility or nothingness. In all those cases the best remedy and the only specific is the opposite truth. Here the spiritual teacher and the physician meet and become one. Of this we have the highest illustration in the life and work of Jesus the Christ.

Every thought which has truth for its foundation, or has its root in the one and only Reality, has in it the life of God; just as a particle of water proceeding from the ocean by emanation or evaporation, is a miniature sea, a microscopic ocean, and has all the properties of the Atlantic, whence it came. Hence, a thought, a truth, whose inward essence is always Divine, has in it the very life of God, and must have the highest therapeutic virtue of anything in the universe. The mind is the only life of the body, and the only real and enduring thing in human nature. No one ever dies of what is called disease, as has been said in a previous chapter. It is only when faith, hope, and imagination lose their hold upon the organic structure, and the soul relaxes its grasp upon the body, that it yields. Then it goes down like a scuttled ship in a storm. It is only kept afloat by the buoyancy that the mind imparts to it, and when the connection between it and its life-preserver is sundered, it goes under the waves to rise no more. When the correspondence between the mind and body ceases, the body dies as a lamp expires when the oil is exhausted.

Thought is the grand characteristic of man, and belongs to the essence of the soul. The word man, according to Max Müller, is an ancient Sanscrit word meaning to *think*, and is the root of the Zend word *manthra*, speech. Man may be defined as the being who thinks and speaks. This separates him by a wide chasm from all the orders of animals below him. A change of thought, or of a fixed mode of thinking, must of necessity modify the state of the soul, as the very *existence* of the soul is identical with thought, and it creates the body into its own image and likeness. It is easy from this to see how much it must have to do with health and disease.

If love is the life of man, as Swedenborg affirms, thought is the existence, or outward manifestation, of that vital element or principle, and the quality of that existence must depend upon the character of his thoughts. The mind always thinks, and must as long as it *lives*. It was the opinion of Kant, expressed in his Anthropology, that we always think when we sleep; that to cease to dream would be an extinction of our life. He also says that we can dream more in a minute than we can act in a day, and that the great rapidity of the train of thought in sleep is one of the principal causes why we do not always recollect what we dream. He elsewhere observes that the cessation of a force to act is tantamount to its cessation to be. With the above view Sir William Hamilton agrees. (*Bowen's Metaphysics of Sir William Hamilton*, p. 220.) Long before Kant, Cicero, the Roman philosopher and orator, affirmed that the mind is always active. He says: "*Nunquam animus cogitatio et motu vacuus esse potest,*"—the soul can never be destitute of thought and activity.

Being or life comes to its first active manifestation in thought. In the beginning—in the first principle or pure being, as the original term means,—was the Word or Thought of God. (John i: 1.) By this all things were and are created. So in man, who is the image of God, thought is the first manifestation of the living principle in him, or that by which being (in German *seyn*) goes forth into *ex*-istence (*daseyn*) and into a bodily expression. When we say that a man's thoughts are employed on business, or trade, or government, or art, or philanthrophy, we mean the current of his life tends to that form of activity. It is *set* or *fixed* (which is the radical meaning of the word think) in that particular direction. The same is true of disease, its inmost essence being a *fixity* of thought in a false position. Especially is this true when the morbid condition becomes chronic. Our life always flows out into manifestation in the direction of our thoughts, and disease is only a *state*, or, as the word etymologically signifies, a standing still of thought, in other words, an immovable fixedness of a morbid way of thinking. But as our varying modes of thought are, to a certain extent, under the control of the self-determining power of the will, so to the same extent health and disease are under the dominion of the mind, or the voluntary exercise of faith and imagination.

If there is any power resident in human nature which possesses a creative energy and a modifying influence over the bodily condition, and one that lies within the compass of the God-given abilities of the soul so to exercise as to change the morbid mode of thinking, that is, the spiritual essence of disease, let us search earnestly among our faculties to find it. The practical value of the discovery will be a full reward for any sincere effort that may be expended in the quest.

CHAPTER X.

The faculty of imagination, in the estimate of the popular mind, and even among those who pass current in the world for scientific men, has been greatly undervalued. It has been degraded to a lower level among our intellectual powers than by divine right belongs to it. It is really one of the highest and most influential powers of the soul.

We have been educated to believe that an *imaginary* disease, or one that owes its origin and continuance to an abnormal action of this mental power upon the body, is an unreal one. It is supposed to be the magnifying into undue proportions of what has no importance, or the creation of something out of nothing. This is false in philosophy and untrue in fact. The imagination, or, as Fichte calls it, the fancy, is the formative power of the body. It has in it a creative potency. God created, and perpetually creates, the world by some power that answers to imagination in us. And how much of our life do we spend in a world of our own making! The creations of fiction are as real as those of history, and there is as much *truth* in the one as in the other. Fiction, in the etymological sense of the word, is that which the mind makes. Poetry, from a Greek word of a similar meaning, has the same signification. They are mental creations. The imagination is the image-making faculty, or that which forms an idea that it can so project outward as to view it outside of the being of the mind. It creates the world in which we *really* live, and the body by which the soul enters into the limitations of time and space, and where we temporarily dwell. We wish to elevate this most important faculty from its degradation in mental science and the estimation of the world to its native Divine dignity and importance.

The imagination is a spiritual *force*, and a creative power. An imaginary disease is not an unreal one, for we cannot fancy a thing that has no existence. " What the populace say about imagination presenting images that we mistake for reality is, like popular philosophy in general, pure nonsense. No man ever imagined or can imagine anything that has not reality *somewhere*, and this whether waking or sleeping." (*Life: Its Nature, Varieties, and Phenomena*, by Leo H. Grindon, p. 415.) The creations of the imagination are as real as our own bodies, or any of the objects that come to our perception through the senses. To cure a disease of mind or body by this power or force is not to heal a person of what never ailed him, or of what had no actual existence. The very fact that a man imagines himself sick is a proof that he is so; for the disease is only the effect of an abnormal action of this *creative* power.

The imagination is both an involuntary and a voluntary power of the mind. In its involuntary and preconscious action, it builds up the organism, heals its wounds, reacts against every abnormal condition, and carries on all the physiological processes and so-called automatic movements. But the will or self-determining power of the soul, guided by an instinctive intelligence, may take all these processes under its control, and what is called the vital force — which can never be distinguished from the action of the mind upon the body — can be precipitated upon any given point of the organism for the modification of its condition, and the production of a desired sanative result.

Could we trace the mental history of every disease, we should see how much it was the product of this power; and if we could see the hidden influences that were at work in every case of cure, we should perceive how much was owing to the productive spiritual force of the imagination, combined with faith in effecting the therapeutic result. In these two spiritual forces, or agencies, we have the most important of all curative devices. They ought to be more profoundly studied, as they possess a higher sanative value than all that the Materia Medica has given us. Nowhere do we find their efficiency so fully illustrated as in the life and practice of Jesus the Christ. By him they have received the seal and sanction of the Divine method of cure.

From what has been said above we see why the "irregular," or unauthorized, practitioner is so often successful where the "learned ignorance" of the regular physician has failed. The first somehow brings into action the divine principles of faith and imagination, and directs their force upon the body; and the world accepts the result as almost if not quite miraculous. The time may come when there will be an entire revolution of public opinion, and the now unorthodox physician, who appeals, whether he knows it or not, more directly to the two principles that in the highest degree influence the bodily condition, will be accepted as the man who is legally authorized to prescribe for "the ills that flesh is heir to." He who can best minister to a mind diseased, and control and direct these mental forces so as to modify the corporeal condition, is the best physician; and if he is "constrained by the love of Christ," or the same benevolent impulse that actuated him, he is in the regular line of apostolic succession, even though no mitred priest has laid hands upon his head, and consecrated him to a work the importance of which the ecclesiastical functionary understands but little or even nothing.

If what has been said above is true as to the real principle of cure, then the only rational design in prescribing material remedies is to furnish aids to *faith and imagination*, which are the efficient cause of that alteration of the bodily and mental condition that we call recovery from disease. If a patient's faith is so weak that it cannot walk alone, give him a drug to be a cane on which a saving and healing faith may lean for support; or prescribe for him some pharmaceutical preparation, homeopathic or allopathic, as a crutch, by the aid of which the imagination may hobble along in the direction of health and happiness.   But blessed is the man who has passed the infantile state of his existence and been weaned of his dependence upon material things, and who can walk erect in the Divine dignity of his spiritual nature as an image of God, and whose faith brings him into living contact and conjunction with the Central Life.

If it be true, as has been admitted by the intuitive reason of mankind, and has become an axiom of philosophy, that *inertia* is a property and necessary condition of matter, or, in other words, that it can neither move nor effect any change in its state unless it be acted upon by some force outside of itself and distinct from it, then it follows that there are no automatic or self-originated movements or changes of the material organism.   Every change in the bodily *status* in the direction of disease or health is an effect for which medical philosophy must find a cause that is not in the body itself, and I verily believe and, without hesitation, affirm that the only efficient cause is some action of mind.   The body, in all its varying conditions and changes, is only an outward manifestation, a material and sensible expression, of the state of the soul. This is, under God, the creative power of the body,— it speaks and it is done.   The mental forces that originate and modify the condition of the body are *faith and imagination.* These may act preconsciously, or voluntarily and with conscious effort.   Thus, the whole science of medicine, through all the ages of its history and all its conflicting schools, may be condensed into a single sentence, in which they are all reduced to an essential unity,— *if you would cure disease, call into active operation the principles of faith and imagination.*   All curative devices that do not effect this are powerless.

As Prof. Krauth has said in his annotations on Berkeley's "Principles of Human Knowledge:" "No theory of the human body is worthy of attention which does not acknowledge the *soul* as the controlling force of the body." The psychical is first. The mind is the conditioning power of the material. It is the organizing force that lifts the organic out of the inorganic. In its relation to the body the mind is a sort of vice-creator, or secondary formative power; and this productive and constructive energy is something very like what we call imagination. I as firmly believe as I do in my own existence that there is here a principle of vast practical importance, and one that contains the seed of a valuable and efficient system of phrenopathy, or mental medicine.

The things seen by the imagination are called phantoms, by which is meant unreal appearances. That they are so is an assumption not capable of proof. They *may* be as real as the objects of the external world. We have the same evidence of the reality of the one that we have of the other, as both are seen only in the mind. When I assert that heat is in the fire, it is a phantom or fallacious appearance, for the real truth is that it is a *sensation* in me. When one says that he has a pain in some part of his body, as in his hand, his head, or his stomach, that is a phantom, for the body has no sensation, no feeling. The pain is no more there than when it is felt in an amputated limb. But we can imagine a pain until we feel it; and we can imagine and fear a disease until, by the creative power of these mental forces, we really have it. So the same is true of health. By a voluntary and intelligent use of faith and imagination, we can effect a cure of disease in ourselves and others.

I know of no writer who takes a higher view of the imagination as a creative force than Jacob Behmen, the theosophist. Instead of looking upon it as an impotent faculty of the mind, dealing in fiction and airy nothings, he viewed it as the greatest power in nature. All outward power that we exercise over the things about us is but a shadow in comparison with that *inward power* that resides in imagination and will. It communicates with eternity and coöperates with the Divine Creative Life, and nothing is impossible to it. It was considered by him as one of the chief instruments of conversion and regeneration, and its use was recommended as such; and he might just as well have said as much of its influence in the cure of diseases of the mind and the body had he traced its influence in that direction.

Van Helmont declares that there is an inner power of the soul whence the mightiest events, the deepest impressions, and the most decisive effects proceed. He says: " I have hitherto avoided revealing the great secret that the strength lies concealed in man *merely through the suggestion and power of the imagination,* to work outwardly, and to impress this strength on others, which then continues of itself, and operates on the remotest objects." (*Ennemoser's History of Magic,* Vol. II, p. 246.)

Ennemoser, who had a clear perception of the influence of the mind upon the body, says of the power of the imagination, that an intensely active imagination transforms the ideas of fancy into permanent shapes, which even obtain a certain plastic firmness in the body. " The soul creates and the body forms, and in fact only to that shape which has been held before it. The imagination is the creative and inventive power of the soul, which endeavors to reproduce outwardly that which it inwardly believed ; and this succeeds more especially when the body is in a passive condition, and the outward senses are dormant." (*History of Magic,* Vol. II, p. 101.)

Imagination is an element in an act of saving or healing faith, as was recognized by Behmen. The person of an active or strong imagination is one whose faith is the " substance of things hoped for." It gives life and reality to faith. Stewart, the Scotch metaphysician, came near expressing this truth. It was his opinion that " the exercise of the imagination is always accompanied with a belief that the objects of the imagination exist." Prof. Ferrier remarks of this opinion of Stewart that it appears to him to be founded in truth. (*Ferrier's Philosophical Works,* Vol. III, p. 515.)

Imagination is the power by which the thoughts, the ideas of the mind, are projected outward into an actuality in the body. In connection with faith in God, the ever-present and ever-active creative Force, the body is moulded by it into the external expression of what the mind conceives and desires as a state of physical health. It is a power when properly educated and conjoined with faith that brings the soul, in its curative effort, into communicative contact with the Immeasurable Life, and thus feeds and augments our noblest powers from their Eternal Source. It is in us the image, or finite expression, of God's creative energy, and, consequently, when used under the guidance of a spiritual intelligence, is the greatest healing power in nature.

Imagination is only a mode of thought, and its power is only an illustration of the influence of thought. What passes in the Church parlance under the name of "conversion," or "a change of heart," is effected by this transforming power. The doctrine of justification by faith, which is the central idea of the Pauline development of Christianity, and which, after having been buried out of sight by the ritualism and externalism of the Papal Church, was restored as a saving power to the Christian system by Luther, and which was again dropped out of the creed of the religious world until revived by the Wesleys, and then became a saving power to millions of souls, *owes its efficiency to the imagination.* The penitent comes into the idea or belief that he is condemned of God, and is burdened with the sense of guilt, which is called *conviction.* He is now willing and desirous to be saved, and is taught to *believe*, that is, to think or imagine that God now forgives and saves him. This is only a belief of the truth (as God forgives all and condemns none), and then his burden of self-imposed condemnation rolls off, his self-torment, doubt, and mental turmoil cease, and, coming to an inward sense of justification by faith or imagination, he enters into a solid and enduring peace. (Rom. v: 1.) But *imagination* has much to do with this, as was taught by Behmen, and as anyone can see who can analyze the mental process involved in the change of the spiritual *status* of the convert. But I charge the reader to bear in mind that the change is none the less *real* by being effected mainly by the transforming power of the imagination. In a connection with the Church for more than forty years, and by an unbiased study of the psychological phenomena of revivals, I know that the mental metamorphosis, called conversion, has often in it the element of permanency, and the soul by it becomes anchored in the Divine Life. The same remarks will apply to the cure of all diseases of the body and mind, which constituted the fullness of the idea of *salvation* as it existed in the mind of the Christ, and is expressed in the Gospels.

CHAPTER XI.

We have seen that there is a two-fold life of the soul, which manifests itself in the two forms of conscious and unconscious mental action. The preconscious life and activity of the mind is seen in the building up of the organism, and in carrying on all the physiological processes. These mechanical and *geometrizing* effects seem to be under the control and direction of the highest and most unerring intelligence, though acting unconsciously so far as our voluntary mental action is concerned. But all the *instinctive* actions of the mind belong to this region of our mental nature. There is a dignity and importance attached to these that have been but poorly appreciated in philosophy, in religion, and in the science of medicine.

Instinct may be defined as an original impulse of the soul, impressed upon it by the author of our being, toward a certain form of thinking, feeling, and acting. Hartmann, who represents the latest and, at the present time, is the most popular exponent of the idealistic philosophy of Germany, defines instinct to be acting in conformity with a purpose, without any consciousness of that purpose. (*Bowen's Modern Philosophy*, p. 437.) Archbishop Whately says "Instinct is a blind tendency to some mode of action independent of any consideration on the part of the agent of the end to which the action leads." . But in the phenomena of instinct we see an exhibition of the highest intelligence, and, though it may act without our volitions and even without our consciousness, it can with no propriety be called *blind*.   Sir William Hamilton's definition of it is still worse.   According to him, "Instinct is an agent which performs blindly and ignorantly a work of intelligence and knowledge."   If this was true, the wonder is that it should make no mistakes, or, if any, so few.   Dr. Paley's definition of it is better, because blindness and ignorance are not attributed to it, but it is still defective.   "Instinct," he says, "is a propensity prior to experience, and independent of instruction."   It is an inborn predisposition and tendency towards a given form of action by which God perpetually acts upon and in the human soul, and, when yielded to without obstruction and without any depraved perversion, leads us, by an unconscious thinking and by an intelligence originally and continually impressed upon the mind by the Father of spirits, unerringly in the right direction.   It is not confined in its action to the wants and demands of the lower nature, but its influence is felt in the highest regions of our spiritual being.   What we call conscience is only an instinctive recognition of what is right and wrong, accompanied by a Divine impulse to do the one and refrain from the other, analogous to what occurs in all animals when they are seen spontaneously to reject in their food whatever would be injurious to them. This they do without any knowledge of the laws of physiological chemistry, which gives us light as to the adaptation of food to the needs of the animal economy.   *Appetency* is an innate *seeking* for something, a desire or reaching out of the mind for that which will supply a conscious need.   It is a prescription of what we call nature, —which is only another name for the God-life within us,—of what the mind and body require for their nourishment, their growth, and happiness.   It relates more to the department of feeling than to that of pure intellect.   If this department of our nature could be relieved from the ban of a false theology, and the unnatural system of ethics that grows out of it, and could become a subject of education as much as the reason and the memory are, it would become a guide in duty and morals far nearer infallibility than the mandates of popes or the decisions of ecclesiastical councils. If we derive our being from God, then the fundamental laws of our nature are expressions of the will of God, and our spiritual instincts have the sacredness of the utterances of Sinai. Either this or atheism is true. Instinct being an original and ante-natal predisposition of mind toward a certain mode of action is as much a Divine law in the human spirit as gravitation and chemical affinity are in the realm of external nature. A genuine instinct, not modified by a false education, is a revelation from God and a mode of knowing the Divine will as much as is the Decalogue. Kant, with all his cold, intellectual scepticism, is compelled to exclaim "Instinct is the voice of God." Hartmann in his "Philosophy of the Unconscious," attributes it to that mysterious power of the soul for which we have no name,—in German, *hellsehen*, in French, *clairvoyance*,—which is considered by him as Divine, as it transcends the ordinary conscious, voluntary powers of man. This takes it from the dunghill of total depravity and the compost heap of things rejected by an unreasoning theology and unnatural moral philosophy, which excludes God as an active and ever-operating force from human nature, and places it on a throne among the princes of the earth. It is no longer an outcast and a condemned and banished criminal driven into a hiding place, but it sits at the gate among the rulers of the land.

The relation of this department of the soul to health is a most important one. No one will be disposed to deny that the almost uniform health of the lower animals, especially when their life has not been interfered with by man, is owing to their following the law of their nature and the guidance of their instincts. These are "a pillar of a cloud by day and a pillar of fire by night" to lead them to the promised land of their highest destiny,— the *summum bonum* of the animal soul. So, in human society the highest state of health of mind and body will never be realized until our instinctive nature is allowed to have a voice in the regulation of our lives, and walk side by side and hand in hand with our more fallible reason. Then every man's best physician will dwell in his own heart, and can be called from the Divine depths of his own nature to prescribe for his bodily ills and mental ailments. Animals when sick are often observed to seek for plants which when in health they reject as food. But in man there are all the instincts that there are in the lower orders, and these, when properly educated, would furnish a better treatment of disease than all the medical libraries of the world contain. In the preconscious region of the mind there are spiritual instincts by which men are much more influenced than by their boasted reason. One of the deepest and divinest of these is the tendency of the human soul to return unto God, from whose being it issued into conscious individuality. As all rivers seek the ocean whence they came, and as "fire ascending seeks the sun," so all souls tend back toward their Source. However far we may be removed from Him by a voluntary or involuntary spiritual remoteness which, in its essence, is a moral unlikeness to Him, we shall by a divine elasticity inherent in all human souls, rebound from the point of greatest distance and return to union with Him. As instinctively as the newborn infant seeks the mother's breast, so the soul of man, when left to its own Divine tendencies, and to the pressing nature of its inmost needs, is drawn to God to seek spiritual nutriment from the bosom of the Infinite Life. There is something in the soul, especially in the religious element, which is deep-seated in human nature, which spontaneously tends to vent itself in prayer and pour out itself in supplication to God.

There is an instinct of worship. The history of the race proves this. The universal prevalence of some form of adoration can be accounted for only in this way. It is an instinctive movement of the Divine life that is concealed in the depths of all souls. The Divine Life is not something imported into human nature from without, as we have shown in a previous chapter, but is there already as the inmost ground of our being; and complete separation from God would be an annihilation of our individual existence. This Divine element of the soul expresses itself in worship, — not necessarily in the pomp and ceremony of cathedrals, but in the devout silence of adoring love in the sacred stillness of the soul, the hallowed solitude of our own hearts. A genuine religious life, when left to act for itself without obstruction, will create its own forms of manifestation. It is a law of our being that all the feelings of the soul tend to ultimate themselves in some outward expression. To confine all religion to a stereotyped form, and to limit its manifestation by the enclosure of a liturgy, is to deposit the life of Christ in a sepulchre, and lay a stone upon the door of it, which can be rolled away only by an angelic influence.

With regard to the instinctive action of the mind, we may remark that it is intuitively true that whatever is perfectly natural is Divine. This is self-evident, if we admit God to be the Author of nature and the ever-present Force whose uniform action constitutes the laws of nature. And to live in harmony with what is Divine within us is healthfulness, holiness, or wholeness. If there is such a thing as the voice of God in man,— which you may call, if you will, the dictate of nature,— it is found in that range of mental action which has been denominated instinct. Here God speaks as plainly as on the tables of stone. The word comes from the Latin, and means "*inwardly moved.*" But it is the Divinity within that is the moving force. We may then say in the language of Pope,—

"And *reason* raise o'er *instinct* as you can,
In *this* 't is God directs, in *that* 't is man."

There is in nature a Divine, Intelligent Life. What we call instinct is the action of this intelligent, living principle. The actions commonly denominated instinctive are exhibitions in a wider form of the same creative energy which moulds the various organs of the body, and maintains them in their integrity and functional activity, and which we have called preconscious mental action. This intelligent Life in nature impels the bee to construct its cell, the beaver its dam, and the bird its nest. In plants it is the controlling influence in their formation and movements. So marvelous are the phenomena exhibited by plants, so similar to what we see in animals, that Empedocles, among the ancients, and Darwin and Dr. Percival, in more recent times, have supposed them susceptible of pleasure and pains, emotions and ideas. Descending to the mineral kingdom we still trace the action of an Intelligent Life. In man, besides all the instincts which he has in common with animals, it is seen to coalesce with his voluntary powers, and rises to the highest exhibitions of artistic genius in music, poetry, painting, architecture, and every department of mechanical skill. It even becomes intuition, and an interior, Divine Word. But in each and all these cases it is the operation of the same Intelligent Life and Thought that govern nature in her three grand departments or kingdoms.

As an eloquent writer and accomplished scholar has said: "God is the organizing framer and preserver of the world of living things; instinct is the method by which his energy takes effect. It is the general faculty of the entire living fabric, underlying and determining all activities which transpire, either invisibly in the organs themselves, or as played forth to observation, thus bearing the same relation to the general structure which the constructive chemical forces bear to the crystal. Instinct, in a word, is the operation of LIFE, whether promoting the health, the preservation or the reproduction of an organized frame, or any part of such frame, and whether animal or vegetable. (*Grindon's Life: Its Nature, Varieties, and Phenomena*, p. 510.)

"Instinct," says Dr. Mason Good, "is the law of *the living principle;* instinctive actions are the actions of the living principle pervading and regulating all organized matter. It applies equally to plants and to animals, and to every part of the plant and to every part of the animal, so long as such part continues alive." (*Book of Nature*, Series 2, Lecture IV.) Virey affirms that "internal impulses of life constitute acts of instinct in plants the same as in animals." The distinguished physiologist, Dr. Laycock, remarks: "Inherent in the primordial cell of every organism, whether it be animal or vegetable, and in all the tissues which are developed out of it, there is an intelligent power or agent which, acting in all cases independently of the consciousness of the organism, and whether the latter be endowed with consciousness or not, forms matter into machines and machinery of the most singular complexity with the most exquisite skill, and of wondrous beauty, for a fixed, manifest, and predetermined object,— namely, the preservation and welfare of the individual, and the continuance of the species." He also affirms that this wonderful principle exhibits a knowledge of all that is known in human science,— in chemistry, electricity, magnetism, mechanics, hydraulics, optics, acoustics, — far transcending the limited knowledge of the human intellect. This intelligent living agent that presides over the construction of organs directs also in the use of the organs constructed. This intelligent and benevolent principle and force, call it by what name you will, — Brahma, Osiris, Zeus, Allah, Jehovah,— is the Life of God in nature, which perpetually creates and unerringly governs the world and all it contains. It was said by some of the ancient philosophers, *Deus est anima brutorum*, God is the life of brutes He is also the life of every vegetable organism, from the lichen on the granite boulder to the *Washingtonia gigantea* of California. Virgil somewhere says that the bees have in them a portion of the Divine Mind. Addison, in the Spectator, declares that these intelligent operations which we call instinct come not from any law of mechanism, but are an immediate impression from the first Mover, and are only the Divine energy acting in the creature. Newton, in a scholium to the Principia, considers the actions of animals — and the same would be true of man so far as he is an animal — as the constant, direct, and immediate operation of the Deity Himself. Lord Brougham, while admitting that this doctrine exhibits the finger of God as perpetually working before our eyes, and that it brings us constantly into His presence, respectfully. and, as it seems to me, unsuccessfully, attempts to combat it. Either Christian theism or atheism is true, as there is no position that is logically tenable between them.

In concluding the discussion of the subject of instinct I desire to call the attention of the reader to one remark. *This Divine principle always acts towards a given end,— the highest health and happiness of the individual.* It gives an impulse as certain in its action as the law of gravitation towards the right use of the organs it constructs. We should examine the depths of our inner consciousness to find this Divine propulsion or tendency, and yield to it, as pointing by the finger of God in the direction in which wholeness and health lie. With this view of it Fichte says: "The highest within me independently of consciousness and the immediate object of consciousness is the *impulse.* The impulse is the highest representation of the intelligence in nature." (*The Science of Rights*, p. 497.)

An unperverted instinct being the operation of the Divine Life in man, and including in it the highest intelligence to point out the right way, and an *impulse* to walk in it, is the most unerring guide to health and happiness. It could become to us as the clew of Ariadne to conduct us, in our bewilderment, out of the labyrinth of disease and trouble, if we had the faith and courage to follow it, and if our spiritual vision were not so blurred and clouded as to render it difficult for us to discern it.

CHAPTER XII.

THE HIGHER FORMS OF MENTAL LIFE AND ACTION, AND THEIR CURATIVE INFLUENCE.

The preconscious range of the mind's activity is not confined to the formation of the tissues nor to the carrying on of all the involuntary movements of the organism, nor to the instinctive operations of the soul, but manifests its phenomena in all the higher workings of the mind. It often exhibits phenomena which far transcend its ordinary conscious powers, and above and beyond anything that it can accomplish by any volitional effort, and thus demonstrates its native divinity and its celestial citizenship. As God is immanent in human nature, there is something infinite in the capacities and possibilities of every soul. It sometimes asserts its Divine freedom, rises above the range of the senses, breaks loose from their trammels, and operates in a way analogous to that of angels and spirits *without organic conditions.* "For," as Morell has said, "as the conscious life of the soul links us by numberless gradations to the sense-world, so the preconscious life of the soul brings us into a series of relationships with the spiritual world." Man is spiritually an *amphibia,* or exhibits the phenomena of a double life. While possessing faculties and organs that adapt him to a life on the world that is manifested to the senses, he has faculties and powers, often only in an undeveloped rudimentary state, that connect him with a range of life on a higher plane of existence. The younger Fichte, after a long and

225

patient study of these higher phenomena of the mind's action, has discovered the central fact, the underlying principle, that explains them all. He comes to the conclusion that they exhibit a different relation of the soul to its own organism from the ordinary one; and that " besides the ordinary states of consciousness, demonstrably connected with the nerves and brain, there exist others also, the constitution of which leads us to the necessary admission that the soul developes them out of itself while in a condition relatively or absolutely free from the influence of the body. These latter states demonstrably distinguish themselves by a preponderating vivacity, rapidity, and intensity." (*Contributions to Mental Philosophy*, p. 69.)

If the mind can, and sometimes does, act in the present state of existence free from the external apparatus of the body, and independent of organic conditions, then we find here an unerring prophetic intimation of its immortality, at least a philosophical and demonstrated basis for the universally prevalent belief of this, which lies so deeply imbedded in the religious consciousness of the race.

The higher forms of mental phenomena of which we speak in this chapter have been exhibited by all the religions of the world, especially in their earlier history, and constitute a large share of their marvelous and so-called miraculous element, and have given to those religions their currency and access to the popular belief. Among these we may mention clairvoyance, or mental perception, clairaudience, or an internal hearing, second sight, the neo-platonic ecstasy, somnambulism and the trance, the prophetic vision, or a discernment of the future, and all the phenomena of revelation, intuition, and inspiration. These are not, in the ordinary sense, miraculous gifts, but are powers belonging to the nature of all souls, but in most individuals existing *potentially* rather than as a fully educated or developed mental activity. In all these manifestations of the latent powers of the soul we discover in them a greater or less degree of freedom from bodily conditions. This is a fact common to them all. They seem to be the result of an emancipation of the soul from the thraldom of the body. The body which it has formed as its representative on the plane of sense is, as it were, laid aside. Paul had experiences of this independent action of the mind, and was caught up into the heavens, and declared that he knew not whether he was in the body or out of it. (2 Cor. xii: 1–4.) I am aware that Dr. Carpenter, one of the profoundest physiological scholars of this or any age, has attributed many of these phenomena to an *unconscious cerebration.* But this is taking an effect for a cause. There may be a corresponding action of the brain, but it is only the result of an antecedent movement of the mind. But this unconscious cerebral activity is an hypothesis incapable of proof. Fichte is no doubt much nearer the truth in referring them to a preconscious mental action; and it is more than probable that the mind in these exalted states acts independently of the bodily organism, and rises out of its elementary and rudimentary condition, and exhibits an activity and a display of powers premonitory of its higher state in the life to come. Its latent powers come into action, and the soul begins to live eternal life.

These states are by no means to be considered as abnormal, but as natural to man. Their influence upon the bodily condition, when they are reached by a normal and slow process of development, is often most salutary. While the mind is thus freed from the body, it seems to possess an increased power over it, and disease is often relieved or wholly cured by these higher experiences. In this state of emancipated and heightened intelligence, we come to the perception of the " soul of things." The mind is raised to the realm of causation; the material world becomes a shadow, and spiritual things the only substantial realities. The body ceases to be the *man,* and we become all soul. Disease is traced to its root in some abnormality of mind, and, being viewed as spiritual, is brought under the control of spirit. We are no longer sensebound, but rise to the perception of truth in its reality, and above the fallacious appearances of the senses.

How we may attain to this more exalted range of mental life

and action is a question of great practical importance. We must acquire the habit of forgetting the body that we may become spirit. It is a state that has been called by the writers on the higher forms of religious life and experience a state of *recollection*, and by Bernard of Clairvaux was denominated *contemplation*. The mind is recalled into itself. The external sense-world is shut out of thought and perception. All voluntary and conscious mental action is suspended, and in this state of passivity, or, as Madame Guyon called it, *quietism*, we come at once into the involuntary and preconscious range of the mind's activity. Our intuitive perceptivity is quickened by the general sphere of intelligence in the spiritual world. We come into receptive communication with the uncreated Word, the living Light, that has illuminated the prophets of all religions and of every clime. In this condition of abstraction from the world of sense the Spirit is received that "teaches all things" and "guides into all truth" (John xiv: 26; xvi: 13); and inspiration is no longer viewed as an historic fact of the remote past, but an attainable, practicable experience of religion today. In this preconscious range of the mind's action we come into closer interior relations with the Divinity everywhere immanent in the universe. As it was viewed by Bernard of Clairvaux, Kempis, Eckhart, Tauler, Guyon, Fénelon, Behmen, and all the Christian Mystics, the Divine communication, in this interior state, assumes the form of a philosophical necessity. The man, emptied of self and the world, and raised above the fallacious appearances of the senses, is infallibly filled with the Deity and with heavenly light and life in accordance with the old principle that "nature abhors a vacuum." Certain it is, if we are freed from all that is repellant to the Divine Life and Light, and every thing is removed from the mind that is opaque to spiritual truth, and bars its ingress to the soul, we come into a state where our individual life is mingled with the Divine Existence, and our soul acts in harmony with the Over-Soul, like the sound of two musical strings vibrating in unison and flowing together in one concordant strain. This exaltation of the intellect and harmonizing of the disturbed emotional nature cannot but give a quickening influence to every department of our being, and God's "saving health" permeates and pervades the entire man.

In this more exhalted range of the mind's activity, communication with the world of angelic life becomes its normal condition, and the soul goes to it as instinctively and naturally as the new-born animal to its native element. It is the dawn of immortality. The present conscious attainment of eternal life is one of the truths taught by Buddhism, but more clearly in the sublime spiritual utterances of Jesus the Christ. "To know God is eternal life." "He that believeth on me hath everlasting life, and shall never die." (John xvii: 3; xi: 26; iii: 15.) When we rise above the life of sense to the true life of the spirit we attain to immortality, and lay hold of eternal life. We come to the attainment of a resurrection this side the grave, for the *anastasis*, of which Jesus speaks, is not the resuscitation of a dead body in the graveyard, nor an ascent in space, but an ascent in the scale of life from a natural, sensuous existence to a spiritual mode of thinking, feeling, and perception. The resurrection is a state attainable in the present life. It is the liberation of our spiritual powers and faculties from their material thraldom. "The supersensual world is no future world; it is now present; it can at no point of finite existence be more present than at another, nor more present after an existence of myriads of lives than at this moment."

"It is not necessary that I should be first severed from the terrestrial world before I can obtain admission into the celestial one; I am in it and live in it even now far more truly than in the terrestrial; even now it is my only sure foundation; and the eternal life, on the possession of which I have already entered, is the only ground why I should prolong this terrestrial one. That which we call heaven does not lie beyond the grave; it is even here diffused around us, and its light arises in every pure heart." (*Fichte's Vocation of Man, Popular Works*, pp. 345, 346, 351.)

That heaven and eternal life are states of the soul to be

unfolded here and now, and not to be reached by locomotion through space to some distant stillar orb in the material universe, and at some indefinite future time, is one of the plainest teachings of Jesus the Christ. According to him, immortality is already in man, and "the kingdom of the heavens is at hand," that is, within our present grasp.

On this subject Schleiermacher says in the conclusion of his second Discourse on Religion: "The final aim of a religious life is not the immortality which many wish for and believe in, or only pretend to believe in,—not that beyond time, or rather after this time, but yet in time,—but the immortality which we can have immediate in this temporal life. In the midst of the finite to be one with the Infinite, and be eternal in every instant,—this is the immortality of religion."

In this resurrection state, which Christianity makes attainable on earth, the soul is not dependent upon the bodily senses for its perceptions, but—

"Like naked lamp, she is one shining sphere,
    And round about hath perfect cognizance —
Whatever in her horizon doth appear ;
She is one orb of sense,—all eye, all touch, all ear."

CHAPTER XIII.

Happiness, which may be defined as the satisfaction resulting from the harmonious gratification of all the powers and faculties of the soul, is a spiritual healthfulness, and, by a necessary law of cause and effect, this state of the mind will ultimate itself in the outside circumference of our being, or what we call the body. Its echo will be heard there and recorded in the physical organism. Fichte affirms that life is itself, and in itself, blessedness,— that the two cannot be distinguished, but merge into one. Happiness is an essential and inseparable property of all true life. Swedenborg more than a century ago gave utterance to one of the profoundest axioms of a spiritual science when he declared in his philosophical work, Divine Love and Wisdom, that life is love,— an idea which may be made evident to anyone who will give to it any earnest and patient thought and attention. Love is of itself a state of blessedness,— satisfaction with itself, joy in itself; and therefore love and happiness are one and the same, and consequently all true life must be blessed, since life is love. Thus life, love, and blessedness, and, we may add, by necessary inference, health, are intimately connected, and are identical and always go together, so that one cannot exist without the others. All delight, or emotional bliss, arises from love, that is, from life. It is an ebullition and overflowing of vitality. The man who is not happy, who has not attained to blessedness, does not in reality live. He only

231

appears to live. His existence is only a *seeming* and not a Divine reality. It is an undesired, unwelcome, and unsatisfactory state, which is endured rather than enjoyed. His highest enjoyment is a negation of misery, which he attains only in sleep, the image of death.

A religion, whose central principle is fear, cannot make the soul happy, and does not bear the seal and impress of Divinity. God's infinite Life is love, and love is blessedness in itself. To consciously live in God, to share his Life, to be made one with Him, and thus be made a partaker of the Divine nature, is to live in the order of our creation, and to move in the element in which we were made to exist and to act, and out of which there is no real life and blessedness. Let it be remembered that happiness and health are most intimately, if not indissolubly, associated. The man who is happy, not by transient gleams of spiritual sunshine, not by a casual gay surface-coloring of his existence, but by a blessedness *all through his being*, is not, in the proper sense of the word, diseased. The radical idea of the term disease — without ease — is inconsistent with this state. Let us remember that life, blessedness, and health are one. He who is not blessed, who is not happy, does not really live. He does not realize the full idea of what we call life. The wheels of life move, if they move at all, with friction, and labor, and effort. All action in the line of duty is an up-hill exertion, and not a spontaneous vivacity.

An unhappy man cannot in the full sense of the word be a healthy man. *Much of what physicians treat as physical disease is only a mental unhappiness.* It follows from this that the best physician is he who blesses others, who makes other souls happy by the Divine sunshine of his words and presence. The sphere of his beneficent life is a contagious peacefulness and undisturbed tranquility. He ministers to minds diseased, calms their fears, allays their anxieties, solves their doubts, quiets their forebodings, removes the gloom of dispair, supplants their self-condemnation by a sense of pardon, and aims to pluck from the heart every rooted sorrow. Such was Jesus the Christ, who came to comfort those that mourned, to give them beauty for ashes, the oil of joy for mourning, and the garment of praise for the spirit of heaviness. The good physician is a *doctor* or teacher. His first inquiry is not what ails the body, but what are the more real and interior needs of the soul. By attending to the body alone, he would only work at the circumference of our being; by giving his attention to the mental and spiritual state, he begins the curative process at the center of our existence, and, according to an established law of Divine order, works from within outward. The spiritual disturbance, the mental abnormality, has priority in time, and is first in importance, for the reason that in the mind is found the cause of all bodily changes. We should then search for the spiritual symptoms first, and look at the tongue, feel the pulse, and examine the excretions afterwards. The divinest and most Christ-like man in human society is the good physician,— he who, from the overflowing stores of his spiritual intelligence and goodness, is governed by an irrepressible impulse to impart life, health, and peace to others. He is God's messenger, God's prophet of good, an inspired herald to announce and inaugurate the good time coming to the sorrowing and suffering. He follows more closely in the footsteps of Jesus the Christ, the Divine Man, than does he who clothes himself with the spirit of an imaginary, priestly dignity to give his solemn sanction and official seal to a soul's salvation.

God is supremely happy, because He is a boundless, changeless, irrepressible, and everlasting Love. But love is life, and love in us is the life of God in the soul of man. It is an exalted blessedness to lay the hand on the heart and feel it warm with the vital flame of heaven. But it is a *supreme* bliss of the soul to be the organ of its communication to others. We then become partakers of the Infinite tranquility,— the peace of God that passeth understanding,— and the soul in unruffled serenity floats on the waveless, stormless ocean of the immeasurable Life of God.

The final end of man's creation was to share the bliss of God. Even our sorrows serve to fit us for this.

"Here grief and joy so suddenly unite
That anguish serves to sublimate delight."

Our sorrows are usually only transient moods that are succeeded by heightened joys, as beneath the warming sun the vapors vanish and leave a lucid sky.

"Catch rich, grand thoughts from fountains pure above,
Then pour them out with thine own thoughts in love.
Mark every place with flowers where thou hast trod,
And let thy path lead always towards thy God."

Hypochondria, which consists in *melancholia*, and the conse quent dyspepsia accompanied with gloomy ideas of life, dejection of spirits, a loss of faith that blurrs the bright picture that hope paints on the canvass of the future, like clouds obscuring the glories of sunrise, and all this accompanied by an *indisposition to activity*, is a more general characteristic of disease than physicians have recognized. For all this class of ailments, an hour of supreme bliss, or even the slightest taste of the soul's *summum bonum*, or highest good, is the specific remedy. Under its influence, with a magical efficiency and Divine celerity, the bodily disease vanishes and becomes a *nihility* or nothingness. It passes into the realm of oblivescence, or forgetfulness, and is annihilated by ceasing to be an object of *thought*.

CHAPTER XIV.

THE TRUE IDEA OF SIN, AND ITS RELATION TO DISEASE.

There is a lurking suspicion in the human mind, and has been in all ages, that somehow disease is the result of *sin*. There are traditionary traces among most nations of a time when man was pure and holy, and was consequently free from disease, and life was greatly prolonged beyond its present term. This may have some foundation in historical fact, but is probably greatly colored by mythical additions. Yet it shows that there is in the mind of man an instinctive recognition of the principle that holiness and health, sin and disease, have an important relation to each other, even though they may not express the absolute connection of cause and effect.

Christ, after the cure of disease, often said to the restored patient: "Go in peace, and sin no more." Here the causal relation of sin to disease seems to be implied, if not directly stated. The same is implied in what he said to the paralytic: "Son, be of good cheer; thy sins are all forgiven thee," where the remission or removal of his sins is equivalent to the cure of his disease. According to Jesus the Christ, holiness — which, according to Swedenborg, expresses a right state of the intellect or the thoughts — is spiritual health; and disease, so far as it is an abnormal condition of the bodily organism, is only the externalization of an anterior mental or spiritual disturbance, or inharmony. Sin is a moral evil or disorder. It is a divergence from that mental order

235

which expresses the will of God in relation to man's well-being. It is in the mind before it can become an external act or outward condition, as was taught by the Christ; yet by an invariable law of correspondence it translates itself into an outward effect upon the body. Disease, then, as was affirmed by Swedenborg, and which is in harmony with the teaching of Jesus, is always an *impure* state because it corresponds to evil. It is the echo in the body of some form of spiritual disorder. Following the lead of Jesus in his dealings with it, we would not affirm by this that a sick man ought to be *punished* here or hereafter, but that he ough to be *cleansed* from his leprosy (which may lie deep within), and to be made whole or holy,—the two words having the same radical or etymological meaning.

Paul gives a comprehensive and general definition of sin as "a transgression of the law," by which he means, or ought to mean, to include something more than the Decalogue. It is a divergence from the spiritual and moral order of our being, which expresses to us the law of our nature and the will of God. In the metaphorical expression "transgression," or a crossing over, the law is symbolized as a straight line. To pass over it or diverge from it on either side is a sin. But unfortunately for most or all of us, we were born on the wrong side of it. By the law of heredity, which means the tendency in the mind and body of an individual to develop in the likeness of his progenitors, we inherit a predisposition to many forms of evil. This is often nourished and strengthened by what is called in philosophy our environment, by which is meant the sum total of the physical and moral conditions and influences that surround us,—the ambient world of matter and spirit. In the present state of the world it is not strange that there are so many sick people and sinners. It would be a *miracle* if it were otherwise. I am fully persuaded that much of what is called acute disease and nine-tenths of all chronic disease is the result of an hereditary predisposition to it. We are born morally and spiritually out of joint. This is what Dr. Chalmers calls "the great unhingement" of human nature. But is there do deliverance, no redemption for us? Did Jesus the Christ introduce into this world of moral and spiritual darkness, disorder and disease, a plan of salvation, a method of cure for both soul and body? Can we be rescued from the effects of this hereditary taint, whether it be in the direction of theft or rheumatism, of covetousness or consumption? If it is our misfortune not to have been born aright in our first start in life, can we, in any proper sense of the word, be born again? Is there in every human being, however sinful or diseased, a hidden germ of a new and higher life that can, by a Divine spiritual and celestial influence, be, as it were, impregnated and developed into a new *man*? Is this whole Christian doctrine of salvation a baseless phantom, or is there an underlying practicable truth in it? I affirm that Christ, whose patronymic name was Jesus, or Joshua, which signifies a *savior*, or health-giver, was sent into the world to save his followers from sin, and thus redeem them from the spiritual seeds of disease. In the grand system of cure which he inaugurated, spiritual truths and influences are the restorative and healing agencies. In his Divine therapeutics faith is of more value than pharmacy, contrition than cathartics, and instruction is shown to be more efficacious than ipecac. In his hands this spiritual system of medicine was adequate to the cure of the worst forms of bodily malady. Before the power of the Word and the Spirit, which found in him a willing instrument and organ of communication, all disorderly spiritual influences fled, and disease and death retired. I dare not affirm that his life was a succession of miracles, in the ordinary sense of the word, as a departure from the laws of nature, but we should recognize in his beneficent career the knowledge of a higher order within the realm of nature. Miracles, as even Prof. Phelps in his work on the New Birth has acknowledged, are not the grandest disclosures of Omnipotence. (*New Birth*, p. 26.) The means by which the curative results recorded in the Gospels were effected by the Christ are still available. They belong to the very essence of Christianity and to the established law of the relation of the soul to its bodily manifestation, and are not mere transient devices.

The same system of treatment and method of cure can today save
to the *uttermost* our disordered human nature — soul, spirit, and
body — for time and eternity.

It is an idea deeply imbedded in the religious consciousness of
the world, as I have before said, that disease is the effect of sin.
This instinctive or intuitive truth seems to have been incorporated
into the system of Jesus the Christ.   In saving men from their
sins, he delivered them from disease.   But it is a question of great
importance — what was the idea of sin as it existed in the mind of
Jesus?   We must lay aside all theological definitions and go to
the language in which the New Testament was written, or in which
it comes to us.   The word used by Jesus to express the idea of
sin is ἁμαρτία (hamartia).   The first, and consequently radical,
meaning of this word is given by Robinson in his Greek Lexicon
of the New Testament as *an aberration from the truth, an error.*
It is a word borrowed from archery where the arrow does not hit
the mark.   In John viii: 46, it is used in opposition to ἡ αλήθεια,
the truth.   Donnegan defines it *a mistake, a mistaking.*   This
shows that the natural remedy for it is truth, a spiritual intelligence.   Prof. Austin Phelps, in his work on the New Birth, which
is intensely orthodox, affirms that truth is the instrument of regeneration, and that truth is a spiritual power, in accordance with the
passages of Scripture which he quotes, — " Of his own will begat
He us with the word of truth," and " The law of the Lord is perfect, converting the soul."   He might have quoted with greater
effect the words of the Christ, where he intensifies truth as a sanative and saving power, when he prays for his disciples: " Sanctify
them through thy truth."

Sin as the cause of disease is an error, a wrong way of thinking, feeling, and acting.   It is a great *aberration from the truth*
to suppose that the body has life in itself, that disease, properly
so called, is in the physical organism, or that the condition of the
body is ever anything but an effect of which the mind is the cause.
Christ came to convince the world of this sin, — this grave mistake.   (John xvi: 8, 9.)   He came to make known the truth on

this subject, and to demonstrate its efficiency as a curative and saving agency. It was his grand remedy, a panacea for human ills. He demonstrated, as no one had ever done, the medical value of an idea, the healing power of spiritual truth, the sanative virtue of instruction, and its ability to overcome the error, the mistake, the *sin*, that was the root of disease. He left behind him a system of cure which the world has been slow to understand, and too dull to comprehend, and it has gradually dropped out of the life of the Church, being overlaid and smothered by an external ecclesiasticism. But a future spiritual science of health and disease will restore it to the world. Truth, like Milton's angels, is immortal in every part, and cannot die. In Christ's miracles, or marvels of healing, there is no infraction of the laws of nature; we only witness the predominance of a higher over a lower law, — of spirit over matter, of the mind over the body, — but all in the domain of what we call nature. This we often witness. When I raise my arm, a spiritual law or force neutralizes or overcomes the law of gravitation. The lower yields to the higher. This is a miracle. So those chemical laws or forces that induce decomposition in animal substances are continually overpowered and held in check by that spiritual something which is called in physiology the *vis vitæ*, the vital force, which is only another name for the unconscious action of mind. It is one of the highest laws of nature that the physical, the material, should be under subjection to the spiritual and controlled by it. This is illustrated in the life of Jesus the Christ.

The Saxon word *sin* or *syn*, in its primary or radical sense, means the same as the Latin-English word *error*, a wandering. In the Confession of the Church-of-England Liturgy, "We have erred and strayed from thy commandments," we have the exact signification of the word. The Latin *peccatum*, a mistake, a blunder, has the same signification as the English word *sin*, and the Greek term (ἁμαρτία) used by the Christ. The fundamental idea of sin in most, if not all, languages is that of an error, or mistake, an aberration from the truth. It is the result of ignorance. Any other meaning attached to the word is a sort of theological veneering that is put over the word, and that does not belong to it by Divine right. Many of the terms used in religious parlance have had other meanings pasted over them besides the true one. These must be removed in order to get at the Divine idea. In the Scriptural sense of the term, sin is a want of knowledge. It is the result of ignorance. The remedy for it is truth, or knowledge in its reality. Prof. Ferrier, in his Institutes of Metaphysics, has established a consoling doctrine in regard to it. In the second part of his work, entitled Agnoiology, or the Theory of Ignorance, which is a novelty in philosophy, he has demonstrated that we can be ignorant only of that which *can* be known. For instance, we cannot be ignorant that two and two are five, or that a circle is a square. He affirms that we can be ignorant only of what can be possibly known, or, in other words, there can be an ignorance only of that of which there can be a knowledge. Consequently all ignorance (and, by inference, all *sin*) is remedable. (*Institutes of Metaphysics*, pp. 410–412.)

CHAPTER XV.

THE NATURE OF REGENERATION AND ITS INFLUENCE UPON THE BODILY STATE.

I use the word regeneration not because it is a scriptural one,—for the term never occurs but once in the Gospels (Mat. xix: 28), and then it is not used in the sense given to it in theology,—but because it is a term in common use in religious literature to express the idea of a certain spiritual metamorphosis, or mental transformation, from a lower to a higher condition of life. There is a vast amount of mystery thrown around the subject of regeneration which does not rightly belong to it. If it be a radical change in the mental or spiritual *status* of an individual, it may be clearly defined to the consciousness, and intelligibly described, so that he who seeks it may know for what he is searching and striving to attain. To seek for a regenerative state of our powers is not or ought not to be like a process of algebra where we aim to find the value of an *unknown* quantity.

As our natural or first birth is an introduction into the natural life, and into a mere sensuous range of thinking and feeling, so to be "born from above" marks the incipiency of the *spiritual* life. All progress beyond this is a spiritual growth, and not a new birth. Regeneration is the commencement of that higher mode of thinking and feeling which we call spiritual. To think *spiritually* is to think independently of the testimony and fallacious appearances of the senses. It is to rise out of the trammels of a mere sense-bound existence, and to discern truth in its reality. To *feel* spiritually is to be elevated above the region of a mere sensuous selfishness, into which we are all born, and to act from the love of others,—the love of the neighbor.

It is a question of much importance whether the state of our powers, which we call regeneration, or to use the expression that has the sanction of the Christ, being "born from above," is not an orderly development, a natural evolution, from the condition in which we first enter upon life. Under the proper conditions, all souls come to be regenerated. A seed may remain long without germinating, but when subjected to the proper influences of heat and moisture it springs into life at once. Is regeneration effected by a miraculous interposition, or does it not enter into the Divine plan of creation? Is it not as natural as the unfoldment of the bud into the flower, or the development of childhood into mature manhood? When I affirm that it is a natural and orderly evolution I do not exclude a Divine power and causation from it, for God is immanent in nature and the laws of the human mind. I mean only that he has established and maintained the order expressed by Paul, that that which is spiritual is not first in the development of man, but that which is natural, or on a material plane of thought; afterwards comes that which is spiritual. (1 Cor. xv: 46.) It seems to me that to regenerate or *spiritualize* the nature of man, or to raise the soul from a sensuous way of thinking and a selfish mode of feeling and acting, enters not only into the plan of creation but is the constant aim of God's providential dealings with us.

Every human being has within him the germ of a truly spiritual life, although it may now be overlaid with a deep covering of externality. These spiritual powers may exist only potentially, like the oak in the acorn, or they may be dormant or latent, yet they are capable of being so unfolded as to be the predominant power in our life here and hereafter. Progression upward from a state of sensual selfishness, and the bondage of the intellect to the lower and sensuous range of its action, is in its nature an evolution. It is not progression onward in an uninterrupted straight line, but an ascent to a higher stage of life,—another plane of conscious existence. Hence, it is called a new birth, a being "born [or borne] from above." It is being born of the spirit, that is, our spiritual powers are emancipated from their latent state, analogous to what takes place in our natural powers at our first birth.

But that with which we are more particularly concerned is the question, How does this affect the bodily condition, the physical *status* of the individual? The soul being the organizing principle of the body, and that which imparts to the external organism its only vital force,—for the body without the spirit is dead (James ii: 26),—it always impresses its own inner changes by its inherent, plastic power upon the body, which is its outward expression. If the body has no life of itself, but is only an effect, the cause of which is found in the mind, then the new order or state of mental life which is called regeneration ought to record itself in some corresponding change of the outward organism. It must be translated into a bodily expression, as all spiritual states seek an external manifestation. According to the laws of Divine order, a genuine spiritual life is outwardly expressed by what is called in the New Testament, and in the language of the Christ, wholeness or health.

After twenty-five years' practice as a physician, I am satisfied that much of what goes under the name of chronic disease, especially of a nervous type, has its root in selfishness,—at least, a purely unselfish man or woman, with the consequent tranquil happiness, I never saw who was a nervous invalid. Such a state is usually the result of an over-estimate of their own importance and value in the universe, and a desire to make every one *contribute* to them, instead of *sacrificing* themselves to others, according to the Christ-principle. The best prescription for such persons is in the words of Jesus: "Give, and it shall be given." To love something outside, or beside, ourselves, and to be actuated by an irrepressible desire to be of use,—to do good to others,—gives a strength and tenacity of life that in some cases seems to border on the miraculous. I have known some persons whose ruling passion was to do good who have carried with them through many years an amount of suffering that would have crushed out prematurely many a less unselfish life. In their case their diseased condition did not subtract a single unit from "the days of the years of their life." He who consecrates himself to the good of universal being, and thus becomes an organ of communication between the Divine Love and human needs, is immortal until his work is done. If God's life is love, and all life is from Him, then he who *loves* the most really exhibits the highest degree of life, and God's eternity contributes to his longevity.

It is to be remarked that regeneration, or the being born, or *borne*, from above, is not a *constitutional* change, that is, it creates no new powers or faculties in the human soul. All that it can do is to take the man as he is, and regulate and direct the powers that he receives and possesses as an hereditary inheritance. No new *creation* is possible or is needed, as there is no faculty of the soul that is wrong *per se*, or in itself, but only in its activity in a wrong direction. The legitimate use of all our powers, and of every native instinct, sentiment, and faculty, is in accordance with the will of God, and is to us the law of health and of God. Every man has in himself the germ of a true spiritual life. Without this he would not be a man, but only an animal. Leibnitz introduced into German philosophy, where it has ever remained, the doctrine of unconscious intelligence, or *latent thought*. This hint was taken up by Sir William Hamilton, as before remarked, and has been unfolded by other writers into the now accepted doctrine of preconscious mental action. This has been pushed by the philosophical systems of Schopenhaur and Von Hartmann to an extent that borders on atheism. We may carry the idea of Leibnitz a step further than he did, and assert that there are in human nature latent and dormant spiritual *feelings* that, by the vivifying touch of a spiritual influence and instruction, may be awakened into conscious activity. This is what regeneration does for us. It erects a new superstructure on the old foundation, or rather it emancipates the spiritual manhood from its chrysalis state. Many of the higher and diviner powers of our nature exist potentially rather than *in actu*, and must be evolved from their occult and inactive state.

In the philosophy of Swedenborg he introduces an important distinction between reformation and regeneration, based on his doctrine that the intellect is the *form* of the love. Reformation is of the understanding; regeneration is a state of the will, under which term he includes the whole affectional and emotional nature. As long as anyone sees and acknowledges in his *mind* that evil is evil and good is good, and thinks that good is to be chosen, so long that state is called reformation, or rather re-formation. It is only an intellectual theory, an outside form, an external shell of an inward life, and one not adopted by the affections, that is, incorporated into the life. But when he wills to shun evil and do good, which implies a desire and volitional striving, the state of regeneration begins. It is to be feared that much that passes current in the religious world for the new birth goes no further than an intellectual reformation. It is a *theory* of duty, a mere intellectual system of ethics, rather than a being born from above, or a being *borne* upward to a higher plane of spiritual life. (*True Christian Religion*, 587.)

On the relation of the soul and body Swedenborg is clear and explicit, and greatly in advance of the age in which he lived. According to him, the body is not the real man, but is perpetually derived from the soul; all the things in it are appendages of the soul, and receive from it life and motion, for the body does not act of itself, but from the spirit; it is the *form* or external boundary of the spirit, and that by means of which the soul enters into time and space. (*True Christian Religion*, 103, 224, 156.) The word form is derived from the Greek δραμα, and means that which is seen. When we say that the body is the *form* of the soul, we express the idea that the physical organism is the soul made visible. The matter of which the body is composed is in itself dead and *inert*, yet the connection between the soul and its outward form or manifestation is such that a mental state translates itself into a bodily expression, and sometimes with instantaneous celerity, as, for instance, in a sudden fright, or the blush that attends a feeling of shame. Hence, regeneration, or a change from a mere natural to a spiritual mode of thinking and feeling, must effect a modification of the bodily condition. The new spirit, as Swedenborg teaches, makes for itself a new body, or external form. It not only translates itself into new modes of external activity, but renews the body itself as the passive instrument of the changed interior state. The reformed inebriate, the sensualist, or the glutton soon *looks* like another person. As my friend Rev. E. H. Sears, in his valuable work on Regeneration, has said, "It is spirit that appropriates matter, and makes it flexile to its uses." The immortal soul-principle gives to the body all its life and power. It is the vital, formative, organizing, and governing principle in the organic material. Hence, the fact so often brought to our notice in the Gospel narratives, that *the conversion of the soul and the cure of disease* went together in the practice of the Christ, so that the new spiritual state might have a solid basis of physical health on which to permanently rest. The changed soul makes for itself a new bodily condition, or outward expression, in harmony with its altered spiritual *status*. This is no more a miracle than it is when the emotion of fear or the feeling of melancholy, or the sense of guilt and shame, record themselves in the face. In fact, the science of physiognomy of Lavater, and of Dr. Gall's phrenology, are based on this relation of the soul to its body. The renewal of the body by regeneration is effected in accordance with the same law, and by some force far different from that which is the producing cause in all mere chemical changes and phenomena. It is the result of a spiritual chemistry, a mental dynamic force, certain in its action, but poorly understood.

To effect a renewal of the body by regeneration, or an elevation of the soul from a material to a spiritual range of thought and feeling, requires no more time, and not so much, than intervenes between our conception in the womb and our birth. In fact, during a period of nine months, the corporeal organism could be made over anew more than once. But the disciple of Gall will confront me with the question, Will the organs in the brain of the mental faculties be altered in size? Meeting him on his own ground, I answer: As none of them are wrong in themselves, they do not so much need to be annihilated, or changed in size, as to be changed in their mode of action. I should not expect that a pugilist or champion prize-fighter, if regenerated, would exhibit a diminution in the size of his hands and arms, or in the strength of his muscular system, but only that he would put them to a better use. If the soul is *borne*, or impelled, from above, it will elevate the body to a higher plane of life, and a diviner form of activity.

> "We must be here to work;
> And men who work can only work for men,
> And, not to work in vain, must comprehend
> Humanity, and so work humanly,
> And raise men's bodies still by raising souls,
> As God did first."   MRS. BROWNING.

CHAPTER XVI.

It is a doctrine clearly taught in the Scriptures, especially in the first chapter of the Johannean Gospel, that the world was created by the Logos, or the Divine Thought. (John i: 3.) It is also certain that it is revealed only to thought. What we call sensation arises from within, though at first glance it might seem otherwise. Before we have a perception of an external object, we have an antecedent thought or image of it, without which the sensation could not exist. The eyes may be open, and directed towards an object, and yet we do not *see* it, unless the attention, that is, the thought, is fixed upon it. Without this the world would be to us a blank, an empty void. Ideas may exist antecedently to thought, as these are the thoughts of the Divine Mind. Hegel, the philosopher *par excellence* of Germany, says: " We have mental pictures of objects before we think them: and it is only through these mental pictures, and by having constant recourse to them, that the mind goes on to know and comprehend in the strict meaning of thought." (*Hegel's Logic*, Introduction, p. 1.) The prevalent materialistic systems of philosophy affirm that thought arises from sensation, and is suggested by it. But this is only an *apparent* truth. The Idealists teach that no sensation, whether of sight, hearing, feeling, taste, or smell is possible except it is preceded or accompanied by thought. On this subject Fichte observes: "The whole outward sense, and all its objects, are founded upon universal thought, and a sensible perception is possible only in thought, and as something thought, as a determination of the general consciousness, but by no means in itself and separate from consciousness." (*Popular Works*, p. 423.) Even Sir William Hamilton affirms the same when he lays it down as a fundamental truth that without attention there is no consciousness; and that attention is to consciousness what the contraction of the pupil is to the eye. (*Lectures on Metaphysics*, p. 172.) It was the fundamental idea of Schelling's philosophy that the subject and object are identical, or, in other words, that the thought of a thing and the thing itself are not distinguishable, but are in their inmost reality one and the same, and can never be separated.

Hegel has unfolded the doctrine of John into a systematic statement. His Logic (a word derived from Logos) may properly be characterized as the philosophy of thought. To him, as Sterling in his Secret of Hegel has said, "Whatever *is* is thought." In his system thought is the inwardness, or as it were the kernel, of the world. This is only another way of expressing the doctrine of Berkeley. Hegel calls nature the system of unconscious thought, or, to use the expression of Schelling, a *fossilized intelligence*. Thought forms the indwelling nature or substance of external things. It is also the universal substance, the groundwork, of all that is spiritual. In all human perception thought is present; so thought is the universal in all acts of conception and recollection,— in short, in every mental activity, in willing, wishing, and the like. All these faculties are only additional specifications of thought. When it is presented in this light, thought has a different part to play from what it has when we speak of a faculty of thought, one among a crowd of other faculties, such as conception, perception, and will, with which it stands on the same level. When it is seen to be the true *universal* of all that nature and mind contain, it extends so as to embrace all these faculties and becomes the basis of everything. (*Hegel's Logic*, by William Wallace, pp. 38, 39.)

This is the " Secret of Hegel," to possess which, according to his disciples, was to hold the key to the profoundest knowledge, and have the means of the highest happiness. It takes us to the *Ultima Thule*, the utmost boundary of all that the mind can know. In his system thought is not a mere mental faculty; it is the very substance, the basis, of the mind, and that which is universally present in every mental act and state. To *think* is a necessary condition of our existence, and of the existence, or, at least, the manifestation to our consciousness of everything in the universe. To cease thinking is all the same as a termination of our individual existence. It is a suspension of our being. It is equivalent to an annihilation both of ourselves and of everything else, or, as the German philosophy would express it, the ego and the non-ego. Thoughts are *things*. This is evident from language. Thing is but another form of think. The words are the same at the root. A thing is that which has existence to our minds by being the object of thought. In their inmost reality, things are objective thoughts. Creation, or what we call nature, is a permanent manifestation of the thoughts of God, and we perceive an outward world only so far as we think in concert with Him. All that we know of a tree or a flower, or can *think* of them, measures the extent of our vision of them As one has said : " In the world of man and nature we have simply to do with the thought of God. We cannot suppose that God made the world as a carpenter does a house. It is sufficient that God think the world." (*Sterling's Secret of Hegel*, p. 83.) Hence, the universe is an expression, a manifestation, an ultimation of the ideas of the Divine Mind. As we live in God, so we think in and from Him. " We are not sufficient of ourselves to think anything as of ourselves; but our sufficiency is of God." (2 Cor. iii : 5.) Hegel's doctrine is not pantheism but more properly panlogism, or that which is taught by John, the intimate disciple of the Christ, that all things are created by the Logos, which means the Divine Thought. Thought is the groundwork of all reality. It is that universal principle that underlies all existence. Take away the thought of a thing, and it is to us annihilated. It becomes as nothing. It is a fundamental and intuitive truth that what is out of thought is to us out of existence. When we do not think of a thing, it is all the same as if it were not. This is as self-evidently certain as any of the axioms of geometry. Existence is manifested being, and an entity of which we have no conception, no idea, no thought, neither has nor can have any existence to us for the time being. When we think of it, we again, as it were, create it or give it reality. If there were no mind to perceive, as Berkeley maintained, there would be no universe, for all things are created by and revealed only to thought. Forgetfulness of a thing, a putting it out of mind, a banishing it from thought, is to us its annihilation. If it has *being*, it has no *ex*-istence, or *standing out*, as the word signifies. The celebrated philosopher Immanuel Kant was able by the strength of *thought* to forget the pains of gout. It required, he says, a great mental effort, but never failed to afford relief. When John affirms of the Logos that all things were made by it, and without it was not anything made that was made (John i: 3), he means that thought is the active principle of creation, for a word, Divine or human, is in its essence only a thought.

Is the philosophy of Hegel of any practical value? Can it be made available in constructing an efficient system of phrenopathy, or mental-cure? Spirit is the *substance* or underlying reality of matter, and thought is the creative power of the mind. We have shown in a preceding chapter that all we know, or can know, of a material world and of the human body is in ourselves. Their externeity is only apparent, not real. The same is equally true of disease. Taking thought, as was done by Descartes, to be all that of which we are conscious, we may safely affirm that disease is only in the mind, that is, in our thought. One thing is certain, being confirmed by our experience, that a pain, if it is not thought of, is not *felt*. It is thus made a nihility, a nothingness. For we repeat, that which is not in thought has to us no existence. When we think of it, it passes from nothing to something, for it is only by this that it comes to have any reality to us. Disease without this would be as nothing, for it is only a wrong way of thinking, or, if you prefer it, a false belief. Banish it from thought and it no longer exists. Just to the extent in which this is done it is annihilated. As long as this is done the mind triumphs over it, and it is cured. Here is the grand remedy, the long-sought panacea. It is a fundamental principle in the phrenopathic method of cure. Grasp the idea in all its fullness, and you have a remedy as certain as anything can be,—an infallible and universal specific.

On the effect of thought upon sensation Dr. Carpenter remarks: "The acuteness with which particular sensations are felt is influenced in a remarkable degree by the *attention* they receive from the mind. If the mind be entirely inactive, as in profound sleep, no sensation whatever is produced by ordinary impressions; and the same is the case when the attention is so completely concentrated upon some object of thought or contemplation that sensations altogether unconnected with it fail to make any impression upon the perceptive consciousness. On the other hand, when the attention from any cause is strongly directed upon them, impressions, very feeble in themselves, produce sensations of even painful acuteness; thus every one knows how much a slight itching of some part of the surface may be magnified by the direction of the *thoughts* to it, whilst, as soon as they are forced by some stronger impression into another channel, the irritation is no longer felt." (*Principles of Human Physiology*, p. 855.

The most important inquiry in relation to this phrenopathic mode of cure remains to be considered. How can we get disease out of our thought? If this cannot be done, the system, although theoretically true, is of no practical value. It is said, in objection to the view given above, that as long as one feels a pain he cannot avoid thinking of it. There is a show of truth in this assertion. But it is equally certain that as long as we *think* of it we shall *feel* it; and if by any means we can get our thoughts away from it, so that it is utterly out of thought, we no longer *feel* it. Here is a contest between feeling and thought. Which has the right of dominion? Which one shall govern and control the other? It is a well-established principle in mental science that our thoughts are under the control of our volitions, but the feelings and emotions are not so. There is a self-determining power of thought, which we call free will. We can change the *direction* of our thoughts as readily as a sailor can alter the course of his vessel by varying the position of the helm. But in the mind the department of the feelings lies beyond the direct action of the will. These cannot be changed or suppressed by any direct volitional effort, but only mediately through the thoughts. If I am in pain, or unhappy, or diseased, it is *possible* for me, at least, to think of something else, and in proportion as this is done relief is gained. Invalids are often recommended to travel. and they gain great advantage to themselves by so doing, because, by seeing and thinking of so many other things, the attention is diverted from themselves. But why should this have any therapeutic value if their thoughts have nothing to do with the inception and progress of their malady? In proportion as their disease and their trouble are out of thought they become non-existent. A chronic disease being a fixedness of thought, a morbid steadfastness of a false idea, in this condition a new idea, a radical change in the mode of thinking has great remedial efficacy. It may fall as silently upon the soul of the sufferer as the dew upon a fading flower, but has the vivifying power of the archangel's trump to raise the dead, for ideas are the only things that really live.

It may be considered as an established principle, a demonstrated truth, that we can change the *direction* of our thoughts. We can think of something besides the pain or the disease. This, if not a cure, is a relief. But we can go a step further than this, and institute a line of thought that runs counter to the disease, and will neutralize it with as much scientific certainty as an acid coming in contact with an alkali will change it to something else. Some of the most deadly poisons can be rendered harmless by the chemical action of an antidote. They are commuted at once into an innoxious substance, a harmless compound. So it comes within the compass of the powers of our minds when in pain and disease to *think* that we shall recover.   Such a thing is manifestly conceivable.   We can think this as easily as we can say it; for we could not say it even as a repetition of the words of another unless it was first a thought in the mind.   We can also think that we *now* are getting well, that a cure is inaugurated, and that the pain, or the disease, or the unhappiness, *is passing away.*   It is quite possible and practicable to *think* this, and if we continue this quasi-belief, we shall soon in a degree begin to *feel* it, and it becomes so far a reality, for it is only thought that gives a real existence to anything in the universe.   The feeling added to the thought makes it an act of faith.   For faith is not a mere intellectual belief, but a *feeling* that a thing is true, and thus, according to Paul, it becomes the substance of things hoped for, the evidence, the convincing proof, of things not seen.   (Heb. xi: 1.) All the operations or modifications of mind are reducible to thought and feeling.   Thought and feeling are the essence of the soul, and the sum and substance of all mental activity and soul-life.   They include and bound our very existence.   Without them we should be as nothing.   If I subtract them from what I call myself, my individual being, there is no remainder.   When these are arrayed against disease, my very being is in antagonism to it, and the malady is withered at the root.   Here is the antidote to that abnormality of mind, that morbid *thinking*, that is the cause of disease.

If our mental force has become weakened, and the mind has become fixed in its action in a wrong direction, and in our unaided strength we are not adequate to the instituting of the proper line of thought and feeling, we may receive help from others.   Here is the highest office, the divinest function of the physician.   Unless ne can by some means inaugurate a new mode of thinking and feeling, with which the disease cannot coëxist, he is of no use. Faith makes us whole now as it did in the days of Jesus the Christ, for the reason that it is inconsistent with the mental state that underlies the disease and supplants it.   It is a spiritual medicine, having the nature of an infallible antidote. It is a new mode of thinking and feeling that comes in to overpower the morbid mental state, which is the original cause of the malady. The influence of thought in the inception of disease, and in its cure, is unconsciously and instinctively recognized in common parlance. It is often said of an invalid that he is well if he only *thought* so, and after recovery the remark is frequently made that he could have recovered sooner if he had sooner come to think so. This is true, though its expression is often tainted with a lack of charity. To change the morbid thinking is precisely where the difficulty in the cure lies.

. He who would assist the invalid to rise out of that material range of thought and sense-bound state of mind that are the ground of the disease must not address himself or his remedies merely to the body of the patient, for that is adding weight to the mill-stone that is already drawing him down. He must be taught to forget the body and become spirit. The body is. in itself. lifeless, motionless, and sensationless. It has neither thought, intelligence, nor feeling. All these are in the soul. To perceive this is a long step towards recovery. What we call the physical organism is the most unreal part of human nature. This must become to us an ineffaceable conviction, and be so inwrought into our very being as to change our mode of thinking, feeling, speaking, and acting. In addressing the invalid, the body should be ignored, and we should speak as a soul, and from the soul, to the soul of the patient or sufferer. We then speak from the Divine realm of causation, and have a power over disease that cannot be gained by occupying any other standing ground. The man who is bound with the iron fetters of sense, and is in the underground dungeon of materialism, can afford but small aid to another in the same condition with himself. To possess the divinely-ordained power of mind over matter, and of soul over body, he must be himself unshackled and born into the true liberty of the spirit. He must be elevated above that range of thought and plane of cognition that are limited to a mere sensuous seeming and the *appearance* of truth to the discernment of the spiritual reality of things. Much that passes current for science is only the semblance of truth, and not a *spiritual intelligence*. This is a Divine healing force,— the power of God and the wisdom of God unto salvation. It constitutes in us a point of attachment between the soul and the creative Thought, and repairs the broken link which has disjoined us from God. The utterances of such a person will be the echo of God's ideas, and have the authority of Divine oracles. His mind vibrates in harmony with the Infinite Mind, and his thoughts become one with the Power that created and upholds the world, and is perpetually exhibited in nature's laws.

The spiritual physician, or he who heals the body by touching the springs of life in the soul of the patient, should speak and act from the Divine realm of his being, as did Jesus the Christ. "The words that I speak unto you I speak not of myself; but the Father that dwelleth in me, He doeth the works." (John xiv: 10.) Man is the highest manifestation of God in the universe. In a broader and more comprehensive sense than the Church has ever recognized, God is manifested in the flesh. (Eph. iii: 16.) We have *being* in Him; He has *existence* in us. Paul affirms that what may be known of God is manifested *in* man (Rom. i: 19), which implies that outside of ourselves we have, and can have, no knowledge of God. To find God there, and identify our life with His Life, is to be invested with a power over disease like that which was exhibited by the Christ. The same language might be used in relation to the Christ. What is meant by that term in the Christian system is not the Jesus of history, the mere son of Joseph and Mary, who has ever been the object of worship in the Christian Church. This has been the great mistake of the religious world. The real Christ is to be sought *within*, where alone he can be found. He represents and personifies the principle of *spiritual life and intelligence*, and is identical with it. In harmony with this view, Paul speaks of the sublime mystery, or arcane doctrine, of Christianity as being that of "Christ *in* you, the hope of glory." (Col. i: 27.) And, in the deepest prayer ever uttered by the lips of man, Jesus as the Christ says of his disciples or scholars of every age, "I in them, and Thou in me, that they may be made perfect [or complete] in one." (John xvii: 20.) For, as a principle of spiritual intelligence, his life may be mingled and blended with ours into a unity. Of this Paul speaks when he says: "It is no more I that live, but Christ liveth in me." (Gal. ii: 20.) In this state of the soul, the powers of the individual man, the personal *Ego*, become augmented and re-enforced, like the addition of an ocean to a drop of water. In union with the Christ, when thus viewed, we come into a fellowship or community of life with the collective man,—the *maximus homo*,—and with all the fullness of the God-head, and "are *complete* in Him who is the head of all principality and power." (Col. ii: 9, 10.)

CHAPTER XVII.

The doctrine of a *vis medicatrix cogitationis*, a healing power of thought, discussed in the preceding chapter, is based on the Hegelian principle that thought is a creative force. The fundamental idea of Hegel's philosophy is that everything in its last analysis, or when we come to its inmost reality, is only a *thought*. What we call the external world and the human body, which is a part of it, are the thought of God, and we come to know them only so far as we think of them. They are revealed to us by the same power that creates them. Disease, like every other *thing*, is created, or, at least, has an *ex*-istence only by thought. In the phrenopathic method of cure, it is a fundamental principle that thought is the ground of all reality. The words real and reality come from the Latin *res*, which is an exact equivalent of our word thing, and means that which is an object of thought. This is recognized in the Hebrew, where the term for word means also thing, as a word is only an expressed thought. That which is out of thought has to us no *conscious* existence, for consciousness is only a mode of thought. A thing, a world, a disease, comes into our consciousness only when we think of it. To be unconscious of a thing is all the same as if it were not. To bring disease into the realm of unconsciousness is to make it unreal, or, in other words, to cure it, for to be diseased and not know it, or think of it, or be conscious of it, is equivalent to being without disease.

In disease we feel weak. This is implied by the terms that are used to express it in all languages. All maladies are called infirmities, or weaknesses. The same want of force or vigor is implied when we call the sick person an invalid (from *in*, not, and *validus*, strong). Feebleness is a fundamental idea of a diseased condition, and the woman healed by Jesus is a representative of this aspect of disease. She was "bowed down with a spirit of infirmity for eighteen years," where we do well to mark the Hebraism in the use of a genitive for an adjective. An *infirm spirit* was the root of the malady. In this enfeebled state of the will and of the power of thought to enter into a combat with disease in our unassisted strength seems like an effort to lift a mountain from its base. Is there any help that is always available and effectual? Can we come into union with the everywhere-present Power that creates and governs the universe, and join our weakness to the Divine Omnipotence in our curative effort? There is in our nature a psychometrical or sympathetic sense, the higher use of which is communion with God and all higher intelligences. By means of this, in a perfectly natural way, we may "be strong in the Lord and the power of His might." (Eph. vi : 10.) We have seen in what precedes the wonderful power of thought over the bodily organism, but our thought may be re-enforced by an alliance with the Infinite Mind. God created and still creates the world and all that is in it by thought. We can so come into direct and immediate communication with Him that his creative energy shall be added to our cogitative and volitional power, so that there shall be a confluence of the two into a unity and harmony. Where is God, and how may I find Him? We look for Him in the distance, and thus miss him. Says the astronomer Lalande : "I have swept space with my telescope, and found no God." And simply because he did not look for Him where alone the soul can find Him. We do not discover God as we do a new planet in the heavens. He is revealed to us in the New Testament, and demonstrated by the intuitive reason, as a Spirit, and a spirit is to be found and known by thought only, and not to be seen by the sen-

suous eye of the body. Jesus the Christ introduced into the
thought of the world two important ideas — 1. That God is our
Father, and that consequently we are his sons. This implies that
we derive our life perpetually from Him, and live in Him. There
is in us an unbroken and ceaseless vital connection with Him.
2. *God is inward to man.*   Before this grand disclosure, He was
worshiped, and adored, and sought unto as an indefinable Being,
and at an obscure, if not unlimited, distance from men. Jesus
taught us where to find Him. We are to seek Him within the
enclosure of our own being.   "The Father is in me, and I am in
the Father."   (John xiv: 10, 11.)   We no longer seek the
thoughts of God from external signs, or from outward oracles, as
that of Delphi, or the Urim and Thummim of the Jews.   Paul in
an inspired moment gave utterance to one of the profoundest
truths in the universe of mind, — the grandest verity within the
compass of human thought, — "*In Him* we live and are moved and
have our being."   As certainly as the unborn infant's life is that
of the mother, so it is divinely true that somehow God's Life
includes ours, and we live because he lives, and shall live as long
as He exists.   Our being is comprised in His, so that if we could
suppose the Divine Life to come to an end, ours would terminate
with it as surely — to compare great things with small — as a
stream would cease to flow when its fountain is dried up. My
existence may be *distinct*, but never separate from His.   In the
hidden depth of the soul there is somewhere a point where our
individual being comes in contact with God, and is identified with
the Infinite Life, as a bay meets the ocean.   This great truth may
not now cross the threshold or door-sill of our consciousness, but
we may nevertheless be as certain of it as we are of the Divine
Existence, or of our own.   Swedenborg calls this deific point, where
God and man meet within the soul, the *Divine internal*, and the
entrance of God into man, and affirms that it is by virtue of it
that we live at all and live forever.   (*Arcana Celestia*, 1999.)

When we cease to think of ourselves as *separated* from God,
and come to view our being as comprised in His, as a bay, how-

ever far inland it may extend, is not disconnected from the ocean, then we kindle anew the smoking wick of our candle of life from a Divine and quenchless flame.   When we *see* this truth in disease, in pain, in unhappiness, the incoming tide of the ocean of the Divine Existence flows back into the river of our life, fills its banks to the full, turns its current in another direction towards the uplands of health and blessedness, and causes it to overflow to others.

A large proportion of diseases are of a so-called nervous type, or, in other words, are purely mental.   It is an uneasy or dissatisfied state, as the word signifies, or perhaps there is a combination of more or less painful sensations, or a functional disturbance of one or more organs.   All these conditions are under the control of the power of thought.   But how is it in cases of organic disease, or when there is an actual lesion, or loss of continuity in an organ?   In this case the mental state that acts as a cause is more fixed, and harder of removal; but to put the trouble, whatever it is, out of *thought*, to forget it, to ignore it, to think of something else, to institute a line of thought that is inconsistent with it, and to think in harmony with the unconscious effort of what we call nature to repair the lesion, is the best prescription for it.   There is such a thing as a soul in nature,—an intelligent Life operating everywhere, in the mineral, vegetable, and animal kingdoms.   The old doctrine of an *animus mundi* is not without some foundation in reality.   There is an intelligent principle recognizable by its constant action in every part and particle of the universe,—in the grain of sand, in the flower, and in the stellar orbs.   Nature is not unintelligent, as Spinoza taught.   There is an infinite current of living thought that runs through the whole of it.   The numerous marks of design, the skillful adaptation of means to an end, which we see everywhere and in everything, indicate with logical certainty the continual presence and action of intelligent thought. This is not the mind of man, but must be the Over-Soul, the Universal Mind, the Absolute Thought.   There is a divinely-intelligent force at work in the human body.   It seems to be the same intelligent Soul-Principle, the identical God-Power, that cease-lessly operates in the world at large. When we receive an injury or a wound, this benevolent and intelligently-active principle goes to work in the most skillful and artistic manner to repair the dam-age. This *vis reparatrix*, or reconstructive force of nature, which is only a gleam of the operation of God's omnipotent Life in man, is the only remedy that can heal or relieve the injury,— heal, if it comes within the range of possibility, and, if not, alleviate the suf-fering. The soul-principle in us, especially in the preconscious range of its action, has a close relationship to the soul in nature, *and we can assist and greatly accelerate its curative action by thinking in concert with it.* This intelligent principle in nature always acts unerringly in the right direction. Our thoughts, our faith, our fancy, our remedies, can only be tributary and auxiliary to it. If our thoughts form an alliance with it, and their force is augmented by it, the most inveterate diseases yield to the com-bined therapeutic power of the finite and Infinite Mind. The *vis medicatrix naturæ* is something of God in man. It is the same power that creates and governs the world. It is the Logos, the Divine Intelligence and Thought, of which nature is a permanent expression. God's thoughts are always in the direction of our highest good,— the healing of our diseases and the removal of the causes of our unhappiness. "For I know the thoughts that I think toward you, saith the Lord, thoughts of peace and not of evil, to give you an expected end." (Jer. xxix: 11.) In other words, God's creative thought always coöperates with ours in every curative endeavor of our minds, to cause us to realize the end at which we aim. An act of faith in this divinely-intelligent, creative, and repairing power places the plastic action of our minds in alliance with it. We enter into a copartnership, a fellowship, a sympathy, a community with it, and the cure is at the same time *phrenopathic* and *theopathic*. It is a confluence of our thought and our imagination in their volitional healing effort with the Force that created, and ever creates, our bodies and the world in which they dwell. It places the soul-principle in us in apposition and conjunction with the creative Word and the plastic Spirit. This has not retired from nature, but is still there as an intelligent *conatus* to heal all our diseases, though its silent action in the human body does not come within the grasp of consciousness. That which created the world and our bodies is never absent from them, for, as Bishop Sherlock demonstrated, preservation is a continued creation. To find the Divine Life and Power in their manifestation as a creative force, we need not go to the temple of worship, much less back through all the ages of human history to a time when the solitary Deity was seized with an impulse to make a world out of nothing, for it is nearer to us than the world on which we tread, because it is the hidden spring of every physiological movement. It is the secret and mysterious virtue of every medicine or curative device. When, by an act of faith and imagination, I think in the same direction, and in concert with this intelligent and Divine *conatus*, to repair my injury, to heal my wounds, or to cure my disease, and no longer by my *thought* obstruct its therapeutic and saving effort in my behalf, its action is intensified and accelerated. As one has said: " There is surely a piece of the Divinity in us; something that was before the elements, and owes no homage to the sun. Nature tells me I am the image of God, as well as Scripture. He that understands not this much hath not his introduction or first lesson, and is yet to begin the alphabet of man." (*Sir Thomas Browne's Religio Medici*, part 2, Sec. 11.)

There is more than a *spark* of the Divinity in us; and this life of God in man has more to do with our restoration from disease than even religious people ever dream of, though it is a clearly taught doctrine of the Jewish sacred writings that it is God " who healeth all our diseases." (Ps. ciii : 3, cxlvii : 3; Jer. xvii : 14.) Cure by any of the prevailing methods is, in its inmost nature, a *theopathy*. It is always the Divine in nature, and in man, that heals. As we have shown, there is a wonderful *vis reparatrix*, or repairing force, inherent in our organism. In some of the lower forms of animal life it is still more manifest than in man, as a segment of a limb is sometimes replaced by it. Hartmann calls it the action of the Unconscious, by which he means a sort of blind impersonal intelligence and will that govern the world. I see no good reason why we should not call it God, or, if you prefer it, the Logos or Word of God. With this modification of the meaning of the term, which takes it from what seems to border closely upon atheism, and brings it into harmony with a Christian theism, I can adopt his language when he says: "After poisoning their patients with drugs, the doctors have come at last to know their business better, and now generally stand aside, or attempt only to remove obstacles which ignorance or accident have put in the way, so as to leave free course to the curative agencies of the Unconscious, which alone can restore the patient to perfect health." (*Bowen's History of Modern Philosophy*, p. 439.)

What we call nature — a term introduced into philosophy by Hippocrates — is only the Deity under another name. God's uniform mode of acting is what we call the laws of nature. Because a thing takes place in harmony with law does not exclude the idea of a Divine causation from it. God is not included in the world, nor excluded from it. The visible universe is in God, just as an imaginary scene of beauty, though it seems to have an external existence, is really in our minds. Nature without God would be as powerless as a body without a soul. There is not a point or particle of the globe that is isolated from Him. He did not roll up the vast orbs that compose the universe, and toss them away from himself like balls into empty space. He did not once, in a week of creative energy, make a world and then retire from it. *Creation is not a historic fact, but an ever-present reality, a thing He is perpetually doing.* Man, including a soul and its manifestation in a body, is not something that has been dropped out of the Divine Existence, as a pebble falls out of your hand, or a coin from the mint, and after that has no connection with it; we are still in Him and He in us. He did not make a world, or a human body, and wind it up as you do a watch, and leave it to run down without Him. He winds it up continually, and without a moment's intermission, and is ever the hidden spring of all its movements. The Force that created is never inoperative. God is neither an idle spectator of his universe nor a useless appendage to it. He has not left the world and the human body, which is a part of it, to develop themselves without his presence and interference, or, as Goethe somewhere ridicules this common belief, he does not "sit aloft seeing the world go."

It is neither hard to find God nor difficult to commune with Him. The cumbersome and bungling machinery of the Church, invented to elevate us to Him, or bring Him down to us, is of no use to the spiritual man. He is as near to us as we are to ourselves. His being in its infinite and endless compass includes ours. In us He somehow comes to a self-limitation. We have *being* in him and he *ex-istence* in us. He becomes man, and we become as gods. Jesus approved the use of this appellation in its application to human beings, as where, in the Old Testament Scriptures, we read: "I have said ye are gods; and all of you are children of the Most High." (Ps. lxxxii: 6; John x: 34.) It is a sublime truth that gives dignity to human nature that in us God is manifested in the flesh. To realize this in some degree of the intenseness with which Jesus the Christ was perceptive of it is to be conscious of a power that we otherwise cannot possess. In us also the Word is made flesh and still dwells among us, for it is our life, and that life is the light of men. It is the true light that lighteth every man that cometh into the world. In saying this we do not undeify the Christ, but elevate human nature at large. In common language we call a priest or clergyman a *divine* I affirm that other men are equally entitled to the appellation. The Word of God is not a person, much less a book, but the perpetual out-going and expression of his productive and enlightening Thought. This Word dwells in every man as the light of life, and invests us with a creative potency, for all things are made by it. It is God's Thought, and when our minds are in unison with it in our struggle with disease, we are invested with a fraction of God's omnipotence. Here is realized a *theocrasia,*

as it was called in ancient philosophy, a mixing with God. When
we thus act, the boundary line between our individual effort and
God's creative energy is obliterated, and they become merged into
a unity, as when a child and a strong man lift a rock from its
place, the strength of the two is mingled into one force. Jesus,
who became in so high a degree receptive of the illuminating and
creative Word,— which made him the Christ,— did not look upon
his own being as separated from that of the Father, but as included
in it. "Believe me, the Father is in me, and I am in the Father.
The words that I speak unto you, I speak not of myself; but the
Father who dwelleth in me, he doeth the works." (John xiv : 10.)

The secret of the cures and all the marvelous works of Jesus is
given by himself in John v : 19, 20, 30. He declares that it was
given him distinctly to see and clearly to recognize the Divine
operation in nature. In disease he saw a Divine power, a *vis
reparatrix* at work to cure it. He identified himself with God,
and coöperated with this Divine healing *conatus* in the human
body, and thus greatly intensified its therapeutic action. In raising the patient from disease to health, he lifted in the same direction and in concert with God. He plainly asseverates that he
did nothing of himself, but only what he saw the Father *doing*
(ποιοῦντα). Why may not a sincere disciple of Jesus become
in this a copy of the Master, and do the same? By acting in
unison with the Divine power in nature, which is perceived already
at work in the case, we may be empowered to restore the sufferer
to his normal state,— *mens sana in corpore sano*, a sound mind
in a sound body. This is effected not by a miracle, but, as in
the case of the cures wrought by Jesus, by an accelerated process
of nature. All the wonderful achievements of modern science
and the useful arts — as telegraphy, photography, and the ten
thousand results of machinery — are effected in the same way. *In
all human endeavor, conformity to nature is union with God.*
But there is a higher realm of nature than that whose laws we
generally recognize in our superficial sciences and shallow philosophies,— an almost unexplored region of law in relation to the

action of spirit on matter, and of the soul upon its body.   If, in the effort to cure disease, I can find out how God *is doing* it, and conform my healing endeavor to the Divine method, I come into line with Him, and march behind the veiled God-head to the desired result.   I can conform my effort to the Divine creative Thought here, as I can act in concert with the Divine law of gravitation in bringing the water of a spring on the mountain side into my habitation.   In either case I do nothing of myself, but only what I see the Father doing.

There is an interior gravitation of all souls towards God, their proper center.   The wandering soul, disguise it as it may, is home-sick for its native land, and for rest on the bosom of the Infinite Love.   Conscious union with the One Life, and an identification of our being with the only Reality, is the goal toward which we are running.   These soul-longings are not only worship but an unerring prophecy of what we are to be.   We are all on the route that leads to God, where all life begins, and in which it should forever *consciously* act.   The brooklet that rushes down the mountain side, sometimes by a *fall*, then in a calm and tranquil flow, is unceasingly on its way to the ocean.   So the soul of man came from God and is returning to Him, but so as to retain forever the freedom of its individuality in God.

The soul that longs for communion with God need not search long to find him.   "Accustom yourself," says Madam Guyon, "to seek God within, and you will find Him."   There is a Life within us, a living Force and intelligent Thought, that pervade the bodily organism.   It is the Soul of our soul, the Life of our life, the Spring of all our knowledge.   As Bishop Berkeley puts it: "There is a Mind that affects me every moment with all the sensible impressions I perceive.   And, from the variety, order, and manner of these, I conclude the Author of them to be wise, powerful, and good beyond comprehension.   The things perceived by me are known by the understanding, and produced by the will of an Infinite Spirit.   And is not all this most plain and evident ? Is there any more in it than what a little observation in our own

minds, and that which passes in them, not only enableth us to conceive but also obligeth us to acknowledge?" (*Berkeley's Works*,
Vol. I, p. 308.) This brings God very near to us. This Universal Mind and Spirit, in which is included all knowledge, all
truth, all life, and all blessedness, perpetually acts within us. It
thinks for us when we cannot think for ourselves. It works in
us to will and to do when our individual wills are powerless or
quiescent. When we cease to row, we float in the infinite current,
and always unerringly in the right direction. When we cease from
our own working, we do the will of God, or, in other words, God's
will works for us and in us. The greatest possible attainment, the
summit of our highest aspirations, is the conscious identification of
our individual life with the One Life. Our unhappiness, our
misery, our restless craving for an unrealized good, our unsatisfied
yearning, and our *disease*, arise from our seceding from the Universal Life, disjoining ourselves from it by the rebellion of what we
proudly call free will, and setting up for ourselves. If we would
leave the strings of our harp to vibrate from sympathy with the
music of the Universe, instead of fingering them ourselves, and
trying to play a different tune, or on a different and discordant
key, we should be happy and well. He who attains to the blessedness of a life in God, as did Jesus the Christ, lives well and
forever. His spiritual stature reaches from earth to the heavens.
He has mounted upward to immortality in this present time, and
lives eternal life on the earth. Disease and death are vanquished,
and his individuality is merged, without being destroyed, in the
all-comprehending LIFE.

In consequence of this indwelling of God, the common Life of
the universe, in us, recuperation is natural to the human body
and to all living things. There is a Divine energy inherent in the
system that immediately and with omniscient skill reacts against
every disorder of mind or body, and exhibits itself in a psychical
and physiological effort to restore harmony. When a crumb of
bread enters the trachea or windpipe, with what divine violence
all the muscles that expel the air from the lungs contract to blow

it out. This spasmodic action of the abdominal muscles and the diaphragm is not a disease, but is a curative effort of the organism to cast out a foreign and deleterious substance from the lungs. When a speck of dust, or a grain of sand, enters the eye, the lachrymal glands are stimulated to increased action, and the eye is suffused with a flood of tears to wash it out. In the case of poison or unwholesome food in the stomach, the first effort of the Divine Life, or what we call nature, is to induce nausea and vomiting. The action of the stomach is inverted so as to eject its injurious contents at once. If this does not succeed, the next resort of the Divine healing energy is to increase the peristaltic action and vermicular movement of the stomach and intestinal canal, so as to rid the system of it as soon as possible by a diarrhetic discharge. No mother's love, enlightened by all that medical science can give, could prescribe with such alacrity and skill as does nature, that is, the God-life in us, in this and all other emergencies.

In the case of all wounds and lesions, from the prick of a pin to the fracture of a limb, a curative effort of nature, by which can be meant only a Divine energy, acting according to an established order we call law, exhibits itself in a skillful endeavor to heal it. Witness the suppuration of the flesh around a splinter that has pierced the hand. The pain in a sprained ankle is, as Romberg poetically but truly expresses it, the prayer of the sensory nerves for more blood, and the Divine Life of nature answers the prayer by crowding the surrounding parts with blood, and its swollen condition is the result. Very much that passes under the name of disease is only an effort of the Divine Life that is in us to cure the real malady. In the case of a sudden cold, where the pores of the skin are closed, nature throws the heat of the body to the surface, because, according to a fixed law, heat expands the contracted pores and opens them, thus restoring the suspended perspiration. The feverish condition of the body is not a disease, but only a curative device of nature. Instead of checking and obstructing this healing endeavor, we should coöperate with it, and, so far as our therapeutic devices go, we should aim to accelerate its action, as did Jesus the Christ.   In our individuality we are endowed with free will, and, to use a Scriptural and not wholly inappropriate form of expression, we may "come to the help of the Lord" in his Divine curative effort.   How we may do this in harmony with the laws of our being, it will be the object of the remaining part of this work to show.

PART III.

PSYCHO-THERAPEUTICS,

OR

PRACTICAL MENTAL CURE.

"It is the spirit that maketh alive; the flesh profiteth nothing."—JESUS THE CHRIST.

"As the state of the mind is capable of producing a disease, another state of it may effect a cure."—JOHN HUNTER.

"If the imagination fortified have power, then it is material to know how to fortify and exalt it."—LORD BACON.

"I hope the medical reader may be induced to employ Psycho-Therapeutics in a more methodical way than heretofore, and thus copy nature in those interesting instances, occasionally occurring, of sudden recovery from the spontaneous action of some powerful mental cause, by employing the same force designedly instead of leaving it to mere chance."—DR. DANIEL HACK TUKE.

CHAPTER I.

ON THE METHOD OF COMMUNICATING A SANATIVE MENTAL INFLU-ENCE.

All the mental operations are reducible to thought and feeling, or, if you prefer the form of expression, to intellect and sensibility. All modifications of the mind refer themselves to one or the other. All existence, all life, in fact, the very essence of the soul, consists in either thought or feeling. Some, of whom M. Destutt Tracy, a follower of Condillac, is an example, make *feeling* to be identical with individual existence. He is a fair representative of the sensational school of philosophy, and in him it received its best logical expression. He says: "The faculty of feeling is that which manifests to us all the others, without which none of them would exist for us, whilst it manifests itself that it is its own principle to itself; that it is that beyond which we are not able to remount, and which constitutes our existence; that it is everything for *us;* that it is the same thing as *ourselves.* I feel because I feel; I feel because I exist; and I do not exist but because I feel. Then my existence and my sensibility are one and the same thing." (*Political Economy*, p. 42.) The idealists, as Fichte and Hegel, affirm that sensation is not possible except it be accompanied and preceded by thought,—that whatever is out of thought has no existence in feeling. Swedenborg makes the essence of the human soul to consist in the union of thought and feeling, or, as he puts it, the conjunction of the wisdom and the love. The ques-

273

tion which is prior and which is posterior, or which is cause and which is effect, I shall not here discuss. It will be my aim to show that both, as states of mind, are communicable to other minds for the modification of their spiritual and physical condition. In this the cure of disease consists.

It has been shown in the preceding chapters that thoughts are *things*. I do not mean by this that they are material, but substantial realities, and are that which gives reality and existence to everything else. Thoughts and ideas are not as they are usually supposed, mere shadows or abstractions, but are manifestations or modifications of the substance of the soul, and are more real than material things, for these have no properties that are not reducible to sensations and thoughts in our minds. Thoughts are the most substantial of realities, and are in fact the only real things in the universe. But they are *transmissible entities*. They can be transferred from one mind to another. This fact is put to a practical use in the pulpit, and in all our systems of education. In it is found the power of the press in modern civilization. In it also I shall show lies the power of the physician to an extent never recognized by the prevailing schools of medicine. If thought and existence are identical, as has been shown in the previous chapters of this volume, then it follows that to change our mode of thinking is to modify our existence.

Thoughts may be excited in the minds of others through the medium of words. This is by an external way, and is comparatively imperfect, for words have not exactly the same meaning to any two minds. This common mode of communication, which is adopted in our ordinary social life, is of no use unless there previously exists in the mind which you address an idea corresponding to the word you utter. Words can only excite latent thoughts in another's soul, and never originate them. If you speak in an unknown tongue, you excite only a sensation of sound which has no meaning. A person may talk to us all day in a language which we do not understand and give us no idea. The same may be said of written language, which is addressed to the eye instead of the ear. In the case of words, as a medium of communicating thought to the mind of another, it is through the principle of *sensation*, either that of hearing or sight, that the ideas they represent are excited. Yet words have a spiritual potency in them when addressed to one who understands them, or can be made to feel their meaning as we do. Then his soul, his inner being, is made to vibrate, as it were, in harmony with ours.

But words, either spoken or written, are not absolutely necessary to the communication of thought from one mind to another. There is a more direct and spiritual way in which it may be done, even through sensation. You ask me a question, and I answer it in the affirmative by a nod, and in the negative by a shake of the head, and you perfectly understand me, though no words are used. So does a child, for the recognition of the meaning is instinctive and intuitional. But cannot this be done through the sense of *touch* as well as through the sight or hearing? This sense is the most spiritual and interior of all our senses. It is that to which all the others are reducible, and underlies them all. Without it no sensation would be possible. This is a doctrine of Swedenborg's psychology, and is manifestly true. There is a tendency in the minds of two persons who are in *tactual* contact towards a oneness of thought and feeling. This takes place through a universal principle of human nature denominated psychometry, but which I prefer to call the *sympathetic sense*. If I wish the person sitting or standing next to me to move away, a slight push of the hand excites in him both the thought and the impulse to do so. It calls into action in him all the muscles concerned in the movement. This is, when carefully examined, a marvelous phenomenon. It is only because it is so common that we cease to wonder at it. I communicate to him by my touch a thought of a complicated muscular movement and a tendency toward it. But is it out of the range of possibility to affect, by the same hand, the natural action of other organs,— as the heart, the lungs, the kidneys, the stomach, the liver, or the peristaltic action of the bowels? There is no good reason why an *impulse* cannot be transmitted on the wings of an invisible thought as a messenger to those organs. It is in itself no more unreasonable than that your feeling of approval is communicable to another by a pat of the hand on his shoulder, or a feeling of disapproval by a blow proportioned in force to the degree of your displeasure. A pressure of the hand signifies friendship. It has that meaning to everybody. There is a sort of instinctive Masonry by which our thoughts and feelings are communicated to others by the touch, and which all souls understand. I use these only as examples, or illustrations, of the transference of thought and feeling from one mind to another through the medium of the hand and the sensation of touch. When the hand is placed on the head of a patient, at the point of impact your mind comes into contact, as it were, with his mind, for sensation is not in the external body, but in the spiritual organism. If he is receptive, or in any degree impressible, your thoughts and healthy emotional states can be transmitted to him, or more properly excited in him, as they do not pass out of your mind in coming into his. An impulse towards a healthy action may in this way be imparted to any organ of his body. This has been established by experiment. Here is the philosophy of the method of cure by the imposition of hands, which, as the primitive, instinctive means of cure, is again being restored to the healing art. It was practiced by Jesus the Christ and his disciples or scholars, which ought to be enough to give it currency among those who assume his name, and profess to copy his life. The hand was used in order that through the sensation of touch (which is only in the mind of the patient) your thought, to which is given a healing intention, may be communicated to his soul, and through this affect the body. In this condition of mental contact with him the physician *thinks, imagines, and believes* for the patient, and if he is highly susceptible his mind will *vibrate* in harmony with yours; if not fully impressible, it will create a *tendency* towards your line of thought and feeling. It is like what we witness in the material world when a body in motion communicates its movement to another body, and both move onward in the same direction.

There is a still more interior way of communication between the mind or spirit of one and the mind or spirit of another, by which thought may be transmitted and an influence imparted. No actual physical contact is necessary to it. The eye is an organ of thought in an eminent degree. Every one knows there is a meaning in a look, a hidden signification in a glance, as much as in a word. Vision may be a passive state or a voluntary act. The same is true of hearing, which is often without effort on our part. But to listen or hearken is an act of will. It requires attention or a concentration of thought. To gaze at another is an act of will, and a determination of thought towards the object. It gives a definite direction to thought, and brings the whole power of the mind to a focal point. The thought, to use an analogy, or to speak according to appearance, goes forth from the eye, and enters the mind of the patient through this aperture of the soul. There is such a thing as a spiritual eye, or "eye of the mind," as Mr. Atkinson denominates it. As a phrenologist, he locates it just beneath the organ of comparison. "It seems," he says, "to split off into the senses, as light divides off into colors, or sound into notes, but to contain within itself *the power of mind concentrated.*" (*The Laws of Man's Nature and Development*, p. 76.) This cogitative gaze, this look with fixed attention, and concentration of thought, was employed by Peter and John in the cure of the lame man at the gate of the temple. In the brief report that is given of the case it is said: "They *fastened their eyes upon-him*, and said to him, '*Look on us*,'" and then commanded him to rise and walk. With the word was communicated a power to do it, for a thought imparted to another may be made to enclose a feeling. It may be, as it were, the outward wrapping of an emotion or *impulse.* Also this same power of mind concentrated, this cogitative gaze, may be made to act at a distance. And why not? Is there anything incredible in it? If the sound of an uttered word, or a sentence, may be transmitted on an electric wave for hundreds of miles through the telephone, why may not a mental force, which acts independently of material restraints and limitations be conveyed to any distance? Distance between minds is more an internal feeling than a material measurement.

Thought may be *directly* impressed by one mind upon that of another. As Paul and Swedenborg both teach, thought is *entheal*, that is, it comes from God and is something of the Divine Life in man. (2 Cor. iii : 5 ; *Arcana Celestia*, 1707, 2004.) It is this that gives such power to our thoughts both over ourselves and others. It is this that makes them — to use an uncommon but proper word — *entheastic*, or having in them the energy of God. As has been said in a previous chapter, thought has in it a creative force. The words of Byron can hardly be viewed as a poetic exaggeration, --

> "The mind can make
> Substance, and people planets of its own
> With beings brighter than have been, and give
> A breath to forms that can outlive all flesh."

By the productive power of thought and imagination the Divine Mind made, and still makes, the world. We, being in his image, and thinking from Him, make our bodies, which are *our* world, in the same way. A state of *theopathy*, or sympathy with God, invests us with the power of *theurgy*, or of doing Divine works. Every true manhood might properly, though in a mitigated sense, be named Immanuel, or God with us. (Mat. i : 23.) The Greeks in their beautiful and expressive language spoke of certain persons as *theophoroi*, or as carrying a God within them, and also of others as *theophron*, that is, having a divine mind, or as being divinely wise. This is more or less true of all great and wise men. But when we speak of God as within man, we must be careful not to take a material view of it. We do not mean the same as when we say that one body is enclosed within the spatial limitations of another, like an idol in a temple. That God is inward to man involves the idea that God's Life is the One Life of the universe, and that our life is bound up in a necessary unity with his. (1 Samuel xxv : 29.) There is in reality no finite life, as all in heaven and earth live by an influx from the Universal

Life. For the same reason, there is no finite intelligence and thought. All that I know, or can know, or even think, is from the uncreated fount of knowledge, and I am only a recipient of it. To think in harmony and concert with God is to fully realize this when we think. This brings our thought into unison with the action of the Divine Mind, and gives to it a Divine and saving efficacy.

When a patient is in a passive, and consequently impressible and receptive, state, *and with his eyes closed*, so as to shut out from his mind all sensational images of external things, our thoughts may be imparted to him, or at least we can change the character and direction of his thinking. This can be done either when in actual tactual contact with him or at a distance. In addition to a state of passivity, he should be in a state of *sympathy* with the physician. These conditions being fulfilled, his mind becomes a *tabula rasa*, or clean slate, on which our thoughts may be written, and even without the intervention of spoken words. What we imagine, and believe, and think, will be transferred to him, for the stronger and more active mind will control the other. Thought is an interior speech, or inward word. It is the proper language of souls, the universal language of spirit. As God's thoughts can be imparted to us by *inspiration*, so we can impress our ideas and feelings upon the minds of others, and inspire them with them. The physician who does this to the invalid, and infuses into him his faith and hope and courage, or, in other words, a better mode of thinking and feeling, has touched the interior spring of his existence, and is, in the true sense of the word, a *doctor* or teacher. It was in this office that Jesus the Christ cured the most inveterate diseases. He was a guide of men's thoughts, an instructor of their souls. In the Gospels, wherever he is called master in our English translation, in the original Greek it is teacher. (Mat. xxiii: 8, 10 ; John xiii: 13.) Hence, his followers were called disciples or learners. By thus modifying the inward spring of existence, he changed the position of the helm of the soul, and put it on a new tack in the voyage of life ;

and, by a Divine law, the inner change was translated into a bodily expression.

If it be true, as Swedenborg affirms, that all power is in *ultimates*, because the spiritual force is then in its completeness and fullness, then it follows that thoughts, expressed in their appropriate words, may have an added potency, and their effects may be made thereby more permanent; but it should never be forgotten that the spiritual idea, which is as the soul of the word, is that alone which gives to it a healing and saving efficacy. Without this, an uttered word or sentence is only an empty sound. It is only a frozen corpse, and not a living spirit in whom is the breath of a Divine Life. It is the idea, the thought, that imparts to a word a sanative virtue. "It is the spirit that maketh alive: the flesh profiteth nothing. The words that I speak unto you are spirit and are life." (John vi: 63.) Feuerbach eloquently speaks of the healing power of the word. "Man has not only an instinct, an internal necessity, which impels him to think, to perceive, to imagine; he has also the impulse to speak, to utter, to impart his thoughts. A divine impulse this,— a divine power, the power of words. The word is the imaged, revealed, radiating, lustrous, enlightening thought. The word is life and truth. All power is given to the word. The word makes the blind to see and the lame to walk, heals the sick, and brings the dead to life, — the word works miracles, and the only rational miracles. The word is the Gospel, the paraclete of mankind. The word has power to redeem, to reconcile, to bless, to make free. We know no higher spiritually operative power and expression of power than the power of the word. God created the world and all things by the word, so that to God it is no more difficult to create than it is for us to name." (*Feuerbach's Essence of Christianity*, pp. 111, 112.)

A word, an uttered sentence, into which is concentrated the soul-life and heart-life of him who pronounces it, and which is animated by a Divine thought, a living truth, has in it a healing virtue above anything in a material drug. The right word at the right time can reach the inner life of man and make us whole. It can change the whole current and quality of a human life. "He sent his word and healed them, and delivered them from their destructions." (Ps. cvii: 20.) He who has to do with the diseased in mind or body need not talk much, but should pray for the *right* word, and should put the energy of faith and love into its expression. It is more powerful against our spiritual foes than the spear of Ithuriel. There is some word that lies as a silent thought in the Mind of God, the Infinite Spirit-Presence. It is what God would say to the unhappy and diseased one were He to break the sublime silence in which He dwells and speak to him. In it is a message freighted with life, and health, and peace. Let us hold our soul passively open and upward to receive it, and give it utterance. It has in it the power of God, and the wisdom of God unto salvation. Many a longing soul is *feeling*, if not saying: "Speak the word only, and I shall be healed." (Mat. viii: 8.) It was by the power of the right word and the spirit that Jesus healed disease. He condensed into a brief sentence the whole force of his inner life,—his faith, his love, his benevolent healing intention, his desire and volition,—which was sent forth as an assertion or a command. It was like the creative fiat, *lux esto*, let there be light, and the living, all vitalizing light of the heavens flashed upon the diseased mind. It reduced its chaos to order and Divine harmony, and a body in ruins was restored to wholeness and health. We ought to ascertain, so far as practicable, the precise nature of the disordered mental state, or fixed mode of thought, that is the spiritual root of the patient's malady, and which has crystalized, through the law of correspondence, into an organic expression in the body. This should be attacked by the psycho-therapeutic force from every point of approach. The patient should himself freely aid in the spiritual diagnosis of his case. The Roman Catholic Church maintains the Divine order when it makes confession a necessary antecedent of absolution, or a being released. (See also James v: 16.) The sin—the error, the falsity, as the word means—should be remitted or sent away

In order to this he should be like clay in the hands of the potter, to be transformed by the divinely-established dominion of mind over matter, and of the soul over the body. In a state of passivity, or mental inertia, the mind acts only as it is acted upon. This state can be assumed at will, and is one of great impressibility or susceptibility to impression from the thoughts and emotions of others, as a vessel without a helm is driven before the wind. In assuming this condition before the good physician, the patient becomes like a ship that has lowered its sails and is being towed by a steamer into a safe harbor. The secret of the influence of what is called magnetism is the influence of the thought and will of the operator over the mind, and through the mind, over the body of another. When the patient is passive and, consequently, impressible, he is made to fix his thought with expectant attention upon the effect to be produced. In addition the physician *thinks* the same effect, tranquilly and strongly wills it, and believes and imagines that it *is being done.* The mental action of the patient, augmented by that of his assistant, and conjoined with it into a harmonious and sympathetic unity, is precipitated upon the body, and becomes a silent, transforming, sanative energy. It must be a malady more than ordinarily obstinate that is neither relieved nor cured by it.

The power of thought in modifying the bodily condition and affecting the functional action of an organ may be shown by a single fact. "Although it is well known," says Dr. Tuke, "that powerful emotions act strongly upon the uterine functions, it is not so well understood how marked an influence an ideational faculty, in the form of concentrated attention, exerts over them. A striking case is reported by Mr. Braid which illustrates this fact very clearly. The effect took place, moreover, in a state of the system *not* rendered susceptible at the time by his special method,—that of hypnotism. He had, on a previous occasion, relieved a state of amenorrhœa by a mixed method, partly hypnotic and partly mental, but it then occurred to him that, inasmuch as he attributed his success in her case entirely to fixed mental attention with a predominant idea (and faith in the result), he might succeed by the psychical process alone, *without sending her to sleep*, —in fact, while she was wide awake. He tried the experiment, addressing her thus: 'Now, keep your mind firmly fixed on what you know should happen.' In the meanwhile he allowed his own will to be passive, and read a book. At the expiration of eleven minutes the experiment ended, and the desired result took place within that period. The same treatment was adopted when required on subsequent occasions, and with the same success." This case speaks volumes of the power of attention, or concentrated thought, combined with faith and imagination, over every organ of the body. (*Influence of the Mind upon the Body in Health and Disease*, by Daniel Hack Tuke, pp. 393, 394.)

CHAPTER II.

THE INFLUENCE OF THOUGHT ON THE BODY, AND A PRACTICAL USE OF IT IN THE CURE OF DISEASE.

To think and consciously to exist are one and the same, as was affirmed by Descartès in his celebrated proposition, *cogito, ergo sum*, I think, therefore I am. Mr. Worcester defines thought to be " the exercise of the mind in any way except sense and perception." The exception here is not necessary, as neither sensation nor perception is possible without thought. I prefer the view of Descartes, followed by Hegel, that all mental action in its last analysis is a mode of thought, and it is equally certain that mental action is the only life of the body, in fact, is the highest form of vital activity. Bodily movements are the *expression*, or pressing outward, as the word signifies, of a mental activity which is reducible to some form of thought. Thought is universally present and underlies every act of the mind. Spinoza affirms that God is *Thinking Being*. In the philosophy of Descartes, the mind, which is an image of God, is a *thinking thing*. As we have said above, thought and existence are identical. We cannot love unless we love something of which we think,—something that must first come into thought. We cannot remember, or imagine, or believe, or doubt, or perceive, or conceive anything that does not first become a thought. We cannot will anything, or determine upon any action, unless it is first presented to the mind as an object of thought, and becomes an object of desire. We cannot

284

desire that of which we have no pre-existing thought or idea.
Take away from us the power of thought, and all mental activity
and conscious life disappear with it. The body also would become
sensationless and motionless, a deserted and closed temple of God
in which divine service is over. This view of the relation of
thought to life and existence will render intelligible what will be
said as to its influence upon the bodily condition. It was a grand
conception of Hegel, that as God creates the world by thinking it,
so it is governed and progresses according to the laws of thought
or logic. This is the central idea of his Philosophy of History.
The same is true of the human body, which is the external world
which the soul creates for its manifestation and as the theater of its
activity. Its conditions of health and disease are formed by thought
and governed by its laws. Physiology and pathology are a living
logic As there is a "logic of events" in the history of the
world at large, so there is in the varying conditions of the human
body the same unbending order of sequence, — the same law of
spiritual cause and physical effect.

Ideas, which are the images and inmost reality of all created
things always tend to an external or material manifestation. If
the mind forms an idea of a change in the bodily *status*, and holds
itself steadily and tenaciously to that idea, it originates, or at
least intensifies, an effort of nature, that is, an unconscious action
of mind, to express itself outwardly, and to form the body after the
pattern of the preëxisting idea. All outward things are but the
exteriorization of ideas. The world, with all it contains, is only
the realization, or actuality on the mental plane of sense, of God's
thought, and our bodies sustain the same relation to the creating
soul. If God, as an Infinite Spirit, creates the universe by thought,
as Plato, the apostle John, Swedenborg, Berkeley, Fichte, and
Hegel all essentially agree in teaching, then thought is the primal
force and the greatest power in the world. It is that from which
all things exist and subsist, or have continued being.

We have a proof of the influence and power of thought over the
body in the way in which *suggestion*, directed to the mind respect-

ing the action of the organs, operates upon them. Says Dr. Wil-
kinson: "By touching the abdomen over the colon, and suggest-
ing the effect, we can, in susceptible persons, produce the results of
aperient medicines, and abolish constipation for years. This
order of facts has an important bearing upon the origin as well as
cure of disease, rendering it probable that a large number of ills
come directly out of the patient's mind; for if alteration of fancy
heals, this suggests that fancy first engendered the complaint."
(*Human Body, and its Connection with Man*, p. 374.)

Few persons ever become aware of the influence of thought
upon the *body*, though they see how much it has to do with our
mental states. "Surely, as I have thought, so shall it come to
pass," is an expression of the law of our being, as an image of
God. (Isa. xiv: 24.) The thought of a thing is a spiritual
touch or contact with it,—it is an ideal and real creation of it.
To think of a dishonorable act will excite a feeling of shame,
which will inject the capillaries of the face with arterial blood, and
a blush is suffused over the countenance. The thought of danger,
either as a memory of the past, or an anticipation of the future, or
even as an imaginary peril, will quicken and weaken the action of
the heart. But a real danger that is not an object of thought and
consciousness has no effect upon us. The sword suspended over
the head of Damocles by a single hair affects him not if he does
not think of it. I knew a lady who safely passed a bridge, that
was undergoing repairs, on horseback, one dark and stormy night,
and on a string-piece, but who fainted on being told of it the morning after. It may be worth the trouble of inquiring if physicians
do not often create, or at least greatly aggravate, the diseases of
their patients by telling them of them? Where ignorance is both
bliss and health it is folly to be wise. A man may have a valvu-
lar lesion of the heart, and live to be ninety years of age, if he
does not know it, or think of it. But the knowledge of it soon
proves fatal. It may sound harsh to say it, but it is perhaps true,
that the shallow medical science of the young practitioner may
become almost a fatal mental poison to his patient, especially if

he makes an ostentatious display of it in telling of a disease of which the patient never thought before.

The law of association, by which ideas become so connected together in thought that to think of one suggests or calls up the other, is one of the widest in its action and one of the most important of all the laws of mind. It is the key that unlocks many of the more mysterious phenomena of the mind, but is one of the least familiar of the mental laws, being generally overlooked by the great majority of psychologists. I know of no writer on mental science who gives to it anything like the importance that belongs to it except Mr. James Mill. It is one of the fundamental laws of thought, the influence of which is constantly felt in all forms of mental activity.

Disease is often kept in thought, and consequently in existence and consciousness, by the law of association. The morbid condition becomes connected in idea with certain disagreeable sensations. Whenever these are felt we think of the disease; and the thought of the disease calls up and brings into consciousness the unpleasant sensations, just as the sight, or thought, of a surgical instrument revives the idea of the pain it once caused us, and in a degree we feel the pain again.

What we should aim at in the treatment of disease is to break up this association, this morbid concatenation of thought and sensation, and form a new one to take its place. In painful affections a counter-irritant is sometimes employed, which, by creating a new pain or discomfort, diverts the attention from the original one, and puts it out of thought and consciousness. Whatever course we may take, the thought of the disease must be supplanted by the idea of a remedy that has given and still gives relief. This association must be made equally strong with the other. The new association becomes the means of the oblivescence, or forgetfulness, of the disease; and in proportion as a disease is out of thought, or we become oblivious of it, it is cured. The word cure, from the Latin *cura*, care, implies that we no longer care for it, or, in other words, we cease to think of it, or be anxious about it.

In the work of James Mill—Analysis of the Phenomena of the Human Mind—it is shown, in the chapter on the Will, that all action in the body is the result of the contraction of fibres, and these fibrous contractions are effected: 1, by sensations; 2, by ideas. In the early period of life all our movements are reflex, or the result of sensation, which includes what is called irritation. Of a violent muscular contraction and movement generated by sensation we have a familiar example in sneezing. A pungent odor enters the nostrils, irritates their mucous surface, and is the occasion of a certain sensation. Immediately there follows it the spasmodic and violent action of a great number of muscles in the act called sneezing. In drinking water, if a few drops enter the larynx, the sensation occasioned by it calls into sudden action all the muscles concerned in expelling the air from the lungs, which violently contract to eject the foreign substance from them. This is the familiar movement of coughing. Hiccough is an involuntary movement of the muscles, produced by an irritative sensation in the stomach, as is often experienced after swallowing capsicum. The violent contraction of the muscles in vomiting is occasioned by a disagreeable sensation in the pharynx, or stomach. So, the action of the heart and lungs, the peristaltic motion of the alimentary canal, and the functional motion of all the organs, are caused by some irritation that may be expressed by the word sensation, but of which we are not always conscious. But sensation is a mental phenomenon. It is only a conscious or unconscious thinking. Hence, *ideas* as well as sensations are the cause of muscular actions in the body, and have the same effect as sensations. I will give a few familiar illustrations of this. We know that a disagreeable or painful sensation, occasioned by the contact of some foreign substance with the eye, causes the eyelid to close. But if a person rapidly thrusts his finger towards the eye, and near it, we cannot avoid closing it, or, as it is called, winking. Here it is not a sensation, but only the *thought* of one, that produces the effect. The contraction of the muscles follows the thought with as much certainty as it would the sensation if something touched the eye. This, as Mr. Mill remarks, "is not a matter of conjecture, it is a matter of fact. It is an experienced event." It is important to observe that the thought is the last part of the mental operation, and immediately precedes the act. This is not only a fact but a significant fact, as illustrating the power of thought as a motor force in the body. Take that curious phenomenon, which is peculiar to human nature, called laughter. It affects the whole body. It is a remarkable instance of a general muscular action, and of an effect that extends through the organism, produced by thought. We laugh from a ludicrous thought or a ridiculous idea, whether spoken by others or read in a book. Sometimes, long afterwards, when the idea is by any means revived, we laugh again, even when alone. The opposite of laughter is sobbing and weeping. This also influences the whole body. The grief from which weeping springs is the effect of a certain train of ideas, and without the existence in the mind of those antecedent painful thoughts could have no place in us.

Dr. Daniel Turner, a medical writer of a past age, in his De Morbis Cutaneis, says that the bare imagination of a purging potion has wrought such an effect in many persons as to produce a cathartic effect equal to that caused by medicine. He mentions the case of a young gentleman, a patient of his, who, having occasion to take many emetics, had such an antipathy to them that ever after he could vomit as strongly by thinking of them as most persons do by taking them into the stomach. (*Mill's Analysis of the Phenomena of the Human Mind*, Vol. II, p. 341.)

In reading the excellent work of Dr. Tuke, on the Influence of the Mind upon the Body, we should naturally come to the conclusion that a "psychical virus," in the shape of a morbid imagination, was the only cause of disease, which may not be so far from the truth, whatever may have been his aim. Nearly every disease known to medical science is shown to have been caused by it, and to have been a *malade imaginaire*. Prof. Dick, of Edinburg, expresses the opinion of many distinguished medical men when he says " that hydrophobia in man is not the result of any poison introduced into the system, but merely the melancholy and often fatal results of panic fear. Those who are acquainted with the effects of sympathy, irritation, and panic in the production of nervous disorders will readily apprehend our meaning, and, if our view be correct, the immense importance of disabusing the public mind on the subject is apparent."

Müller mentions the instance, by no means uncommon, of a person's teeth being set on edge by witnessing another about to pass a sharp instrument over glass or porcelain; also the production of shuddering by the mere mentioning of objects which, if present, would excite that sensation. In these cases it is simply a *thought* that produces the effect. Similar effects may be produced by what is called a *recollective imagination*. Herbert Spencer says: "I cannot think of seeing a slate rubbed with a dry sponge without there running through me the same thrill that actually seeing it produces." There are few persons who realize the important influence of our thoughts over our bodily condition. Müller has investigated this subject more fully than most physiological authors have done; and, as a condensed statement of all that he has written, he lays down the principle that "the *idea* of a particular motion determines a current of nervous action towards the necessary muscles, and gives rise to the motion independent of the will." But thought is capable of influencing the action of any organ in the body, as well as the voluntary muscles, by determining a current of nervous, or, in other words, of mental, force to it.

We have in a well-authenticated fact, mentioned by Drs. Bucknill and Tuke, a case which illustrates the influence of an idea accompanied by a strong emotion, and directed to a particular part of the body. A lady of intelligence, while passing a public institution, saw a child with his foot in such a position that a heavy iron gate swinging together seemed as if about to crush it. The child escaped unharmed, but the ankle of the lady became so lame that it was with difficulty she could reach home, a distance of a quarter of a mile. The inflammation of the foot was so severe that she was confined to the bed for many days. The truth of the story is vouched. for by both those intelligent physicians. (*Manual of Psychological Medicine*, p. 165.) This fact only exhibits, in an exaggerated degree, an influence that is at work in the generation of most chronic disorders, which are only the bodily expression of a fixed mode of thinking. But would not the same principle — that is, an idea accompanied with deep emotion, and directed to a particular part of the body — act with equal efficiency in the cure of disease? There are numerous facts which show that it can, and often does, as in the case of the cures that are wrought in answer to prayer, and those effected at the tombs of saints. Facts of this kind are as well authenticated as any recorded in the history of man. But do they not give us the glimpse of a law that is worthy of investigation, and one which can be put to a practical use? If, as Iago is made by Shakespeare to say, there are things —

> " The thought whereof
> Doth like a poisonous mineral gnaw our vitals,"

is there not in an idea a therapeutic influence of equal potency?

The influence of thought, or of a change in the dominant idea, in the cure of painful affections is well illustrated by what so frequently occurs with those who are suffering from *odontalgia*, or toothache. How often does it happen that while patients are on their way to the dentist the pain entirely disappears? The mental process of cure in these cases may be a feeling of fear of the dentist, and a dread of the pain attending the extraction of the tooth. This diverts the attention, that is, the *thought*, from the painful tooth, and has the same effect upon it that sleep would have. Or it may be and quite often is this: while on his way to the dentist, the sufferer feels a *wish* that it was not necessary. Then he begins to doubt whether the pain after all is so very bad, and becomes convinced that much of it has arisen from the exaggerating effects of impatience, and is, in fact, no worse than the operation of extracting it. By the time he reaches the office of the dreaded dentist, he has convinced himself that the tooth does not ache at all. And such is the fact, at least for the time, if not ever after. The same mental process would cure us of most, if not all, diseases. In the case mentioned, it is certainly the influence of the mind upon the body that effects the therapeutic result. It is in reality a change of *thought* that does all this. But is it not possible so to discipline our minds that we can by a voluntary effort, through faith and imagination, gain relief and effect a cure in all similar cases? In the case just described, the same principle of cure is equally applicable to most diseases and painful affections. Can a good reason be given why it is not? It is not impossible that we have here, in a brief compass, the germ of a far-reaching and profound spiritual science of healing.

There is no part of the human body that would seem to be more inaccessible and impervious to a mental influence than warts. A wart is defined by Dr. Mason Good as a firm, arid, harsh extuberance of the common integuments, and found chiefly on the hands. Its vital connection with the body would, at first sight, appear to be but little more intimate than the clothing we wear. Yet there are many cases recorded by distinguished physicians where they have been made to disappear under the influence of the trivial, and in themselves inert, devices employed by popular superstition to remove them, and this after caustics and all other orthodox remedies have failed to exterminate them. Lord Bacon records a cure of them in his own case by one of the many means resorted to in such cases by the people, and which was recommended to him by the wife of an English embassador, and which could have had no possible influence over them other than the tendency of an idea towards an external expression in the bodily organism; or it may have been through that mode of thought which we call faith and imagination. But both these are, or may be, voluntary acts of the mind. In so trifling a matter we see an exhibition of one of the most important laws of our nature. The power of thought that causes the disappearance of a wart is available for the cure of a cancer, and most of "the ills that flesh is heir to." *For whatever, as to the bodily condition, we think to be true, either by*

*u spontaneous impulsion or by a tenacious, volitional effort,
becomes to us a reality.* This takes place not by accident or
chance, but by the operation of one of the deepest laws of our
being. This is not a new truth, for Solomon, by a flash of Divine
inspiration, three thousand years ago, said of man, that as he
thinketh in his heart, so is he. (Prov. xxiii : 7.) Jonathan
Edwards, who, as is not generally known, embraced the doctrine
of Bishop Berkeley as to the external world, asserts "that all
existence is mental, and the existence of all exterior things (including of course the human body and its varying conditions) is
ideal." (*Memoirs of Jonathan Edwards*, by Sereno E. Dwight.
Appendix. Remarks in Mental Philosophy.) In accordance
with this doctrine, disease becomes non-existent to the same extent
in which we cease to recognize it in thought and by the will.

Of the power of thought to affect the body Mrs. Hemans
speaks, under the influence of an inspiration as high as that of
Solomon, when she says —

> "Swift *thoughts* that came and went,
> Like torrents o'er me sent,
> Have shaken as a reed this thrilling frame."

The most intelligent medical practitioners are beginning to realize that the mind is the most *real* department of our being, and
are coming to suspect, if not clearly to perceive, that all diseases
of a so-called nervous type arise from some prior mental disturbance, and are only the physical counterpart and outward *expression*, or pressing out, of a spiritual inharmony. By a law of correspondence, the mental abnormality records and perpetuates itself
in the morbid condition of the body, which is always a creation of
the mind into its own image. The mental condition of the patient
is not to be viewed as a mere *symptom* of the bodily disorder, but
is the prime element, the underlying *reality*, of the disease. In
fact, the morbid condition of the body is symptomatic of the
unsoundness of the mental state. There can be no doubt of the
influence of a *fixed morbid thinking* in the generation of a dis-

eased action in the bodily organs, nor of the power and impor
tance of a sound mental activity in originating and accelerating a
cure.

Disease, like everything else in the universe, being a creation of
thought, and having no existence except in thought, or, to express
it in another form, it being the materialization of an idea, it should
be the aim of the physician to banish it from the thought of the
patient, and exile it into the region of forgetfulness. As has been
said in a former part of this work, that of which we do not think
has to us no existence. It is during the continuance of the oblivescence, so far as we are concerned, as good as annihilated.
That of which we do not think does not come into our consciousness. There are many well-attested facts to show that men, in the
ardor of battle, receive wounds of a serious nature without being
aware of them until after a considerable lapse of time. We have
a large amount of unsuspicious evidence of this. A pleasurable
or painful sensation to which we give no attention is not felt. On
this subject Mr. James Mill remarks: "If any man tries to satisfy himself what it is to have a painful sensation, and what it is
to *attend* to it, he will find little means of distinguishing them.
Having a pleasurable or painful sensation, and attending to it,
seem not to be two things, but one and the same thing. The feeling a pain is attending to it; and attending to it is feeling it.
The feeling it is not one thing, the attention another; the feeling
and the attention are the same." (*Analysis of the Phenomena
of the Human Mind*, Vol. II., p. 364.) Attention is only a concentration of thought, or, as it is sometimes called, directed consciousness. Hence, it follows that if attention and pain are one
and the same, if we cease to attend to a pain, that is, to direct our
thoughts to it, we cease to have it or feel it. It passes out of consciousness and out of existence. The same is true of disease and
of every discomfort. Here is a most important and uniform law
of our nature, and one that should never be ignored in our
attempts to cure ourselves or others. It contains within it a price-
less value and a sanative virtue above all that the Materia Medica

has given to the world. It is the curative efficacy of a whole drug shop reduced to a single grain, in which there is a Divine sacramental and saving potency.

We have in the phenomena of dreams, when the soul crosses the imperfectly defined boundary line between this world and the spiritual realm, a striking illustration of the influence of ideas over the body. In disease, when we are dreaming, we often for the time become well. It is one of the circumstances attending dreams that our ideas, or thoughts, are unmixed with sensations from without. In a sound slumber, the five senses are closed; they are impervious and inaccessible to impressions from external things. But our ideas have oftentimes so much vividness as to have all the effects upon the body of sensations. Our thoughts, in fact, become internal sensations. They would do this in the waking state if our minds were equally abstracted, or, in other words, if there were the same degree of inattention to surrounding things. In dreams the invalid becomes to himself well, because ideal things and states become real things and states. It would be well for us to cultivate the faculty of dreaming ourselves into health and happiness while awake.

The influence of thought in shaping the bodily condition is seen in the effects of a " fixed idea." Whenever the idea of an act, or a bodily state, is strongly presented to the mind, there is in it a marked tendency to work itself out into a full actuality. Take as an illustration of this the act of swallowing the saliva. A friend suggests to us that we cannot refrain from doing it for the space of a minute. This presents the idea of the muscular movement so vividly to the mind that we are almost sure to do it. The tendency to work out, or externalize, the idea is so strong that it overcomes the force of the will, which, in the case mentioned, is supposed to be arrayed against it.

Tell a person that there is a fly, or a speck of dust, on his face, and, although there is none, and no sensation of one, yet the idea or thought immediately excites the muscles of the arm, and the act of brushing it off follows at once. Almost all persons in looking from a high tower have the thought of jumping off, and this is attended with a tendency more or less strong to do so. The man who leaped from the dome of the capitol at Washington, a few years ago, probably did it from an impulse generated by the idea of it. Tell a person that he looks sick, or that he has some disease, and if the idea is vividly formed in his mind, and is accompanied with a degree of credence or faith, it will tend to actualize itself, through an invariable law of our nature, in a morbid condition of the body. The disease is the externalization of the thought, the expression, or pressing outward, of the mental state, the physical side or counterpart of the idea. All habitual mental states have their inseparable physical accompaniments. Melancholy, anxiety, impatience, remorse, and all abnormal and depressing mental conditions, with the *ideas* from which they spring, are invisible sculptors that fashion the body into their outward expression. Many diseases arise from a *false idea*, and if this is corrected, the tap-root of the malady is sundered.

The law of the tendency of an idea to a bodily expression works with equal efficiency in the direction of a cure, as in the generation of a diseased condition. Disease being in its spiritual root the fixedness of an idea, and its tendency to an ultimate manifestation or actuality, must be supplanted by the thought or belief of a state of health. This, by a law of correspondence, will tend to actualize itself, or express itself outwardly by an altered condition of the physical organism. In proportion as the ideas suggested by a physician are accepted and mentally appropriated by the patient, they will have their influence in modifying the bodily state. They will tend to kill or make alive. On his words hangs life or death, health or disease. They have a far higher potency than his drugs. A short time ago I met a little girl who was suffering from toothache. I placed a finger over a branch of the fifth pair of nerves, and suggested that the pain was passing away, and would soon be gone. In a moment or two the prophecy became fact, because the idea was accepted and believed. Like all ideas, it tended to a full actuality in the body. The cure, as I learned afterward, was also permanent. If a patient, as may sometimes be the case, is not in a receptive state, and our sanative idea is not transferred to him so as to become his own, if he exhibits a *desire* to recover, we must silently think, believe, and imagine for him, while he is passive and our hands in contact with him. Our thought will then affect him somewhat as his own thinking would, though less in degree. When he gains relief, as he probably will in a brief time, he will then accept and adopt as his own our suggested ideas, and, by a subtle and potent law of our being, they will tend to a full realization in the body.

Hegel says: "Actuality brings immediately to pass the unity of essence with existence, or of the inward with the outward. The idea as being inward tends on every hand to the outward, so that the inner and outer become one." (*Logic*, pp. 221–223.) In the tendency of an ideal state to actualize itself in the body, and to create the body into its own image, we have an almost unused power in the cure of disease. A comprehensive knowledge of this law, and a skillful employment of it as a remedial agent, and the same faith in its uniform action that we have in the law of gravitation and chemical affinity, will render a practical use of the idealistic or spiritual philosophy much more efficient in the relief and cure of disease than the prevailing materialistic systems of medication. It reaches more effectually the hidden springs of life in the body. It penetrates to the center of our being, that may be impervious to the influence of a drug.

The body and the soul are not two separate things, but one and the same, like cause and effect. These are a unity. A cause is in the effect, and an effect is in its cause. This was remarked by Descartes, who refers us to two facts of consciousness to prove the unity of the soul and body. When the body receives a wound we feel pain. The pain is in the soul-principle, but without a state of unity with the body would not be felt when the physical organism is injured So, when there is need of new material in the body to supply the place of the worn-out particles that have been ejected by the excreting organs, the soul experiences a feeling of hunger.

But this mental feeling and the need of new material could not coëxist unless the soul and body were a unity, and acted together. So, in all languages bodily actions are appropriated for the expression of mental energies, as in the French *penser*, to think, which primarily means to weigh. To *attend* or give *attention* is primarily a stretching out, as the hand, toward a thing. All bodily actions and states are a word of which some mental energy is the spiritual meaning. So every idea in the mind tends to an actual expression in the body, so as to maintain this unity and harmony, whether it be in the genesis of a diseased condition, or a state of health. If a person by some means forms the idea that a harmless tumor is a cancer, and the thought becomes fixed, nature, in order to maintain the unity of the body and the soul, actually changes the character of the tumor and transforms it into a cancer. So the idea and the fear that an affection of the respiratory organs (though it is only a slight asthma) is an incipient *phthisis* will, by the power of the idea alone, change it to a consumption. I have known cases where a person supposed that he had come in contact with the poison ivy, the *toxico dendron*, and though it was demonstrably certain that he had not, it produced all the effects of actual poisoning. Such is the wonderful force of that mode of thought we call imagination. But, as was said above, the law works with equal efficiency and energy in the direction of a cure. If in the case of the tumor the patient thinks it is harmless and is passing away, and with a divine obstinacy holds the mind steadfastly to that idea, what we call nature (that is, an ever-present, ever-active God-life in the universe, an all-pervading World-Spirit) goes to work to place the body in harmony and unity with the idea and the inward becomes the outward, and the tumor disappears with a rapidity proportioned to the strength and steadfastness of the thought or belief.

The reader will bear in mind that, with regard to the nature of thought, I accept and adopt the definition of Descartes, who says: "By the word thought I understand all that which so takes place in us that we of ourselves are immediately conscious of it;

and, accordingly, not only to understand, to will, to imagine, but even to perceive, are the same as to think." (*The Principles of Philosophy*, Part I, Sec. IX.) In this sense of the term thought and existence are identical. All action of mind or body is preceded by either conscious or unconscious thought. "Thought is indeed essential to humanity. It is this that distinguishes us from the brutes. In sensation, cognition, and intellection, in our instincts and volitions, as far as they are truly human, thought is an invariable element." (*Hegel's Philosophy of History*, Bohn's Edition, p. 9.)

What is called magnetism, which has proved itself one of the most efficient means of the cure of disease, owes its efficiency to the fact that in its inmost reality it is but the sphere of our thoughts and feelings. This continually emanes or exhales from us. This subtle spiritual principle which is perpetually escaping from us forms an atmosphere around us, which is charged with the living forces of our minds. The Sanscrit word for the soul is *atma*, which is equivalent to the Greek *atmos*, vapor or air, and enters into the composition of our word atmosphere. This emanative *sphere* of our minds, as Swedenborg calls it, having no determinate direction, does not perceptibly act upon those around us, except in the case of those who are highly sensitive. *But it can be impelled by the will,*— because it is only our personality diffused abroad, and is a part of our living self,— and a definite direction can be given to it. The principle which sets it in motion in a given direction exists in our souls in the same way as that which communicates strength to our arm, and its nature is similar; for physical strength is wholly a spiritual force and mental energy. By a gentle impulsion of the will, we concentrate this subtle force into the hands, and through the touch, by the same volitional act, we impress it with a determinate direction to any individual or to any part of his body. By the power of thought and volition, we may direct it to a person in the same room with us, or through many miles of space, even across the Atlantic ocean.

In the human soul reside all the healing virtues and potencies that can be found in medicinal plants and minerals; for all material things correspond or answer to something in the mind. The so-called properties of matter, as has been before shown, are reducible to sensations and other modifications of our minds. Take as an illustration the oak. The English term comes from a root that signifies strength, and originally the oak meant the *strong tree*. In one of the names used to designate this tree in the Latin language this idea is retained. The word *robur*, from which comes our term *robust*, means both an oak and vigorous strength. But this is not a property of any material body, but a quality and force of the mind. Hence, all the tonic virtue of this tree resides in the mind, and may be communicated to another. The same may be remarked of iron, and of cinchona,—so much used as tonic medicines,—and of all botanic and mineral substances. Their curative properties are something in their spiritual essence, which answers to some energy of the soul. These are stored up in a healthy person, ready to be imparted and, in fact, go forth from him in the sphere of his life. Jesus the Christ referred to something like this when, after the woman, having a spirit of infirmity, had touched the fringe of his garment and was made whole, he said that he perceived *virtue*, or a sanative force, had gone out of him.

The hand is the divinely appointed medium through which a sanative spiritual influence is communicated to another. In this way Jesus imparted to the diseased and suffering a healing and saving virtue. (Mat. ix: 18, 19, 25; Mark viii: 25; vii: 32, 33, 35; Luke xiii: 11, 13; Mark vi: 5.) On this subject Swedenborg, more than a century ago, has said in a brief compass, nearly all that can be said. According to him, the touch signifies *communication, transference, and reception*, because it is this in reality. The interiors of man put themselves forth by external things, especially by the touch, and thereby communicate with another, and transfer themselves to another, and so far as the will is in further agreement, and makes one, they are received. Whether we speak of the love or the will, it amounts to the same thing, for what is of the love of man this also is of the will. Hence, also, it follows that the interiors of man, which are of his love, and the thought thence derived, put themselves forth by the touch, and thus communicate themselves with another, and transfer themselves into another, and so far as another loves the person or the things which the person speaks or acts, so far they are received. (*Arcana Celestia*, 10,130. See also 10,023.)

The practice of Jesus the Christ has given dignity to the use of the hand in the cure of disease, and the above extract contains the arcane philosophy of its efficiency, and the sum and substance of all that has been written on the subject of magnetism as a curative agency from Mesmer to Delentze.

The method of cure recommended in this volume is the plan of cure adopted and, with marvelous success, practiced eighteen centuries ago by Jesus. It is the same in all its essential features as his Divine method of healing through faith, and is based on his fundamental maxim, that "it is the spirit that maketh alive; the flesh profiteth nothing." (John vi : 63.) This is a complete inversion of our ordinary way of thinking, and of that which prevails in the various schools of medicine, where the condition of the fleshly manifestation of man is viewed as everything in disease, and the state of the living spiritual principle is as nothing. This view of human nature I believe to be false in philosophy, and deleterious to the highest well-being of humanity, when made the basis of a medical practice. It is an inversion of the Divine order, for God heals the body by saving the soul. Though the spiritual physician of today has to deal with a different class of people from the simple, child-like, trusting souls who came to the Christ eighteen hundred years ago for a cure of their maladies, yet, if his system is based upon a true philosophy of human nature, it can be made effectual today. Instead of an unthinking multitude, ready to be moulded into a new mode of thinking by any superior mind, we have to deal with those who have positive ideas, and have to encounter the pride of individual opinion which is sometimes called science. Yet some of these may become in spirit as little

children, and thus be receptive of the things of the kingdom of
God. The man or woman who can be made to see and understand
the law of our nature, by the operation of which the inward
always tends to become one with the outward, ought to coöperate
with the idealistic or spiritual physician in his beneficent healing
endeavor, and if he is sufficiently *desirous* of being saved, or made
whole, of whatever disease he has, he will do so. If he has no
desire to be healed according to this Divine method, he can be
left, as Jesus would have left him, to go his own way.

COSIMO is a specialty publisher of books and publications that inspire, inform and engage readers. Our mission is to offer unique books to niche audiences around the world.

COSIMO CLASSICS offers a collection of distinctive titles by the great authors and thinkers throughout the ages. At **COSIMO CLASSICS** timeless classics find a new life as affordable books, covering a variety of subjects including: *Biographies, Business, History, Mythology, Personal Development, Philosophy, Religion and Spirituality,* and much more!

COSIMO-on-DEMAND publishes books and publications for innovative authors, non-profit organizations and businesses. **COSIMO-on-DEMAND** specializes in bringing books back into print, publishing new books quickly and effectively, and making these publications available to readers around the world.

COSIMO REPORTS publishes public reports that affect your world: from global trends to the economy, and from health to geo-politics.

FOR MORE INFORMATION CONTACT US AT
INFO@COSIMOBOOKS.COM

❋ If you are a book-lover interested in our current catalog of books.

❋ If you are an author who wants to get published

❋ If you represent an organization or business seeking to reach your members, donors or customers with your own books and publications

**COSIMO BOOKS ARE ALWAYS
AVAILABLE AT ONLINE BOOKSTORES**

VISIT COSIMOBOOKS.COM
BE INSPIRED, BE INFORMED